NOTTINGHAM AND LONG EATON
SPEEDWAY

1928-1967

NOTTINGHAM AND LONG EATON
SPEEDWAY

1928-1967

PHILIP DALLING

Front cover: main image by John Sumpter; top image by Dick Smart.

First published 2007

Stadia is an imprint of
Tempus Publishing Limited
The Mill, Brimscombe Port,
Stroud, Gloucestershire, GL5 2QG
www.tempus-publishing.com

British Library Cataloguing in Publication Data.
A catalogue record for this book is available from the British Library.

ISBN 978 07524 4163 4

Typesetting and origination by Tempus Publishing Limited
Printed in Great Britain

Contents

Nottingham speedway legend Fred Strecker in the 1960s. Fred turned to another form of horsepower in later years and hunted with the South Notts.

Preface

Long Eaton Stadium loomed large in my life as a young journalist in the 1960s. I spent many hours watching the Archers in speedway action, mourned their departure to Leicester in 1968 and welcomed the sport's return a year later.

Always to be found at the same table in the Stadium's clubroom on Tuesday evenings in the 1960s was a vigorous middle-aged man, usually dressed in the sort of tweed suits that gave him more the look of a country sportsman than a short-circuit racing enthusiast. Fred Strecker was closely connected to the stock car racing promotion at Station Road and with his friend and business partner, George Dykes, he had raced the heavily armoured cars of the sport's earlier years.

I associated Fred almost exclusively with the four-wheel sport and our conversations were usually little more than an exchange of pleasantries. I discovered later – too late, as it turned out – that Fred and George had been speedway legends at the old Nottingham Olympic Speedway and its later successor, the White City Stadium.

When, in recent years, the *Nottingham Evening Post* featured a picture of the Trent Lane track in its Bygones series and invited readers to share their memories, the few surviving fans ignored the internationally famous speedway names of the era who had ridden in Olympic and White City colours, including (if briefly) the first-ever English World Champion Tommy Price, England internationals Walter 'Nobby' Key, Les Wotton and George Greenwood, and Australian test stars Billy 'Cyclone' Lamont, Dicky Wise and Jack Chapman. Their memories were of local favourites Strecker and Dykes, and fellow pioneers Charlie Shelton and Joe Gooding.

Fred, George, Charlie and Joe, together with most other stars of the first speedway golden age, are gone now, but in researching this book I have seized with both hands the opportunity I missed in the 1960s to pay tribute to genuine dirt-track heroes. Fred Strecker and George Dykes were also the bridge between speedway at Nottingham in the 1930s and at Long Eaton in the 1950s, where they acted as starting marshal and machine examiner respectively at the start of the Archers' era. Fred and George had always encouraged the local men taking up the sport, including 1949 world number three Louis Lawson of Belle Vue and England, and Lionel Watling of Birmingham and Leicester.

The Archers' era at Long Eaton lasted until 1967. Although, as this book recounts, international speedway riders of the highest class, including World Champions Ove Fundin and Anders Michanek, featured at Station Road in the latter part of the 1960s, the track still produced its local heroes, like Ray Wilson (a world-class rider himself), Norman Storer, Graham Plant and Peter Wrathall.

This book is dedicated to all the riders, from home or abroad, champions or journeymen, who provided so many thrills over so many years on Trentside.

Philip Dalling

Acknowledgements

A great many people both from within and outside speedway have been generous with their time and knowledge during the preparation of this book.

Inside the big family that I believe speedway still represents, help has come from former riders, promoters, officials and the men and women on the terraces – fittingly both the household names and the supporters who keep the sport alive. Riders who have contributed include Guy and Nicky Allott, Erol Brook, the late Ivor Brown, Howard Cole (Kid Bodie), Ray Cresp, Clive Hitch, Johnnie Jones, Louis Lawson, Rim Malskaitis, Ernest 'Pedlar' Palmer, Graham Plant, Eric 'Bluey' Scott, Vic White, Ray Wilson, Archie Windmill, Jack Winstanley and Peter Wrathall. I am indebted to Reg Fearman for his helpful comments on the chapters that cover the 1963-1967 period, when he was promoter at Long Eaton.

The late Dick Smart of West Bridgford retained vivid memories of Nottingham White City up until his death in 2004, and his photographs provide a superb link with a vanished era. Other Nottingham and Long Eaton fans to whom I am indebted include Tony Cooper in Richmond, Ontario, Canada, June Barker (Long Eaton), Frank Hughes (West Bridgford), Chris Lightfoot (Arnold, Nottingham), Chris Lynas (Nottingham), Joe Orchard (Westcliff-on-Sea), Alan Orchard (Banbury), Cyril Parker (Southwell), Cyril Smith (Long Eaton), and Geoffrey Tipping (Edwalton).

The Nottingham riders of the 1920s and '30s and some of the Long Eaton stars of the early 1950s are, sadly, no longer with us. Their memory has been kept alive by their families, without whose willing cooperation this book would not have been possible. My gratitude goes to Fred Strecker's sister Olive, his son Roger and his daughter Ann English, as well as George Dykes' daughter, Judith Linley, Sandra Tipping, the daughter of Charlie Shelton, Brian Hurst, Charlie Shelton's nephew and his family in Hucknall, Steve Coleman and his wife Jeanette, the nephew and niece of Joe Gooding, and Ernest Goldingay, the brother of Lionel Watling. All welcomed me into their homes, recounted their memories, and trusted me with their precious photographs and mementoes.

The late Ray Bennett, a professional photographer who lived a stone's throw from Station Road, took many of the photographs from the 1950s. John Sumpter, a long-term colleague of mine, is responsible for the majority of the 1960s shots. Another former colleague, Lisa Gilligan, worked wonders with many of the older photographs and spent many hours working on restoring photographs and advising me on the illustrations for this book. Mrs June Wrathall, whose father and mother, Arthur and Audrey Rudge, were tireless workers for the Long Eaton Speedway Supporters' Club, provided many photographs from the 1950s, and Archers fan Philip Wells filled in the photographic gaps from the 1960s. I am also grateful to John Somerville for giving me permission to use photographs from the collection of the late Wright Wood.

I would also like to thank all the speedway journalists, historians and statisticians who have generously shared their knowledge and made available much valuable material. Special thanks go to Robert Ozanne, whose database of pre-war speedway statistics, with accompanying notes, on the *Speedway Researcher* website forms an amazing record of the era. Others who helped include Nigel Bird, Graham Fraser, Cyril J. Hart, Jim Henry, Chris Illman,

Alan Jones, Howard Jones, Peter Morrish, Tony McDonald, Ian Moultray, Glyn Price, Mark Sawbridge, Mike Smallman, Barry Stephenson, Allen Trump and Bryan C. Tungate.

In addition, I have consulted the following books, publications and websites: *Speedway: The Pre-War Years*, Robert Bamford, assisted by Dave Stallworthy; *Homes of British Speedway*, Robert Bamford and John Jarvis; *Speedway in Manchester 1927-1945*, Trevor James and Barry Stephenson; *Speedway in Leicester: The Pre-War Years*, Alan Jones; *Speedway in Leicester: The Hunters Era*, Alan Jones; *History of the Speedway Hoskins*, Ian Hoskins; *Speedway at The Firs 1931-39*, Alan Smith; *Stenners Speedway Annuals*, 1946-1954; *Five Star Speedway Annual 1960*; *Speedway Star Digest*, various years; *Speedway and Ice News*; *Speedway Star*; *Vintage Speedway Magazine*; *Backtrack*; *Nottingham Guardian*; *Nottingham Journal*; *Nottingham Evening Post*; *Nottingham Evening News*; *Derby Evening Telegraph*; *Long Eaton Advertiser*; *Speedwayplus*; *Speedway Researcher*; *Opposite Lock*.

Thanks also to Andy Smart and Phil Meakin of the *Nottingham Evening Post*, Dorothy Ritchie and colleagues at the Angel Row Local Studies Library in Nottingham, Mike Jobling and staff at Long Eaton Public Library for assistance and permission to reproduce photographs, the University of Nottingham Hallward Library local studies collection, the Local Studies Library at Irongate, Derby, the Nottinghamshire Records Office, and the British Newspaper Library, Collindale. The illustration on page 15 is reproduced courtesy of Nottingham Historical Film Unit and www.picturethepast.org.uk.

If anyone has been left out of this list, I apologise. My memory is sharp when it comes to recalling Tuesday evenings at Station Road in the 1960s, but not so good when it comes to more recent events!

Finally, a special word of thanks to that prolific speedway author and historian Robert Bamford for his invaluable help and advice in the publication of this book and for his hospitality at the Abbey Stadium, Swindon.

Introduction: Speedway on Trentside

The city of Nottingham, renowned worldwide for its legend of Robin Hood, for Players cigarettes, Boots Pure Drug Company and Raleigh cycles, sits at the heart of England, astride the River Trent, considered by many to mark the cultural divide between the north and south of England. To the west of the city is Long Eaton, a modest little manufacturing town without any of the fame of its big sister, despite the fact that much of the acclaimed Nottingham lace was actually made there, and not in the city centre.

Nottingham and Long Eaton – the latter town actually situated across the county boundary in Derbyshire, marked by the Trent's tributary, the River Erewash – share another common link. For much of the last seventy-nine years, one or other centre has provided an East Midland home for speedway, or dirt-track racing as it was often called. The years of speedway activity along the Trent sadly saw little overlap and there was never a Nottingham-Long Eaton local derby to set pulses racing at either the original Olympic Speedway at Trent Lane, Colwick, its successor, the White City Stadium, or Station Road.

Speedway racing began in Britain in 1928 and Nottingham was the first of the two Trentside centres to host motorbike racing in official short-circuit competition. Auto Cycle Union-licensed grass-track events on a speedway-shaped circuit at Trent Lane in 1928 were followed by the first dirt-track meeting at the same venue in March 1929. Nottingham meetings that year were held under an open licence, although two leagues had been formed: the Southern League (won by Stamford Bridge) and the English Dirt-Track League, for northern sides. A team called Long Eaton entered speedway legend for formally entering the English Dirt-Track League for the 1929 season but never actually riding a match, in a competition which started with seventeen teams but finished with just eleven, headed by champions Leeds. Manchester's Belle Vue, later to become acknowledged as the world's premier speedway club side, were among the sides to resign, alleging slack organisation.

Despite failing to ride league matches, Long Eaton did stage speedway in 1929, although historians are reluctant to confirm just how many meetings actually took place at Station Road. When speedway was tried at Long Eaton at Whitsuntide 1929, it attracted only modest crowds – it may be this that convinced promoters league racing was not a viable proposition. A group of Nottingham riders also tried their hand at promoting at Station Road, but a Saturday afternoon meeting (the greyhounds had priority in the evening) was attended by fewer than 1,000 people.

Another attempt was made in 1930, with a challenge match between Nottingham and Leicester. That too attracted only a modest crowd by the standards of the era.

Nothing more was to be heard of Long Eaton for nearly two decades.

Nottingham itself enjoyed a chequered speedway career throughout the 1930s, experiencing activity of some sort every year except 1932, 1935 and 1939. The end came at White City, after only eight meetings, in 1938 and there was to be no post-war revival at the well-appointed venue, despite efforts by various promoters.

Speedway racing of a kind did take place in the city in the late 1940s, when a local motorcycle club promoted meetings for charity on an oval grass circuit, sanded on the bends, at Highfields, off University Boulevard, to the west of the city. This venture attracted riders of the calibre of Belle Vue's Dent Oliver and Nottinghamshire's Louis Lawson.

The mantle of racing passed to Long Eaton in the sport's second golden age, although speedway was already well established in its post-war boom before a wheel had even been turned at Station Road. An attempt to start racing in the summer of 1949 proved abortive, but an open licence was secured for the new Archers side for 1950.

A successful first season of friendlies, a modest third division debut in 1951 and a late summer resignation from the Southern League in 1952 was the Station Road story, as the increasing availability of television and a punitive entertainment tax, amongst other factors, saw speedway head into decline.

Practice sessions were staged at the track in 1953 and a team labelled as Long Eaton rode in one away challenge fixture. At least three unlicensed 'pirate' meetings were held at Station Road in 1954. That same year stock car racing arrived in Britain, and Long Eaton, together with other defunct speedway venues, provided a natural home.

The stock cars, together with the bread and butter greyhound racing, kept the stadium alive. Along the Trent at Colwick, the Nottingham White City remained largely a greyhounds-only venue, although kart racing is also believed to have taken place.

The success of a new Provincial League in the early 1960s encouraged promoters to look at defunct speedway venues. Long Eaton came to life again in 1963, formed part of the amalgamation into the one big British League in 1965, and survived until the end of 1967, when the promotion team decided to transfer the track licence to Blackbird Road, where the old Leicester Hunters had gone out of business in the autumn of 1962.

Again, the success of a lower league proved to be Long Eaton's saviour, and racing returned in 1969 after just a one-year gap. From that point until the sad demise of the Station Road stadium in 1997, Long Eaton became one of the most stable venues in British speedway, with only the odd year or two out of the sport.

For two seasons in the 1980s Station Road hosted a team called the Nottingham Outlaws, in the hope that the name change would attract more patrons from the city. Curiously enough, a survey in the early fifties had shown that speedway attracted far more customers to Station Road from Derby, ten miles away, than from the much nearer Nottingham! Derby patrons outscored their Nottingham counterparts by an incredible 5-1!

As ever, optimists continue to dream about a return of speedway racing to the banks of the River Trent. There is a suggestion that at least one promoter has taken soundings about the possibility of introducing speedway at the new Nottingham greyhound stadium, located quite close to the old White City venue, at Colwick, in the car park of the Nottingham horse-racing track.

Optimists also continued in 2006 to hope for a revival at Station Road, with a redeveloped track occupying just a part of the former extensive stadium site. Station Road in 2006 was a truly dismal sight, with the stadium and the adjacent Pavilion Hotel totally demolished.

Speedway entertained and thrilled Trentside crowds for a total of forty-two seasons following the first tentative events in 1928. That figure would undoubtedly have been higher had Station Road not fallen prey to the developers. But the dates of operation at Colwick and Long Eaton simply represent the bare bones. Speedway is about people and both venues, at various times, saw the greatest names in the game, produced an assortment of characters and made a major contribution to the not insubstantial sporting history of the East Midlands.

1

Nottingham's Olympic Speedway

The banks of the River Trent in and around Nottingham play host to a remarkable group of sporting venues, of a quality, variety and proximity it would be difficult to equal. Two historic football grounds, one of the world's most famous test cricket venues, a racecourse, a greyhound stadium, and the boat and clubhouses of nationally renowned rowing clubs are all to be found along a stretch of river to the south-east of the city, within a radius of about a square mile.

The hour before the start of play in an England–Australia test at Trent Bridge, or before the kick-off in a Nottingham Forest versus Derby County local derby clash at the City Ground, sees a constant stream of fans heading south of the river across the historic Trent Bridge. On the north bank, Meadow Lane is the home of the Football League's oldest club, Notts County, while eastwards along the river lies Colwick Park, home of horse racing in the city since the move from the original course on The Forest in the early 1800s.

While sport in other cities moves ever further out of town and famous old stadia are demolished, Nottingham clings to its Trentside sporting tradition. But most of the fans making their way to the city's current arenas have little notion that there was once another notable sporting venue on the north bank of the Trent, only yards from the waterway itself.

The area to the north of the river, at Trent Lane, in the eastern suburb of Colwick, next to the racecourse's western boundary, was used for allotments, agriculture and football pitches before the First World War. In 1922, entrepreneur Tom Little laid out more than sixty tennis courts, both grass and hard. The title given to the area at the time of the introduction of speedway, the Olympic Grounds, must date from this development, as earlier maps do not use the name.

Grass-track motorcycle racing was growing in popularity in Nottinghamshire, Derbyshire and Lincolnshire, and the Nottingham Tornado Motor Cycle Club sought a permanent base for its meetings. The result of the club's search was the Tornado Speedway, constructed on the Olympic Grounds, which began life as a primitive motorcycle grass-track venue in 1928, and acquired a cinder surface, safety fence, track lighting and other facilities, together with the new title of Olympic Speedway, in the following year.

But for opposition from local worthies, prospective promoters could have found a ready-made venue for speedway already in place at the Trent Lane site. Detailed plans had been published in July 1927, by a subsidiary company of British Greyhounds, for a 500-yard dog circuit, with track lighting, three grandstands and a total spectator capacity of 12,000.

The whole of the share capital of £13,500 had been subscribed and work was set to start within weeks, with racing – on three nights a week – due to start in the spring of 1928. As it was, local church and civic leaders voiced fierce opposition, led by a lay member of the Nottingham Archdeaconry of the Church of England.

Mr A.G. Hines, chairman of the Nottinghamshire Football Association and a member of the council of the autocratic Football Association itself, declared that greyhound racing was, 'a vicious thing – the most vile thing that has come on earth in my opinion.' The greyhound plans were, for the time being, dropped.

Fortunately, the Nottingham authorities regarded motorcycle racing with more favour. The Tornado Club was able to stage its first meeting at Trent Lane on Saturday 28 July 1928.

Charlie Shelton was one of the original Nottingham Tornado Motorcycle Club members to turn to the cinders. The pipe-smoking Shelton is pictured on his Douglas on the centre green of the original Olympic Speedway circuit.

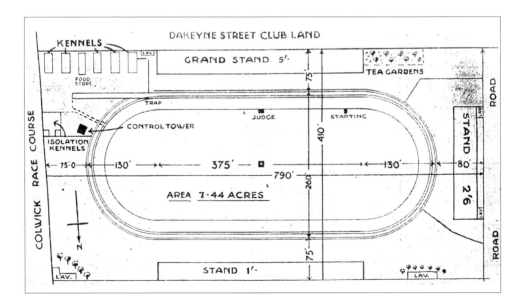

Above: Nottingham could have had a first-class stadium for speedway from the off if the city fathers had not rejected the above plans for a stadium on the Olympic Grounds, submitted in the summer of 1927.

This rare shot from the Picture the Past archive shows speedway-style racing on grass at the Tornado Speedway, Trent Lane, in 1928.

Early meetings of short-circuit motorcycle racing in England used the title 'dirt-track racing', although the Australian pioneers appear to have always preferred the term 'speedway'. The Nottingham enthusiasts were in no doubt about which name they preferred. Although the events at Trent Lane in 1928 were raced on a grass surface, with at least six riders in a race, the advertising urged a thrill-seeking public to visit the 'Tornado Speedway'.

Adults were charged 1s 2d for admission, with children paying half price, and spectators were advised to take the Colwick Road tramcar to its Trent Lane stop.

The local press gave an enthusiastic reception to short-circuit motorcycle racing's debut in Nottingham. A contemporary report said the Olympic Grounds had been the scene of stunt flying and many other exciting sports, 'but none more thrilling than the motorcycle grass-track racing witnessed there on Saturday.' Reports provided plenty of detail for those readers who had not been tempted out to Colwick. The riders, who covered eight laps of a quarter-mile circuit in each race, had 'well studded their tyres in order to prevent skids at the four nasty corners.' The prohibition on riders placing their left foot on the anti-clockwise circuit – a feature of the early Australian meetings staged by legendary promoter Johnnie Hoskins at Maitland in New South Wales – also applied initially at Nottingham.

The anonymous reporter seems to have had some experience of racing on dirt circuits. The races, said the report, 'did not, of course, provide many of the thrills associated with dirt-track racing, but were responsible for several very exciting incidents, notably the duels between Frank Sissons, the crack Hucknall rider, and Les Otter.'

Sissons won three of the four events, riding both a solo machine and a sidecar unit. In the championship race for the twelve fastest riders of the day, he headed home a fellow member of the Tornado Club who was to become a Nottingham legend – the twenty-two-year-old Fred Strecker. Also in the prize money at that first grass-track meeting was another local boy, Charlie Shelton, who went on to ride speedway for Wembley and Nottingham. The venture was a clear success, with the only criticism being one that was to plague speedway (and Nottingham in particular) throughout its early history – false starts and long intervals between races.

Nottingham's motorcycle racing fans did not have to wait for very long before seeing the bona fide dirt-track racing approved by the local journalist. As so often was the case with the provincial tracks, it was local enterprise that promoted the sport, in the shape of the Haslam family from Derbyshire. The Haslams were coal owners based at The Elms, a large house in the mining town of Ripley, which boasted an adjoining field where the family organised grass-track racing. In the winter of 1928/29, W.M. or Bill Haslam, operating as Olympic Speedways Ltd, took over the rough-and-ready Trent Lane circuit.

The grass surface at Trent Lane was replaced by cinders, and initially a simple post and metal rail fence was erected – soon to be replaced by a boarded barrier. Rudimentary cinder banking for spectators was also provided, and press pictures of the first 1929 speedway meeting show a crowd of around ten deep. The safety measures were still primitive, but Nottingham probably compared favourably with the Lundwood circuit at Barnsley, where the safety fence consisted of a mound of turves, on which some of the bolder spectators sat during races!

Ernest 'Dids' Houlton, who became the Nottingham team manager in 1931, was competitors' steward and scrutineer for the first season.

Promoter Haslam must have been encouraged by the fact that several hundred people gathered at the track for the first practice session. The star attraction at the trials was New Zealander Stewie St George, who had arrived in Britain with one of the first batches of riders from Australia. St George believed several of the local riders involved in the practice were capable of wider success, recording faster times than established men who had won Golden Helmet races elsewhere.

Fred Strecker, riding an AJS, and Les Otter were the men singled out by St George. The 'Australian crack' as the local press inaccurately described him, was less impressed with the biting winds blowing off the River Trent than he was with the local talent. He did not ride in the practice session, assuring reporters that he was getting his machine ready for the season. Although wearing a heavy shirt and a leather jacket, he was said to have 'shivered violently' every time he stood still for more than a few seconds.

The opening meeting was scheduled for 23 March on a circuit described as having, 'a coating of cinders and all the safety devices demanded by the sport's governing bodies'. A 'pleasing feature' of the Olympic Speedway was that the cinders were watered. Some tracks were said to be without this arrangement and the onlookers became 'almost as black as the riders'.

Another major innovation enjoyed by the Nottingham fans was an advertised ferry service to the speedway along the River Trent, with boats running from Whitty's wharf and boatyard at Trent Bridge direct to the quayside right next to the track – a facility almost certainly unique in the sport's history.

When the racing got underway, Stewie St George's assessment of the potential of Les Otter proved only too uncomfortably accurate for the overseas star. Otter beat St George in the senior scratch race final, part of a programme which, typically for the time, included both solos and sidecar racing.

The Tornado Club continued with its grass-track meetings, moving to a new circuit at Mapperley, leaving the Olympic Speedway free for a packed season of dirt-track thrills. Promoters across Britain were eager to cash in on the tremendous enthusiasm for speedway. Nottingham was no exception and nearly sixty meetings were staged at Trent Lane between the end of March and the middle of October, with racing for the most part taking place on Thursday evenings and on Saturday afternoons. Track lighting was introduced as the season progressed, although the earliest photographic evidence for this, showing lighting standards similar to those used to carry overhead tram or trolley bus wires, does not appear until the following year.

Nottingham was effectively a year behind other tracks, which had introduced real speedway in 1928 and its meetings, outside either the Southern or English Dirt-Track Leagues, relied on the attractiveness of individual events and match-race clashes between the local favourites, the Australian and American pioneers, and the increasingly popular British stars such as Arthur Atkinson, Gus Kuhn, Roger and Buster Frogley, and Wal Phillips.

Most of the meetings followed the general 1928 pattern, with scratch races, handicaps and track record attempts, with a variety of golden and silver helmets, gauntlets and armlets on offer. Some of the trophies were donated by local businesses, such as the Oscroft garage concern, which was to support the Nottingham track throughout its existence. With so many meetings taking place, a detailed account of racing week by week would occupy a book of its own. Several meetings and individual displays stand out and deserve to be recorded.

Above left: Fred Strecker.

Below left: New Zealander Stewie St George acted as a consultant for the opening of the Nottingham Olympic Speedway in 1929, but his bid to lift the major honours at the opening meeting was thwarted by local man Les Otter.

Below right: Bill Haslam, a member of a colliery-owning family from Ripley in Derbyshire, promoted speedway at Nottingham Olympic from 1929 to the mid-season closure in 1931.

Nottingham Olympic Speedway programmes are much
sought after by collectors and command high prices.

The list of winners of the major prizes reads like a who's who of speedway's golden years. In addition to Atkinson, Kuhn, the Frogley Brothers and Wal Phillips, riders such as Sprouts Elder, Vic Huxley, Frank Arthur, Harry Whitfield, Clem Beckett and Frank Varey left the Trentside with trophies and prize money. George Wigfield from South Yorkshire became a local hero by providing the sternest opposition for the star visitors.

Nottingham fans also caught a glimpse of the women who raced dirt-track machines in the very early days, before the authorities barred them from competing. Fred Strecker raced Eva Asquith in July 1929, winning the series 2-1. In the same month, match races were staged over four heats between English and Australian riders, including future Nottingham star Jack Chapman. England won 20-8, with Gus Kuhn and Wigfield winning two races apiece.

Crowds grew, according to the local press, as the season progressed and the presentation of the meetings became as slick as was possible during an era of faulty starts, unreliable machinery and frequent crashes.

Although Nottingham raced outside the leagues in the first season, there was a reasonable amount of team racing, usually billed as 'inter-city challenges'.

On August bank holiday Monday 1929, Nottingham met Leicester at Trent Lane. The home side tracked Joe Gooding, Fred Strecker, A.E. Lester and Reg Lucas, in opposition to the Leicester line-up of Arthur Sherlock, Alec Bowerman, Neville Wheeler and George Marsh. Nottingham won 20-7, with Bill Henstock stepping into the Leicester side as reserve when Sherlock crashed and withdrew.

Despite not being members of the English Dirt-Track League, Nottingham were invited to enter that competition's knock-out cup, giving fans their first taste of truly competitive team racing. The draw matched Nottingham against South Yorkshire side Wombwell and the home leg on 23 August 1929 brought Nottingham victory by 35-23. The reported crowd of nearly 12,000 included members of the Nottinghamshire and Gloucestershire cricket teams. Notts captain Arthur Carr, who was to lift the County Championship trophy a couple of weeks later, spoke to the crowd.

Sadly, Nottingham made no progress in the knock-out competition, as Wombwell won the second leg 38-24, taking the tie by a narrow 61-59 aggregate score. While Nottingham were riding the second leg in South Yorkshire, a large crowd turned up at Trent Lane despite the absence of the local stars, and saw Sprouts Elder win the Oscroft Gold Sash.

George Wigfield (right) was the first Nottingham local hero to really challenge the top Australian, American and emerging British riders during the early days at Nottingham's Olympic Speedway.

Action pictures of the early Nottingham stars are rare. Former Royal Flying Corps man Joe Gooding loses control of his machine and runs on to the centre green in a 1929 study from Trent Lane.

Reg Lucas Junior, son of a Nottinghamshire garage proprietor, was another Tornado Motorcycle Club man to make a dirt-track impact. This centre-green shot clearly shows the boarded safety fence at the original Olympic circuit.

American Lloyd 'Sprouts' Elder, one of the greatest stars of the early years of speedway in Britain, was persuaded to pose with a group of riders in the Trent Lane pits in 1929. Elder, wearing his trademark cap, is in the centre and Nottingham riders in the group include Reg Lucas (left), Fred Strecker (third from left), Charlie Shelton (fifth from left) and Joe Gooding (with cigarette, fourth from the right).

More rare first-season action from Trent Lane, as Nottingham's Fred Strecker (outside) tussles with Australian legend Vic Huxley.

Track lighting was first used on 15 August and was said to be 'highly effective' against the now white-painted, solid safety fence. Frank Arthur made his first appearance at Nottingham on his Harley Davidson Peashooter and beat Wigfield in the final of another Oscroft Sash.

Throughout their racing history, Nottingham sides often struggled to come to terms with away circuits that differed in shape and size from the 412-yard Olympic track, with its wide bends (reduced to 380 yards for 1933). The Nottingham men had a taste of the struggles to come on 17 September 1929, when a visit to fellow non-leaguers Wolverhampton brought a heavy defeat, by 39.5 points to 13.5. The Wolverhampton riders got home first in each of the nine heats and won six of them by 5-1. Reg Lucas Junior, the son of a Mansfield garage proprietor, dead-heated with a home rider for second place in heat eight and Fred Strecker and B. Stanton – a rider soon to disappear without trace – also managed second places.

The *Wolverhampton Express and Star* was kind to Nottingham in its match report, concluding that the scoreline was really no reflection of the riding ability of the visitors, whose home circuit was very different to the always tricky Monmore Green track. 'After the wide sweeping bends of the Nottingham track, Monmore Green must have seemed a perilously narrow place to scrap on to Strecker and his boys,' said the match report. A local rider called Jim Middleton, from the South Notts village of Bunny, was the fourth member of the Nottingham team.

A great deal of interest was shown in the Scott machine ridden by Fred Strecker at Wolverhampton. This was said to sound 'simply delightful'. But although Strecker was reported to take the bends 'flat out in terrific broadsides', he cut out about halfway along the back straight in each of his rides. The new Douglas being ridden by local star and future Nottingham promoter Arthur Westwood was far more reliable.

Track advantage was also cited when Nottingham visited Cardiff. The writer of subsequent Trent Lane programme notes said the Nottingham boys, who managed only eight points between them in the match, had nevertheless 'performed heroically'. The notes said:

> The moment they saw the Cardiff arena our boys' hearts sank. Scraping around a thin strip of dirt sprinkled on the outside of a rugby football field was a tall order. And when Charlie Shelton on his first try-out scraped a goodly portion off his knee-cap in the process, Nottingham's stock fell considerably below par.

The team racing highlight of 1929 came on 21 September when Wembley were the challenge match visitors. Charlie Shelton, Joe Gooding, Rocky Burnham, Fred Strecker, Wally Humphrey and Bill Henstock lined up for Nottingham against Wembley's Jack Ormston, Charlie Barrett, Alf Foulds, Ray Tauser, Len Reeve and Jack Jackson. Wembley ran out 35-28 winners.

Nottingham's own industrial products made an appearance on the Trent Lane track during the course of the match when Rocky Burnham, already in the veteran stage as a motorcyclist and an in-and-out member of the Nottingham line-up for several years, rode a Raleigh machine.

As was then the norm, the promoters took advantage of the popularity of speedway to run meetings up until the point when the weather was just too bad to continue. For the fans, there was the memory of a spectacular addition to Nottingham's sporting menu to savour throughout the winter, and the prospect of league racing when speedway resumed in 1930.

2

The Southern League Era

Enthusiasm for speedway ran high on Trentside as the 1930 season dawned. Nottingham may have missed out on the initial year of league racing in Britain, but big crowds for the 1929 open licence meetings encouraged the Trent Lane promotion, and there was an apparent determination to make up for lost time.

The extensive Nottingham press of the period – two morning and two evening newspapers – sheds no light on the reasons why the Olympic management applied to the Southern League rather than to the northern-based English Dirt-Track League, re-branded as the Northern League for 1930. The chaotic nature of the northern competition in 1929, with many withdrawals and an uncompleted fixture list, may have been one factor behind the decision.

Travelling and the availability of local derby matches probably also influenced the choice. The northern competition included Edinburgh, Glasgow and Newcastle, and just one Midland club, in the shape of Leicester Super. The Southern League, in addition to the glamorous Wembley and West Ham, provided local clashes with Leicester Stadium, Coventry and Birmingham Hall Green. Birmingham Perry Bar also entered the league, but withdrew after just four meetings.

The best media coverage for Nottingham speedway came from the *Evening News* and its associated morning paper, the *Journal*. The somewhat more upmarket *Evening Post* and its morning stablemate, the *Daily Guardian*, took rather less interest. The *News* boasted a speedway correspondent, who took the pseudonym of Broadsider. Previewing the 1930 season, Broadsider told his readers that the demand from the Trentside public for speedway had been so insistent that the date of the opening meeting had been brought forward:

> Nottingham was a long time taking to the sport but last season crowds of 15,000 to 20,000 people were the rule, and the latter mark was exceeded on several occasions. With entry into the Southern League, and visits from the 'crack' teams of the south, interest in 1930 looks like being intensified.

From a distance of nearly eighty years it is impossible to prove or disprove the attendance levels of the initial period at Trent Lane, always rounded off to the nearest thousand by the press. The photograph taken at an England-Australia representative match in 1930 shows a very large crowd indeed in the background, packed onto the cinder banks that surrounded the track at the time.

In all probability crowds varied enormously from meeting to meeting, depending as always upon several factors, including the weather, the form of the home team and the quality of the visiting attraction. At least in 1930 the Nottingham fans could watch in some comfort, as Trent Lane now had a grandstand, roofed and able to accommodate around 1,000 people. The track management, in days when health and safety regulations for sports grounds were virtually unknown, claimed there was accommodation for a total of 25,000 spectators.

With Nottingham starting a year behind most other tracks in terms of league racing, the riders who had established reputations both north and south of the River Trent in 1929 were either unavailable or beyond the reach of the Nottingham promotion's cheque book.

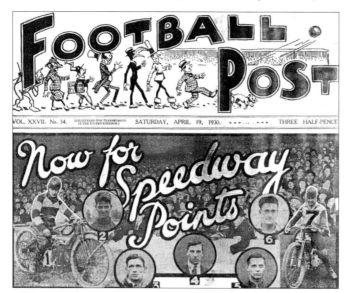

Nottingham's *Football Post* newspaper, still published on Saturday evenings, gave front-page prominence to a preview of the 1930 season, featuring George Wigfield (1), Charlie Shelton (2), Joe Gooding (3), Buster Brown (4), Reg Lucas (5), Rocky Burnham (6) and Fred Strecker (7). As it was, both Shelton and Strecker were to ride elsewhere.

A picture which captures the atmosphere of the Olympic Speedway, Nottingham. Fans pack the cinder banks in 1930 as a representative English team prepares to take on Australian rivals. The English riders are, from left to right: Billy Ellmore, Cyril 'Squib' Burton, Wally Humphrey, Frank Varey, Fred Strecker, Hal Herbert.

Above: A mid-season Nottingham Olympic Southern League line-up from 1930. From left to right: Nobby Key, Bill 'Smiler' Henstock, Joe Gooding, Buster Brown, Wally Humphrey, Billy Ellmore. The picture shows the original Olympic race-jackets with black and white vertical stripes.

Right: Nottingham's team building for the first season of Southern League racing in 1930 included New Zealander Spencer 'Smoky' Stratton, one of the original Sheffield team men from 1929.

Bill Haslam's initial Southern League squad had a decidedly northern and midland look about it, with the exception of Walter 'Nobby' Key, a 1928 original who had gained experience at Wembley. The rest of the team was built around George Wigfield, the South Yorkshireman who had proved a big favourite at Trent Lane in the open meetings and challenge matches of 1929, and Spencer 'Smoky' Stratton, one of the Sheffield pioneers, plus local men Joe Gooding, who had spent the winter of 1929/1930 riding in South America (see International Interludes chapter on page 67), 'Buster' Brown, and 'Smiler' Bill Henstock, from Sutton-in-Ashfield. Juniors Reg Lucas Jr, Rocky Burnham, A.E. Lester, Ellis Blacknall, Rory Moore and George Dykes were also available.

The major disappointment for the Nottingham fans as the 1930 season began was the absence of the two most impressive local products from 1929. Fred Strecker, who had eagerly exchanged the immaculate white uniform of his family's pork butchers shop in the St Anne's Well Road district of Nottingham for leathers, lined up at Manchester White City. Charlie Shelton, who had impressed in a challenge match against Wembley at the end of the 1929 campaign, accepted an offer from the Empire Stadium management.

Both Strecker and Shelton accepted bookings at Trent Lane for Nottingham's first 1930 meeting, an open event. But when it came to league fixtures, the loss of two locally-born riders of proven ability would prove to be a considerable handicap to Nottingham as the season progressed.

In 1930, Southern League matches were run over nine heats with a 3-2-1 scoring system, in place of the 4-2-1 system used in 1929 (and again in 1933). When the Southern League fixtures got underway, the Nottingham fans' introduction to fully competitive speedway produced an anti-climax.

Harringay had arrived at Trent Lane for the historic first league match on 24 April 1930. Nottingham, lining up in black and white vertically-striped race jackets, with the individual rider's team number across the front, between two white stripes, tracked Joe Gooding and Bill Henstock, George Wigfield and Buster Brown, and Spencer Stratton and Nobby Key.

Left: Charlie Shelton was one of the locally-born stars of the Olympic Speedway in 1929. By the time Nottingham entered the Southern League in 1930, he had joined Wembley, and is pictured at the Empire Stadium.

Below: Ferry to the speedway! For this challenge match in 1930, the adverts in the local press promised a river-boat service to the speedway, from Trent Bridge to the wharf next to the Olympic track.

George Wigfield, who was Nottingham's first heat-winner in the first ever home league match against Harringay, had an up and down Southern League career with Nottingham. Injured at a crucial stage of the 1930 season, he was a late starter in 1931 after a dispute over terms with the track management.

Gooding and Henstock faced Australian ace Vic Huxley and his partner Alf Fawford in the first heat and both of the Nottingham men fell twice in the course of the race. Huxley, not surprisingly, became the first winner of a league heat at Trent Lane, with Fawford second and Henstock, who had remounted after his second tumble, third.

George Wigfield and Buster Brown levelled the scores with a second heat 5-1, but Harringay regained the lead when Stratton crashed in heat three, allowing Colin Watson and his partner Stan Spencer to take first and third places, with Key second. Rain was by now falling steadily and the track was starting to churn up, as Harringay's Howard Traynor and Eric Spencer took another 5-1 at the expense of Joe Gooding.

At this point the rain, accompanied by thunder and lightening crashing across the Trent Valley, became a deluge, and the meeting was stopped with Harringay leading 13-9. Before the meeting was formally abandoned, the announcer attempted to keep the drenched crowd happy by playing gramophone records over the tannoy. The *News* reported that, 'asking the drenched supporters to *Tiptoe through the Tulips*' was stretching optimism to breaking point!

The match was re-run a week later, on 1 May, and with no system of re-admission the management announced that those who could produce a programme for the abandoned meeting would be admitted free.

The track's eventual full introduction to league racing proved exciting for the crowd. Nottingham held a narrow lead as the closing heats approached, but in heat eight disaster struck. The pairing of Wigfield and Brown was holding second and third places behind Vic Huxley when Wigfield fell and Brown, close behind, hit his teammate's machine. Both bikes were damaged and neither rider took part in the re-run, giving Harringay a 5-0 and 25-23 advantage.

The last-heat decider looked to be confirming a victory for the visitors. Nobby Key got ahead but the debutant A.E. Lester – in the side because Stratton had failed to arrive – trailed for much of the race in last place. Lester then became the unlikely hero (he failed to follow up on his initial triumph) as he first overtook Harringay's Traynor and then went under Stan Spencer on the last bend to give Nottingham a 5-1 heat win and a winning match score of 27-26.

It was the perfect start to Nottingham's career in the Southern League. Victory from the back, allied to close racing, was and still is the formula for crowd-pleasing speedway. Sadly, the season was downhill for the rest of the way. Nottingham raced a further 23 league matches, but won only one more, with one draw and 21 defeats.

For the team's debut in the Southern League, the track management had provided a rudimentary wooden grandstand for spectators. Joe Gooding is pictured on his Douglas in front of the structure.

It did not take very long for the task facing Nottingham to become glaringly apparent. Reigning Southern League champions Stamford Bridge, with Frank Arthur, Gus Kuhn and Wal Phillips, won 31-21 at Trent Lane on 8 May, and a week later Wembley also took the points comfortably, with a 31-22 success.

Contemporary reports suggested that the Nottingham riders equalled the Empire Stadium stars for power and speed, but were completely outmatched when it came to tactics and racing line. The Olympic men, and particularly Wigfield, taking the bends flat out in 1928 pioneer style, were heavily criticised for going out too wide and allowing the more subtle Wembley stars, Arthur Atkinson and Jack Ormston, to cut inside. The riding of Atkinson in particular was described by the local press as a 'rare treat'. Another Wembley man, George Greenwood, later to become a Nottingham rider in both first and second division racing, had a less than memorable debut at the track, being carried off on a stretcher with concussion after a spill. Charlie Shelton appeared in the Wembley team, recording one second place.

Victory came tantalisingly close for Nottingham when Lea Bridge were the visitors on 29 May. George Wigfield was out of the side through an injury sustained at Sheffield and was replaced by Bill Henstock, but the Olympic still seemed strong enough to see off the visitors, a solid side but one without without any obvious stars. Lea Bridge took a first-heat lead when Osment eased home against Buster Brown and Jimmy Stevens held out Henstock. Nottingham hit back with a 5-1 from Rocky Burnham and Nobby Key in the next race, but it was their last heat success until the end of the match.

Lea Bridge went into the lead in heat three and held on to it for the rest of the match. Nottingham lost a vital point in heat five. Burnham beat Stiffy Aston and Aston's partner, Harold Hastings, dropped out with engine trouble. The Olympic, nevertheless, were frustrated when Nobby Key's machine also packed up. Nottingham needed a 5-1 to win in the last race but, although Joe Gooding was a clear winner, his partner Stratton was held out by Alf Foulds. Rocky Burnham's return of seven points was his best ever league performance, but the rest of the Nottingham side were unimpressive against a team they should have been capable of beating.

Fred Strecker reappeared at Trent Lane on 5 June for a challenge match billed by the Nottingham management and reported in the local press as being contested between 'Nottinghamshire' and 'Leicestershire'. It was, in fact, a straight clash between Nottingham and Leicester Super, the second Leicester-based side, which at the time was competing in the Northern League on Britain's biggest ever pure speedway circuit, the 586-yard Melton Road track.

Leicester Super held a two-point lead going into the final heat and Nottingham were forced to track reserve Ellis Blacknall in place of Nobby Key, who was a non-finisher in his previous ride. Buster Brown won the race and Blacknall followed him home in front of the Super's Fred Hore and Ernest Watts, to earn 'Nottinghamshire' a share of the spoils in a 26-26 draw. Blacknall, like A.E. Lester and Rocky Burnham, enjoyed his moment of glory but never became a team regular, and later took on the role of machine examiner at Trent Lane.

Four nights later, on Whit Monday, Nottingham fell to their worst ever defeat (and one of the worst in the history of speedway), crashing 39-7 at Plough Lane, Wimbledon, in front of a large holiday crowd. The Olympic were still without the injured Wigfield, but included new signing Wally Humphrey from Leicester Super. The match degenerated into farce and in two heats the Nottingham pair – Gooding and Stratton in one case, Brown and Humphrey in the other instance – collided and failed to finish. The fourth heat was declared void, at which stage Wimbledon led 19-4, and Nottingham managed just three more points from the rest of the match. Wimbledon stars Jim Kempster, Billy Lamont, Marty Seiffert and Dicky Case were a class above the Nottingham men, at least at Plough Lane.

The following evening (10 June), Nottingham again had opposition from Leicester when they met the Stadium Southern League team in a special challenge match staged at Long Eaton Stadium (full details in the Long Eaton – the Pioneering Years chapter, on page 41). Top man for Nottingham in a 29-20 victory for Leicester was former Blackbird Road star Billy Ellmore, who had followed the lead of Wally Humphrey in crossing the East Midlands to bolster the flagging Olympic side.

Mansfield-based Humphrey, who had been suspended for a while by the Auto Cycle Union (ACU) for signing contracts for both Leicester Super and Nottingham, was the Olympic's top scorer when Hall Green pulled off a narrow 28-26 victory at Trent Lane on 12 June. Eight of the nine heats proved to be 3-3 draws. The seventh heat was the decider, when Buster Brown and Joe Gooding, who had finished in second and third places behind Hall Green men in their two previous rides, lined up against Bunny Wilcox and Reg Hutchins. Gooding again managed a second place, behind Wilcox, but Hutchins forced Brown into last place, securing the two points that won the match for the Birmingham side and preventing it going into the record books as the perfect draw!

Billy Ellmore made his league debut in Nottingham's 32-22 win against High Beech at Trent Lane on 19 June. Wigfield now looked like being out for the rest of the season, but the addition of Ellmore and Wally Humphrey seemed to make up for the loss. Against a High Beech team featuring Stan Baines and brothers Phil and George Bishop, Nottingham won six of the heats, with Humphrey and Ellmore each recording two race wins, well supported by Gooding, Nobby Key and Buster Brown.

The win meant that High Beech fell behind Nottingham into the Southern League wooden spoon position. The local press hailed the victory as 'the turning of the tide', and confidence seemed to have returned to Trent Lane. Nottingham travelled to Crystal Palace on 26 June in a reasonably optimistic mood, but the confidence was shattered by a 41-12 hammering.

When Triss Sharp and the rest of the talented Crystal Palace team came to Trent Lane for the return league fixture on 3 July, the result was just as confidence sapping, with the Palace side winning 37-16. The home fans were probably relieved that the Crystal Palace match at Trent Lane was followed by three successive weeks of individual meetings – one of these witnessed a strange innovation in starting technique.

The Nottingham press reported that a 'rather curious device' was adopted for the evening's handicap events. The riders were led around the track by a rider 'in mufti', drawing behind his machine a rope which, at intervals down its length, had colours attached corresponding to the riders' colours and their handicap marks, these being assessed in yards and not by time. The riders had to keep alongside their respective colours on the rope until the flag dropped. It would not be the last time that Nottingham made the headlines for starting controversy.

When league racing returned to the track on 24 July, West Ham took the spoils by 30-24. Nottingham suffered early mechanical failures, with Billy Ellmore having plug problems in his first race and then shedding his rear tyre in the second. The visitors took the first two heats by 5-1, with wins for Tiger Stevenson and Arthur Westwood, and the home fans must have feared they were going to see another massacre in the Crystal Palace mould.

After heat six, West Ham were winning 25-11. Then the gremlins turned their attention to the Hammers, and an engine failure for Bluey Wilkinson in heat seven gave Buster Brown and Joe Gooding a chance to hit back with a 5-1.

Although it was too late to save the match, Nottingham at least gave the fans something to cheer about. Stevenson won heat eight, with Nottingham men Ellmore and Lucas behind him, but Stratton and Key got a 5-1 in the last heat to finish the match with a flourish.

A week later, Nottingham gained their final match point of the Southern League season, when they managed a 27-27 home draw against Coventry. Leicester Stadium ruined any hopes of a real revival by winning 32-22 at Trent Lane on August bank holiday Monday, although the gloom was slightly lifted by a 28-26 challenge victory at home against Leicester Super three days later.

Southampton became the latest side to lower the Olympic's colours at home with a 28-26 success at Trent Lane on 14 August. The result was particularly disappointing as the match started so well. Nobby Key, captaining the Olympic for the first time, came out in heat one against American superstar Sprouts Elder. Elder made the gate and held the lead for for three laps. Key refused to give up and gradually cut down the American's lead, overhauling him on the last lap.

Nottingham had a six-point lead at the halfway stage of the match but this was gradually whittled away, with Buster Brown stalling in the last heat to give Southampton the lead, for the first time in the match, and the victory.

A further break from league racing came when Trent Lane staged what was billed as 'England's Big Six versus Australia's Six Stars' – a challenge fixture that the local press (although not the Olympic management) optimistically dubbed a 'test match'. Australia were represented by Vic Huxley (captain), Bluey Wilkinson, Jack Chapman, Max Grosskreutz and Charlie Spinks. Ron Johnson was advertised but did not appear. Nottingham's Nobby Key replaced Frank Varey – who had broken a thumb at Glasgow a couple of nights before – in the England side. Squib Burton was the England captain and Jack Ormston, Roger Frogley, Frank Charles and Wally Hull made up the side. Australia won the match 30-24. A crowd of 20,000 was reported and the press marvelled at the fact that, despite fast times, there was not a single crash in the nine heats.

Sheffield from the Northern League provided another local derby challenge match, on 28 August, winning 28-26 in another close but ultimately unsuccessful match for Nottingham.

Nottingham did enjoy a measure of success in the Midland Speedway Cup competition, run by the Southern League Association on a best pairs basis, with riders from Hall Green, Coventry, Nottingham and Leicester Stadium. The opening round at Blackbird Road, Leicester, was won by Squib Burton and Syd Jackson from the home club, with Nobby Key and Billy Ellmore gaining second spot for Nottingham.

When the second round was staged at Hall Green, Leicester retained their pairing of Burton and Jackson, but Nottingham substituted Wally Humphrey for Ellmore. Leicester again emerged victorious, with Coventry's pairing of Jack Parker and John Deeley second, and Nottingham third, surprisingly finishing in front of a disappointing home duo of Harry Taft and Reg Hutchins.

Leicester continued their dominance in the third round at Coventry, and the final stage of the competition, at Trent Lane on 15 September, was purely a formality for the Blackbird Road pair. As it was, Nottingham took the honours on the night, scoring 12 points to the 9 for Leicester, 8 for Coventry and 5 for Hall Green. The Olympic had done enough to become runners-up overall.

The inaugural season of league racing at home ended on 25 September, when yet another London side, Wimbledon, lowered the Olympic's colours 33-21. The match was notable for the improved performance of future Nottingham skipper George Dykes, who had started the season in junior scratch races. He picked up three points, partnering Nobby Key, Wally Humphrey and Joe Gooding.

During the years when the London clubs dominated speedway, effectively until the mid-1950s, many provincial teams gained a poor reputation for their showings in the metropolis. Nottingham were generally poor away from home and in six 1930 appearances in the capital (not counting Lea Bridge and High Beech as London teams) scored only 77 points, ranging from the 7 recorded at Wimbledon to a high of 17 at Wembley! In twelve away matches, altogether the Olympic team managed 20 or more points on only four occasions. The best road performance was at High Beech, where the Olympic ran the home side to a 29-24 result, and they recorded 23 points at Leicester and 22 at Coventry.

Wigfield's absence through injury for much of the campaign was widely quoted by local journalists and home fans in defence of the dismal league record. But even with Wigfield in the saddle, Nottingham were simply far too weak. Several riders, notably Key, Gooding, Brown, Ellmore and Humphrey, were capable of winning league match heats against all but the outstanding stars from the London tracks. But there was no consistency, and an individual rider's eight-point haul on one occasion would be followed by a meagre return the next time out.

At least the Olympic did finish the season, and the enthusiasm of the hardcore supporters did not flag against the background of constant defeat. When Nottingham visited Leicester Stadium in early August, the Blackbird Road patrons were reported to have witnessed a fanaticism unmatched by any other away fans. Male and female Olympic supporters wore hats decorated with ribbons in the black and white Nottingham colours and made such a racket with their bells, trumpets, rattles and gramophone horns that the announcer had a difficult task being heard above the cacophony.

The 1930 league clashes with Leicester Stadium and challenge matches against Leicester Super could have been the start of a lasting rivalry to match the historic local derby feeling that exists between Leicester City and Nottingham Forest. Sadly, future local derby speedway matches were to be few and far between, as the Leicester tracks struggled for support.

Nottingham's 1930 survival contributed to the enviable stability of the Southern League, with Birmingham's Perry Barr the only casualty, due to complications between the speedway and greyhound managements rather than low attendances. Wembley took the championship honours from Southampton.

This was in stark contrast to the situation in the Northern League, where Barnsley, Manchester White City and Edinburgh all withdrew for various reasons at different stages of the season. Their records were retained in a final chaotic league table, in which teams completed various match totals, from the 21 of eventual champions Belle Vue to the 12 of Edinburgh, Wombwell and Rochdale.

Not only did Nottingham Olympic survive, they returned to the tapes and to Southern League action for 1931. Bill Haslam and his partners had been rewarded for their persistence in the face of poor results by a loyal crowd, large enough to make another season a feasible proposition. Haslam, in fashionable plus fours, is pictured in the *Evening News* preview of the new season, along with pictures of the ten riders he put under contract at the start of the campaign.

The most exciting new development was the return of Nottingham's prodigal son. When Manchester White City folded before the end of the 1930 season, Fred Strecker was transferred across Manchester to Belle Vue. He was declared surplus to the Hyde Road requirements for 1931 and returned to his hometown track. Bert Fairweather, previously with Wembley, was also introduced.

Nobby Key and former Leicester men Wally Humphrey and Billy Ellmore had been retained from the summer before, and when the Blackbird Road outfit withdrew from the Southern League at the end of May 1931, they were joined by Norman Kendrick, who was usually known as either 'Nobby' or Harry. Reg Lucas, George Dykes, Buster Brown, Fred Cronk, A.J. Nurse and Eddie Ford were also available.

The major doubt surrounded George Wigfield, who was in dispute with the Olympic management as the new season dawned. The local press reported Wigfield's decision to retire, a story seemingly fed to them by the Trent Lane management. The rider himself responded robustly to the claim, writing to the *Evening News* to say that 'nothing was further from his mind'. Wigfield claimed that, when approached to ride for Nottingham in 1931, he had offered his services on terms 'very nearly corresponding to those mutually agreed for the previous year'. Management obviously saw the matter in a different light.

Although the side looked only marginally stronger than in the previous season, new team manager 'Dids' Houlton was full of optimism. The new season, he proclaimed, was 'full of promise' for Nottingham, who would relinquish the wooden spoon and were being tipped for success in the new *Daily Mail* national cup competition.

That optimism seemed to be justified when the team travelled to London's docklands for their opening 1931 league fixture against West Ham. The estimated 30,000 crowd at Custom House included hundreds of Olympic fans, again complete with their black and white ribbons, who had made the journey from the Midlands in a fleet of charabancs.

Nottingham took an early lead when home rider Reg Bounds momentarily lost control in heat three and allowed Billy Ellmore to get past. Strecker collided with Tommy Croombs whilst well placed in his second ride and damaged his engine, but the Olympic side was still ahead by the penultimate heat. Sadly, Nobby Key suffered a puncture and Buster Brown fell, giving the home side the advantage. West Ham won the match 28-23, but it was, nevertheless, a huge improvement for Nottingham on the previous season's 39-11 defeat at the same venue.

The Olympic's first 1931 home match was against Stamford Bridge, and the improvement continued. The match got off to a bad start, with Key failing to coax either of his two machines into life in the pits, and out on the track, falls and machine failures threatened to turn the proceedings into a farce, with George Dykes the only finisher in heat one. Stamford Bridge took the first two places in the second race, through Arthur Warwick and Gus Kuhn, but this was cancelled out by a 5-1 for Nottingham in the next heat from Strecker and Kendrick.

Rudge-mounted Fred Strecker, pictured in the Trent Lane pits, rode at Manchester White City and Belle Vue in 1930, but returned to the Olympic for the curtailed 1931 Southern League season, when he was top scorer.

The most familiar of the Nottingham team shots shows the 1931 Southern League line-up. From left to right, back row: Ernest 'Dids' Houlton (team manager), Bert Fairweather, Nobby Kendrick, Billy Ellmore, Joe Gooding, Fred Strecker. Front row: George Wigfield, Reg Lucas.

The glamorous London outfit realised it was embroiled in a fight and, by the start of the final heat, Nottingham had a three-point lead and needed a minimum of second place to clinch the points. Warwick and Kuhn started ahead of Strecker, whose machine seemed underpowered over the first lap. When it picked up, the home rider managed to get past Kuhn to win the match for Nottingham.

Strecker, relishing the return to Trent Lane, topped the Nottingham scorers with eight, beating Frank Arthur in heat six by what a local journalist, obviously tempted by the sport's technicalities, described as 'the [Frank] Varey style of diagonal cornering'. Broadsider of the *Evening News* put the Olympic's improvement down to the influence of 'Dids' Houlton as team manager and coach. Houlton, said the writer, had, 'made himself a pal to all the riders and his influence is being distinctly felt.'

The Nottingham team photograph for 1931 shows the riders without race jackets and with faces that suggest the picture was taken after a hard match, before they had a chance to get to the showers. In terms of public relations, it contrasts badly with the sleek team pictures of Wembley, Crystal Palace and other more sophisticated outfits of the time. But at least there is ample evidence in the body language of the riders to suggest a good team spirit.

Wimbledon were crushed 34-17 at Trent Lane on 17 April, and the local press, now affording speedway almost as much coverage as that given to soccer and cricket, tantalised the Nottingham fans with rumours that the Olympic were attempting to sign Sprouts Elder, currently on his way back to Britain by sea after riding in Argentina.

The week after the Wimbledon match, Lea Bridge were the visitors. A 33-21 win for the Olympic meant that Nottingham had already exceeded their 1930 points total. In the first league table to be published, Nottingham were shown to have won three out of four matches and were lying second to West Ham. Hindsight allows us to judge that this was perhaps the high point of Nottingham's speedway history. Although the Provincial League side of 1937

The Newcastle Arms, Sherwood Street   'Phone 2355

PURE HOME BREWED ALES Brewed on the Premises.

Casks or Jars Delivered Daily.   Proprietor: LEN BROWN

LIST OF COMPETITORS.

No.	Name	Machine	District	A.C.U. Licence
2	E. Watts	Douglas	Notts.	—
3	Bill Routledge	Douglas	Notts.	—
4	Fred Cronk	Douglas	Notts.	—
5	Fred Strecker	Rudge	Notts.	31/595
8	Wally Humphrey	Rudge	Notts.	—
11	Billy Ellmore	Rudge	Notts.	—
21	Rocky Burnham	Rudge	Notts.	—
22	Rory Moore	Douglas	Notts.	31/556
23	A. J. Nurse	Douglas	Notts.	31/631
31	Joe Gooding	Rudge	Notts.	—
47	Bert Fairweather	Rudge	Notts.	—
66	George Wigfield	Rudge	Notts.	—
83	J Starbuck	Douglas	Notts.	31/930
91	P L Simpson	Douglas	Notts.	—
		MANCHESTER.		
51	Chun Moore	Rudge	Manchester	—
54	Arthur Franklyn	Rudge	,,	—
99	S. Gregory	Rudge	,,	—
100	Max Grosskreutz	Rudge	,,	—
101	Charlie Hornby	Rudge	,,	—
102	Indian Allen	Rudge	,,	—
103	Len Blunt	Rudge	,,	—

Points in League Matches have been obtained as follows :—

Fred Strecker	....	....	....	....	93
Billy Ellmore	....	....	....	....	86
George Wigfield	....	....	....	....	43
Nobby Key	....	....	....	....	31
George Dykes	....	....	....	....	31
Nobby Kendrick	....	....	....	....	28
Buster Brown	....	....	....	....	24½
Wally Humphrey	....	....	....	....	24
Bert Fairweather	....	....	....	....	14
Joe Gooding	....	....	....	....	13
				Total	387½

MANSFIELD'S LEADING GARAGE   'PHONE 315

Reg. Lucas, Nottingham Rd

Nottingham programmes in the 1929-1931 era showed a list of all the competitors in a meeting. For this Nottingham–Manchester match in 1931, all the team men on both sides are riding Rudge machines, with the second-halfers loyal to Douglas bikes.

won a couple of trophies, this success was achieved at a second division level. At the end of April 1931, Nottingham, without any major stars, without George Wigfield, and with a team largely drawn from local riders, were matching the greatest names in speedway.

Enthusiasm for the sport was really at a high point in the city. The *Evening News* recognised the strength of interest by organising a weekly speedway competition, with a £5 prize for the correct or nearest forecast by a reader of the results of the next three Nottingham matches.

Riders were in the news for reasons other than their on-track exploits. Reg Lucas was fined two guineas for driving a car in a dangerous manner in Mansfield. The magistrate, well aware of the background of the young man in the dock, said he recognised Lucas's racing abilities, but added that they were out of place on the public road!

Was unfashionable Nottingham on the brink of consolidating a team that could not only win at home but also provide close and exciting racing for the fans at away circuits, including the London tracks with their highly critical fans? Such a development could only have been for the good of the sport as a whole. But speedway is particularly susceptible to the effects of injuries and unaccountable loss of form. The cracks in the Nottingham success story soon began to show as May unfolded. After the Olympic had recorded an unprecedented three successive home wins in the Southern League, Wembley restored reality when they won a close match 28-26 at Trent Lane on 30 April.

During an intensive fortnight of competition in the first half of May, Nottingham put up a respectable performance at Stamford Bridge, losing 33-20, but then left themselves an awful lot to do when they lost the away leg of the 1931 National Trophy in round one, by 59-33 at Lea Bridge, on 13 May. In between the first and second legs of the tie, Southern League leaders West Ham came to Nottingham and won by the comfortable margin of 29.5 points to 24.5.

In the National Trophy return leg on 21 May, Lea Bridge completed the double with a narrow 47–46 victory. Nottingham looked like winning the match when Fred Strecker, with three heat wins already behind him, took the lead in the last race, only to fall and hand the honours to the visitors.

During this period of defeat and uncertainty, there was a minor flurry of transfer activity and speculation. The unsettled Nobby Key, who never really rode to his true potential in Nottingham colours, had failed to turn up for the home defeat by West Ham. Essentially a London-based rider, he now joined Crystal Palace. To offset this, the crowd at the home leg of the National Trophy tie against Lea Bridge forgot their disappointment at the defeat when they were told that George Wigfield had settled his differences with the club and was to return to the saddle.

Although the prospect of a Wigfield return caused excitement, Fred Strecker was also now making major contributions. He could be relied upon for both his spectacular riding and his consistent points scoring, home and away. When Southampton ran up 38 points to Nottingham's 15 on the south coast, Strecker was the only Olympic man who could live with the strong home side, scoring a battling 5 points.

The battered Nottingham men got a breather when the league fixture scheduled for 25 May 1931 was postponed. It should have been away at Leicester, but by this time Nottingham's East Midlands rivals had run into financial trouble and had ridden their last home Southern League fixture at Blackbird Road against Harringay on 30 April.

Amazingly, the Leicester team continued to fulfil its fixtures for nearly a month after being evicted from Blackbird Road, riding away matches in the league and completing a two-leg National Trophy round one tie against Stamford Bridge by riding the home leg at Leicester Super's Melton Road home. Inevitably, Leicester eventually withdrew from the Southern League, and Coventry, which had been operating on a non-league basis, was allowed to take on their fixtures. The switch meant bad business for Nottingham, who would have expected a better crowd against Leicester than was likely to result from fixtures against Coventry.

International Squib Burton, who had started the season late due to an overseas trip, was on the market for some time after the demise of Leicester, and Nottingham reportedly saw him as the man to restore their flagging fortunes. As with the earlier rumours about Sprouts Elder, the transfer talk came to nothing and Burton eventually signed for Lea Bridge.

When the Olympic returned to action at Trent Lane, High Beech were sent packing by 32–24 on 28 May, with Fred Strecker getting a maximum and his now established partner George Dykes securing two seconds and a third. Ellmore scored seven points and Wigfield, on his return, had five to his credit. At the end of the meeting, the victory parade consisted of Wally Humphrey, temporarily resting from track action, driving his Austin Seven motor car on to the track, with the riders clinging to the running boards of the little car as best they could.

A 29–24 home win over Crystal Palace was achieved on 4 June. Wigfield scored a 9-point league match maximum and beat Ron Johnson in a thrilling final heat to clinch the match. George and Buster Brown gated first, but Johnson overhauled Brown and by the end was rapidly gaining on Wigfield, who eventually got home by a length. At the back, Brown and Triss Sharp had been involved in an equally close tussle for the odd point, with Brown just holding off the Palace man.

Nottingham were now in seventh place in the Southern League, with 10 points from 11 matches. But despite the renewed optimism generated by the return of Wigfield and the subsequent home victories over High Beech and Crystal Palace – added to a highly respectable 29–24 defeat when the Olympic appeared at the Palace two nights after the home win – all was not well.

The *Evening News* reported on 18 June that the track management had notified the Supporters' Club that the concession of half-price admission for members to the 3s and 2s enclosures would be withdrawn forthwith. A reduced concession was offered but, according to the *News*, the terms of the letter from the management 'disclosed a serious state of affairs' at Trent Lane.

By the end of the Southern League era, another local man was starting to show good form and was established in the team proper. George Dykes, pictured on the Trent Lane centre green, was the Nottinghamshire-born son of a gamekeeper.

Despite the team having a far better record than in 1930, the Olympic Speedway was not getting enough support. The *News*, however, assured its readers that there was 'no fear' that the track would follow the recent example of Leicester Stadium and Harringay (replaced in the Southern League by a Belle Vue 'Southern' team known as Manchester) and close down. One of Bill Haslam's fellow directors, local businessman W.H. Archer, was quoted as saying that he would carry on himself rather than see the Olympic withdraw from racing.

In speedway, such a declaration was, even then, considered the equivalent of a Prime Minister assuring a cabinet colleague of his full support just before wielding the axe.

The *Evening News* judged that Nottingham's crowds were around the 5,000 mark – with about 3,000 members of the Supporters' Club costing the management 'a pretty penny' in concessionary admission. Unusually, the economics of running a speedway meeting were laid out for supporters to see. Nearly £300, said the *Evening News*, was needed to cover a league match, with the fourteen riders receiving £5 each in appearance money, points money totalling £56. Second-half expenses came to more than £60, and with overhead charges, managerial expenses, wages for ground staff and officials, printing and advertising, the figure of £300 was soon reached.

Promoter Haslam said the withdrawal of the admission concessions was 'just to allow the track to get on its feet' and was by no means a permanent move. But supporters still maintained that overall admission prices were too high, with 1s 2d the lowest.

At the same time as the wrangles over admission, Nottingham's team was being decimated by injuries. Results at home continued to be good, with further June victories over Sheffield in a poorly attended Saturday afternoon challenge match, and a 29-25 success against Southampton, including Jack Parker, in the league.

Parker was in a class of his own, winning his three heats and, in the process, beating each of the Nottingham heat leaders, Strecker, Wigfield and Ellmore. Jack, however, had poor support from the rest of the Southampton team and Nottingham riders were first past the post in the other six races. Ellmore and Wigfield were the Nottingham top scorers, with eight points apiece, but the victory was gained at the cost of a broken collarbone for George Dykes, sustained after he had won his first heat.

As July dawned, time was running out for the Olympic Speedway. The troubles were ironic, for even in away matches Nottingham were by no means the embarrassment they had proved in the first league season, and even with Dykes absent, the team was generally giving a good account of itself on its travels.

Nottingham lost 29-21 at High Beech on 27 June and travelled to Belle Vue on 1 July to meet Manchester, losing 32-22. The following evening, the Manchester side came to Trent Lane and the tables were turned, Nottingham easing home by 28-25. But, again, success on the track was accompanied by injury, and this time it was a serious one.

Billy Ellmore, a rider whose contributions were vital to the balance of the side, and who was seen as one of the steadier men in the Olympic team, was described as, 'for once, being truly reckless.' He entered a bend too fast, lost control of his machine when he hit a bump, fell heavily and suffered massive injuries, including a broken neck, collarbone, pelvis, dislocated right hip and severe internal damage. At that stage, understandably, the injuries were believed to have ended his speedway career.

A week later, on 9 July 1931, with no intervening away fixtures, Nottingham faced the current Southern League basement club, Coventry, at Trent Lane, in what was to prove the final league fixture at the track for nearly two years.

Without Bert Fairweather, Ellmore, and Dykes, Nottingham's line-up had a distinctly patched-up appearance.

The Olympic's last Southern League encounter saw them track pairings of Buster Brown and Nobby Kendrick, Fred Strecker and Reg Lucas (making his first league appearance of the season), George Wigfield and Joe Gooding, with a half-fit Wally Humphrey as reserve.

The line-up proved too strong for a Coventry side led by former Leicester man Syd Jackson. Nottingham won 30-23, to record an unprecedented fifth successive home win in the Southern League. Fred Strecker scored a nine-point maximum, and he was backed up by good contributions from Brown (8), Wigfield (7), and Gooding (5). Humphrey got a single point from a reserve ride and Kendrick and Lucas failed to score. Syd Jackson's eight points – he was beaten only by Strecker – led the Coventry scorechart.

The newly-discovered consistency at home and the fighting qualities displayed on away tracks – all achieved despite a plague of injuries – deserved better support. In the programme notes for the Coventry meeting the writer, identified only by the initials 'RSC', admitted that he had been absent from Trent Lane for the Manchester match, paying a visit to Wembley. He concluded his notes by posing a question to his readers:

> I wish someone could explain a problem that is worrying me. Why is it that 20,000 go to Wembley every week and watch the riders tearing around lonely and detached behind a huge expanse of concrete, while at Nottingham only a mere handful of stalwarts realise the thrill of being right among the roaring wonder of it all. If Trent Lane were in London there wouldn't be enough buses to bring the people here.

The bad news for the 'mere handful of stalwarts' was that their loyalty was not enough. The Coventry match was watched by another disappointing attendance. Management had made a last gesture, announcing that the admission price for future meetings to one enclosure would be reduced to 6d for the next meeting. But it was too little, too late.

Promoter Haslam and his fellow directors felt they had lost enough money. The Southern League home fixture against Manchester scheduled for 16 July was postponed for a week (it never actually took place) and, as a final throw of the dice, the directors made an attempt to sell the Nottingham track, as a going concern, to new promoters who would hopefully fulfil the league commitments. Haslam placed an advertisement in a London newspaper offering Trent Lane for sale, lock stock and barrel:

> Track. Nottingham speedway, fully equipped with stands, lighting, car parks etc, for sale. Suitable for greyhound racing etc. Apply Coope, Chartered Accountant, Albion Chambers, King Street, Nottingham.

The *Nottingham Evening News* comment on the move betrayed a touch of bitterness. The London tracks, said the article, still kept their patrons, adding: 'As they have cornered all the recognised "cracks" [no doubt a dig at the transfer of Nobby Key from Trent Lane to Crystal Palace] they will soon find themselves without competition.' It was a prophetic comment. By 1935, speedway was down to seven league tracks, all based in London except Belle Vue.

The *News* praised the Nottingham management – 'four local gentlemen', who, it said, had 'heroically carried on against financial adversity, hoping that the game would attract a regular clientele. The few thousand regular supporters who have attended have not been sufficient to meet the heavy expenses.'

The national speedway press suggested that the Nottingham closure had been forced by the management's inability to raise a team in the face of a growing casualty list. It was undoubtedly a struggle, but the *Evening News* reported that the promotion had received offers of loan riders from various sources, including former favourite Charlie Shelton from Wembley.

Had crowds justified it, management would undoubtedly have been prepared to keep running. Four tracks had already withdrawn from British speedway at this stage of the 1931 season – Leicester, Harringay, Birmingham Hall Green (after competing in the National Trophy) and Glasgow from the Northern League. The speedway authorities, eager that the sport should be seen as well organised and serious, in contrast to the early circus image, was anxious to hit on the head any suggestions of flagging popularity. The story that Nottingham had pulled out because the track could not raise a team was useful camouflage, especially at a time when journalists were less probing than they are today.

For the hard core of Nottingham fans, the fact that the 'for sale' signs were up at Trent Lane was particularly frustrating in view of the team's early season good form. When it was finally accepted that no fairy godmother was going to step in and save the track, Nottingham's record was retained in the final Southern League table, the team having raced nineteen (exactly half) of the scheduled fixtures. The published final table for the year, not surprisingly, showed Nottingham bottom for the second successive season, Wembley again winning the championship. But at the time of withdrawal, the Olympic were ninth out of eleven teams, with eight wins from 19 matches. Had the track been able to continue, and on the basis of that form, it is likely that the bottom spot would have been avoided.

The individual scorers' chart for Southern League matches, following the Coventry finale, revealed that the three heat leaders, Strecker, Ellmore and Wigfield, were all averaging about 6.5 points a match, with only patchy support from the second strings. The improved league showing could be put down to the fact that the top three men were showing greater consistency.

The 1930 squad members – Key, Gooding, Buster Brown, Ellmore and Humphrey – had often combined a couple of league heat wins with a fall or engine failure in the other of their three outings. In the 19 league fixtures Nottingham completed in 1931, there were five full maximums (three for Strecker and one each for Wigfield and Key).

Off the track, there were developments as July progressed. The Supporters' Club, still claiming 2,000 members, refused to accept that closure was inevitable, and stepped in with an offer to run the league match scheduled against High Beech on 30 July. The club offered the existing management ten per cent of the total takings after the payment of entertainment tax, with a guarantee of £100.

The club accepted that the promoters had been losing a lot of money each week, but hoped 'the sportsmen of Nottingham' would rally around the speedway. The supporters – who said they would buy the Trent Lane track for £500 and run meetings themselves if the terms were not acceptable – realised that they needed to stage a fixture quickly if they were to avoid the riders' contracts becoming invalid.

The Southern League promoters' association, not surprisingly, refused to countenance a track run by its supporters and, moreover, refused to supply contracted Southern League men from other tracks to appear at any future Nottingham meeting. Belle Vue/Manchester manager E.O. Spence did allow some of his riders, contracted to the Northern League, to appear, and on 30 July a final meeting did take place – sadly tinged with real tragedy.

Chun Moore and Charlie Hornby joined the uninjured Nottingham riders Joe Gooding, Buster Brown, Bert Fairweather and Wally Humphrey. George Wigfield was absent riding at Sheffield – a blow to the hopes of a good crowd – and the programme was made up with Nottingham juniors Ernie Watts, Fred Cronk, Rory Moore and A.J. Nurse.

The difficulty in finding sufficient riders to fill a full programme offered, fatally as it was to prove, a first racing opportunity for a young New Zealander, John Garmston – known to his friends as Jack. Garmston had come to Britain with the established rider Alf Matson, who lined up for Leicester Stadium in the early part of 1931. Although he was said to have had experience in New Zealand, the 30 July meeting at Trent Lane was claimed to have provided the novice's first – and last – competitive ride in the UK.

Tragedy struck when Garmston lined up with established team man Joe Gooding, junior Fred Cronk and Andy Nicol, in a heat of a Golden Helmet contest. According to eye witnesses quoted in the local press, Garmston was lying in third place behind Gooding and Nicol when his front wheel touched the rear wheel of the rider in front, throwing the New Zealander heavily from his machine.

Cronk, who was in fourth place, was said to have 'crashed almost simultaneously' with Garmston, although, claimed the reports, this incident was 'in no way connected with the fatal accident'. Garmston and Cronk were both carried off the track on stretchers and taken to the Nottingham General Hospital. Garmston died shortly before midnight. Cronk, reported to have broken a bone in his leg, was allowed home after treatment. When the inquest was opened, the doctor who had treated Garmston said the rider had never regained consciousness after the crash and had died from shock and concussion. There had been severe cerebral haemorrhage and extensive internal injuries.

Garmston was cremated at Wilford Hill, Nottingham, the funeral sadly attracting little public interest. It was poignantly reported that the dead man's ashes were to be sent to his mother and sister in New Zealand. Garmston had lived in Leicester, and evidence of identification had been provided at the inquest by a Mr Frank Cave. Mr Cave attended the funeral, together with Nottingham riders Joe Gooding and A.J. Nurse, the Nottingham Supporters' Club secretary Mr J.P. Middleton and former Leicester Stadium manager Norman Coates. The press expressed surprise that there was no representative from the Nottingham track management and that Garmston's mentor, Alf Matson, was also absent.

Jack Garmston's death was to prove the only speedway fatality at Trent Lane, although two other Nottingham riders were to die in speedway-related incidents during the 1930s. There was no suggestion that the fact that the meeting had been run by the Supporters' Club was in any way connected with the fatality.

The funeral coincided with press reports which revealed that the tragic 30 July meeting had also been a financial failure. The gate was said to have been quite a good one by recent standards, but still not sufficient to cover expenses. The Supporters' Club lost £50 on the deal – a considerable sum of money for ordinary people to have to find at the time.

Although the 30 July meeting was the last speedway at Nottingham for 1931, two of the Olympic riders took part in the final of the *Star* Championship, the forerunner of the World Final, at Wembley on 18 September. Fred Strecker and Billy Ellmore had qualified via an eliminating round at Trent Lane before the shutters went up, but Ellmore was ruled out on the night by the serious injuries he had sustained against Manchester, and was replaced by Kendrick.

The event – won by the sole American competitor, West Ham's Ray Tauser – was run over five heats, three semi-finals and a final. The Nottingham men were eliminated in their heat, Kendrick and Strecker finishing in that order behind race winner Tommy Croombs and Vic Huxley of West Ham. It was no disgrace, as Croombs and Huxley were to finish second and third in the final ahead of Tauser.

The saga of the Nottingham closure ran on for some time in the columns of the local newspapers, with the almost inevitable rumours of a revival. One report claimed that 'a Nottingham business gentleman' had offered to put up £1,000 to revive the Olympic Speedway if two others would do the same, but this offer came to nothing.

The *Evening News* reported that a 'northern syndicate' was interested in taking over the Trent Lane track for greyhound racing, a sport on hold in Nottingham because of the fervent opposition from the local authority and local church people.

By 5 September the Supporters' Club had accepted that there would be no more racing at Trent Lane in 1931. Chairman Wilf Joseph asked members to keep together through social events and to support what he expected to be efforts by a new limited liability company to run speedway at Nottingham in 1932.

Billy Ellmore, still on crutches, attended the 5 September meeting, when it was reported that the sale of postcard pictures of the rider had raised £7 for him. Ellmore was starting in business with his mechanic, Frank Stevenson, aiming to run motor trips from a Nottingham base. Ellmore did recover sufficiently to attempt an ultimately unsuccessful comeback for Plymouth in 1932.

The speculation about the Northern syndicate proved accurate and a dog track was established inside the speedway circuit at Trent Lane. Although unusual, this was not unique, and dogs certainly raced inside the speedway track at Exeter's County Ground. The dirt track was said to be 'undisturbed apart from a little widening, in the hope that speedway will be taken up again next season.'

The greyhound management installed a trolley hare, retained the floodlights previously used for speedway, and planned to run the dogs four nights a week. After one or two cancellations due to fog and frost, the greyhounds actually raced for the first time on 21 December, just in time to relieve unlucky punters of their Christmas bonuses.

The controversy over greyhound racing had not gone away, with both civic and church leaders convinced that the sport was little more than a form of roulette using live animals. On the opening night, among what was described as only a 'moderate attendance', the race-goers were joined by an Inspector Gregory and two detectives from the City police force. The policemen took the names of several bookmakers, apparently with a view to prosecutions under a very old by-law which prohibited betting in the city of Nottingham.

3

Long Eaton – the Pioneering Years

While speedway was becoming an established part of the sporting scene in Nottingham in the years 1929-1930, another Trentside town a few miles to the west and across the border in Derbyshire was writing its own chapter in the pioneering history of the sport.

The small lace manufacturing centre of Long Eaton became a sporting centre of some consequence in the 1880s. In 1884, a private undertaking, the Long Eaton Recreation Co Ltd, was formed and acquired thirteen acres of land between the main road to Nottingham and the parallel Station Road for cricket, football, tennis, cycle racing and bowls.

Three years later, the well-established Long Eaton Rangers Football Club won the prestigious Birmingham Challenge Cup, beating West Bromwich Albion 1-0. Some indication of the importance of the competition can be gained by noting that West Brom reached the final by defeating the powerful Preston North End side, the first ever winners of the Football League and FA Cup double.

County cricket was also played at what became known as the Recreation Ground, or sometimes the Pavilion Grounds, in recognition of the important part played in its development by the adjacent Pavilion Hotel. In July 1887, Derbyshire lost by 54 runs to Lancashire in a County Championship match at the ground. The match, which lasted for just two of the scheduled three days, was played on what was described as 'a fierce wicket'.

The next development was the opening in 1928, on the site of the Recreation Ground, of a well-appointed greyhound stadium. The local building company F. Perks, who constructed the stadium, commissioned a series of photographs of the work in progress, and this has left a splendid record of the original circuit and its seven separate wooden grandstands, offering accommodation under cover, it was claimed, for 10,000 people.

With both dirt-track and grass-track racing proving such a success throughout Britain in 1928, would-be promoters began to cast their eyes on the Long Eaton facilities. However, the first approaches seem to have been rejected by the greyhound management, and in November of that year plans were announced to introduce motorcycle, trotting, whippet and greyhound racing to another Long Eaton venue.

The Long Eaton Race Co was formed to acquire a forty-acre field off Nottingham Road, close to where the River Erewash forms the Derbyshire/Nottinghamshire county boundary. The company directors, who included the licensee of the Royal Hotel in Long Eaton, gave the promoting rights for motorcycle sport at the new venue to the Nottingham Tornado Motorcycle Club, which had already shown its ability in staging speedway-style grass-track meetings at Trent Lane, Nottingham and elsewhere in the locality.

The advent of a rival attraction stung the management of the Stadium's greyhound track into action. The Stadium venue had actually closed for a winter break, but was forced to instantly reopen to meet the competition. The two Long Eaton tracks each advertised greyhound meetings for the same day, Saturday 8 December 1928, with the same start time. Their advertising emphasised the differences between the rival attractions, with the Stadium – operating under National Greyhound Racing Club rules, and with an electric hare – promoting itself as 'the track with a season's reputation'.

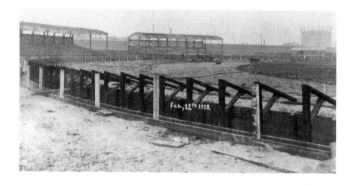

Local building contractors F. Perks left behind a collection of shots of Long Eaton Stadium, Station Road, under construction in the winter of 1928. This example shows the grandstands being built on what would become the fourth (pits) bend of the speedway track. These are now in the care of Long Eaton Public Library.

Another construction shot shows the building of the main grandstand, in front of the Pavilion Hotel which, like the Stadium, has now been demolished.

The new Nottingham Road outfit, racing greyhounds over a straight course, more akin perhaps to coursing, also promised trotting races during the meeting. Press coverage of the opening of the new circuit promised motorcycle racing 'on a dirt track' once that facility had been completed.

The two tracks continued to offer dog racing for some time, but research has so far failed to discover any reports of motorcycle race meetings of any kind at the venue next to the River Erewash. Nevertheless, it was probably the threat of falling behind the new venue commercially that finally prompted the Stadium management to reconsider its earlier opposition to speedway, and allow racing to take place in what was clearly a better appointed arena, suitable for a large crowd.

Whatever the ins and outs of the local politics, a dirt track was certainly laid inside the existing greyhound circuit at the Stadium. The first meeting on what was named the Notts and Derby Speedway took place on Whit Saturday, 18 May 1929. The *Derby Daily Telegraph* described the oval circuit as having four laps to the mile, with the straights 35ft wide and the bends 50ft wide, 'to allow broadsiding at 60mph'.

An aerial view of the completed Long Eaton Stadium in 1928, before the speedway track was added. The shot shows the railway line that ran behind the third and fourth bends, where train crews queuing for Toton marshalling yard got a free view of the racing. The stadium, as originally built, had seven wooden grandstands.

Grand Opening Meeting.
SATURDAY, MAY 18th, at 3 p.m.
NOTTS. AND DERBY SPEEDWAY.
DIRT TRACK RACING
THE TRACK, STATION ROAD,
LONG EATON.
Some of the World's well-known Track Champions will appear in
CHALLENGE RACES AND OTHER EVENTS.
SPECIAL RACING WHIT-TUESDAY at 3 p.m.
Admission 1/2 and 2/4 (including Tax).
Covered Stand for 10,000.   Enclosed Car Park for 2,000.
BUSES FROM ALL PARTS DIRECT TO THE TRACK.

Long Eaton's grand opening meeting was held in May 1929.

The new Long Eaton circuit was a significant track for the former Leicester rider Billy Ellmore. He made his debut for Nottingham at Long Eaton in a 1930 challenge match between the Olympic and the Blackbird Road outfit, and had earlier been the first man to ride seriously on the Station Road track in a demonstration before the first meeting at Whitsuntide, 1929. Later in that first meeting he created the original track record.

The first man to ride the circuit seriously appears to have been the Leicester and future Nottingham rider Billy Ellmore. In a trial before the actual racing began, Ellmore completed four laps in 90 seconds. The opening events did not greatly impress the reporter from the *Telegraph*, who described thrills as being 'few and far between'. His attitude, however, was to change for the better as the meeting progressed.

The line-up for the afternoon meeting depended heavily on Leicester riders, and Ellmore was joined on the track by Stan Baines, Wally Humphrey, Hal Herbert, Al Wilkinson and Nobby Kendrick. Arthur Westwood was the only other notable English speedway pioneer in the line-up, losing out in a match race to Billy Ellmore – the race having been re-started after Ellmore had crashed at the first attempt. Ellmore recorded a winning time of 92.4 seconds – slower than his initial demonstration ride – and this was recorded as the first official track record.

The *Derby Daily Telegraph* described the match race between Stan Baines and Arthur Westwood for the Notts and Derbys Golden Helmet, won by Baines in a time of 95 seconds, as the highlight of the afternoon. The quality of the racing won over the reporter: 'This final, and the challenge races, changed my views of dirt-track racing. With clever men like Baines, Westwood and Ellmore in the saddle, real thrills can be got out of this game.'

Two members of the Derby Pathfinders Motorcycle Club were present that afternoon at Long Eaton Stadium. The late Dennis Dunn put up a creditable performance for an absolute dirt-track novice, taking a second place to the Leicester man Wilkinson.

Dunn had been accompanied to the track by the all-round motorcyclist Alf Briggs, ninety-four years old in 2007, and certainly one of the very few surviving witnesses of that first ever speedway meeting at Long Eaton:

> The Long Eaton track was obviously new and the cinders were very deep and needed bedding in before the lap and race times could come down. It was very spectacular but I decided to stay on the spectator's side of the safety fence that day.

Alf Briggs, very much the all-round motorcyclist and clubman, in fact ventured just once onto a speedway track himself. He was put off the sport when the rider next to him on the starting grid at a Belle Vue practice session promised he would 'do' the Derby man at the first opportunity!

Alf rode in the Isle of Man TT, on the grass and in trials and scrambles, and was later heavily involved in Honda's entry into UK and world motor sport, working for the company for thirty-two years. He did, however, enjoy considerable success against the pioneering greats of British speedway on grass circuits. In the Lancashire Grand National in November 1935, he won the Tyne Cup, competing against a field including Belle Vue stars Frank Varey, Bill Kitchen and Oliver Langton.

A lifetime partnership was forged when an Isle of Man doctor's daughter, already a motorcycle enthusiast, moved to Nottingham and became enthralled by the speedway at Trent Lane. Molly Briggs, as she was to become, bought a machine, joined the Derby Pathfinders club and managed to get the rules changed to allow women to take part in club events.

Molly and Alf eventually married on December 27 1937 – after postponing the scheduled Boxing Day wedding because it clashed with a club scramble! Molly became one of the UK's top women motorcyclists, riding on the grass, in scrambles and in road races, appearing in Czechoslovakia, Spain, Austria and Germany. In 2007 the couple still enjoyed watching motorcycle racing of all kinds on television at their Derby home.

Any new fans captured for the sport by the first Long Eaton meeting did not have to wait very long for a further look at speedway racing. The second meeting on the Notts and Derby Speedway took place just three days later, on Whit Tuesday, 21 May 1929.

The undisputed star of the second meeting was Cyril 'Squib' Burton, the future England star and 1950s Leicester Hunters manager, who in 1929 was attached to the Rochdale side in the English Dirt-Track League.

At the time nicknamed 'Broadsider' Burton, he won all of his races on that Whitsuntide afternoon. Early in the meeting he established a new track record of 91 seconds, beat it in the following race, and then won the Long Eaton Flying Nine event, completing the four laps in 86.1 seconds, as the track settled down.

Syd Jackson of Leicester, later to become a full England international, was also prominent in the meeting, together with Stan Baines, Arthur Westwood and Billy Ellmore. The local press did not mention a crowd figure for the Whit Saturday opener, but the attendance for the Whit Tuesday meeting was reported as being 'about 3,000'. This was low for the era, especially as a grass-track meeting at The Elms, Ripley, on the same day attracted a similar number of people.

Perhaps, with the rival attraction of the grass track – then a major sport in the East Midlands – another speedway meeting over the Bank Holiday at Trent Lane, Nottingham, and a Sprouts Elder versus Vic Huxley match race at Leicester Stadium on Whit Saturday, too much speedway racing was on offer to the local public over too short a period of time.

Little is known about who was behind the promotion of the two Whitsuntide Long Eaton meetings in 1929. The fact that Bill Haslam staged grass-track racing at Ripley on the same afternoon suggests that he had no financial stake in the Long Eaton enterprise. There is no evidence available currently to suggest that anything further happened at Long Eaton Stadium until the late autumn of 1929, when a further attempt was made to promote speedway by a group of the Nottingham Olympic riders.

Cyril 'Squib' Burton, for so long associated with Leicester, was the star of the second meeting at Long Eaton on 21 May 1929, winning the Long Eaton Flying Nine event and beating Billy Ellmore's track record.

It is equally unclear how many meetings took place under the direction of the riders. The programme notes for what is believed to be the inaugural (and perhaps only) meeting under the new promotion, on Saturday 26 October 1929, were full of optimism. Newspaper previews of the meeting trailed the star attractions as George Wigfield and Charlie Shelton – who was at the time on peak form.

The top riders from Nottingham and Bristol had combined to race at the Empire Stadium against Wembley, in one of those curious challenge matches that speedway has regularly contrived over the decades. Wembley won the match 39-24 but Shelton took 10 points from his four rides, beating home stars Buster Frogley and Jack Ormston – a performance which no doubt helped to win the Nottingham man the Wembley contract that later came his way.

The Long Eaton fans were also promised appearances by Slider Shuttleworth of Leicester, Fred Strecker, Joe Gooding, and many of the other Nottingham-based riders. The early Nottingham rider Wilf Joseph temporarily quit racing in order to be the clerk of the course for the meeting.

The track was described as having been, 'too generously laid with cinders which, combined with the effects of a light roller, made full broadsiding a hazardous business.' The early heats saw times of well over 90 seconds, but when Charlie Shelton beat Fred Strecker in the match race final, the surface had bedded down well enough to produce a new record time of 85.4 seconds.

Shelton, as predicted in the newspaper previews, was the most successful rider on the afternoon's showing, although the subsequent reports praised the skill of Joe Gooding, who adapted his normal style to the demands of Long Eaton's 'unusually wide bends'.

Sadly, the venture by the riders to establish the sport in the Derbyshire town did not win support at the turnstiles. It was reported that the attendance was 'considerably less than 1,000'. The counter-attraction of football appeared to be too great to justify regular Saturday afternoon meetings. Saturday evenings, which might have proved a better bet financially, were ruled out as the Stadium was staging greyhound racing.

When a group of Nottingham riders promoted speedway at Long Eaton in the autumn of 1929, Wilf Joseph stepped down from riding to act as the clerk of the course and the main organiser.

The press reports suggested that the promoters intended holding a further meeting on the following Saturday, but no evidence has yet come to light that it actually took place.

Whitsuntide 1930 saw a further attempt to popularise speedway at Long Eaton. The programme for the afternoon meeting on Whit Tuesday, 10 June, again gives no indication of the promoters, or of the officials, but this time it is likely that the meeting was staged by the Nottingham Olympic management. The design and format of the publication is identical to the Nottingham programmes of the time, and it also included the Nottingham Southern League fixtures for 1930. The announcer was the Trent Lane regular W.J. Phillpotts, who rejoiced in the nickname of 'Uncle Birdseed'.

The meeting on offer was a challenge match between the Nottingham and Leicester Stadium Southern League teams, each without star men – George Wigfield of Nottingham was injured and Squib Burton and Syd Jackson of Leicester were riding in an unofficial test match against Australia at Blackbird Road. The programme notes reveal that the promoters did not intend to hold regular speedway at Long Eaton, but hoped to run occasional meetings if the attendance justified it.

Leicester, who finished well above Nottingham in the Southern League in 1930, won the challenge match by 29-20 on what was described as, 'a bumping surface, more fit for a hill climb than for a dirt track.' Times, not surprisingly, were slow, with an incredible 112 seconds quoted for the first heat (where admittedly there was only one finisher), and other races going as high as 99 seconds.

The *Nottingham Journal* said riders could not be blamed for refusing to take risks on a surface where spills were frequent.

The match was raced over nine heats, and Nottingham tracked pairings of Wally Humphrey and Reg Lucas, Joe Gooding (captain) and Buster Brown, and Rocky Burnham and Billy Ellmore, with Bill Henstock at reserve. Leicester were represented by Eric Airey and Bill Pitcher, Bill Hargraves and Cyclone Smith, and Arthur Johnson and Tom Taylor, with 'Slider' Shuttleworth as reserve.

The programme cover for the 1930 Nottingham Olympic–Leicester Stadium challenge match staged at Station Road, Long Eaton.

In heat one Lucas was the first to part company with his bike. Pitcher soon followed suit and Humphrey hit the fallen rider, whose ankle was hurt and his machine damaged. Arthur Johnson coasted home unchallenged for Leicester and went on to record maximum points and clean up the second half.

Billy Ellmore, not long since transferred from Leicester to Nottingham, after blaming loss of form on a re-designed Blackbird Road track shape, was by far the most successful of the Olympic side, recording a second place and two wins.

The *Derby Daily Telegraph* reported that between 6,000 and 7,000 people watched the challenge match, undoubtedly the best attendance so far at Long Eaton, but seemingly not enough to tempt promoters to introduce regular racing.

No further evidence of meetings after 10 June 1930 has yet come to light. Two decades were to pass before speedway became established at Station Road.

4

White City and the National League

Nottingham drew a complete blank as far as speedway was concerned in 1932, the year the rival Southern and Northern competitions 'merged' to form Britain's first national organisation.

The reason for the quotation marks around the word merged is that only two northern sides survived the sport's decline to race in 1932 – Belle Vue and Sheffield. The season was actually divided into two separate competitions, the Speedway National Association Trophy, raced in the first half of the season, and the National League Championship, decided in the second half of the campaign.

Sheffield completed their National Association Trophy matches, but closed down before the National League Championship fixtures got underway, leaving Belle Vue the only survivor from a northern set-up that at one stage in 1929 had boasted seventeen tracks. The northern circuits had declined to thirteen in 1930 and just six in 1931, of which two withdrew during the course of the season.

Stamford Bridge finished four points ahead of Wembley in the National Association Trophy, but the Empire Stadium side won the National League Championship.

All of this activity was of little consolation to the hard core of Nottingham fans, deprived of racing for the first time since the grass-track meetings of 1928.

The situation was no better for the bulk of the riders who had formed the Nottingham squad at the time of the July 1931 Trent Lane closure.

With only ten tracks operating in the National Association Trophy and nine in the National League (following Sheffield's withdrawal), league rides were hard to find. Nobby Key had transferred to Crystal Palace before Nottingham's closure, and he prospered at the South London circuit. George Wigfield rode for Sheffield in the Trophy campaign with some success, but of the others who had featured at Nottingham the previous summer, only Billy Ellmore, whose five matches for Plymouth provided just 5 points before his fitness gave out, and Fred Strecker, with 6 points from two matches for Belle Vue, featured in the averages.

Buster Brown, Nobby Kendrick, Joe Gooding, Wally Humphrey, Reg Lucas, George Dykes, Rocky Burnham and Bert Fairweather either dropped out of the sport or rode second halves at the many non-league tracks still operating. George Dykes is known to have competed at Norwich, and Rocky Burnham rode in pirate meetings at the Leicester Super track.

The late summer of 1932 nevertheless brought a definite silver lining to the clouds hanging over Trent Lane. The Supporters' Club had held together despite the lack of racing, and a specially convened meeting at a city centre hotel was told that the directors of the syndicate which operated greyhound racing at the Olympic track were prepared to finance speedway in 1933 in the National League, running the two sports under a common management.

There was even better news to come, with details of plans for an entirely new stadium. Greyhound racing, after a moderate start, had proved successful at Trent Lane. Fred Parker from Chesterfield, who promoted the greyhounds, was unveiled as the prospective speedway promoter, and it was revealed that under his direction the old Olympic Speedway stadium was about to breathe its last. The final greyhound meeting on the old track was on 17 September 1932, and work began immediately on the transformation into the White City Stadium.

When speedway
returned to Trent
Lane, Nottingham, in
1933, the old Olympic
circuit had disappeared
and had been
replaced by the new
White City Stadium,
pictured in pristine
condition shortly after
completion.

Mr Parker not only transformed the spectator facilities at Trent Lane, but also raised the
level of both the new greyhound and speedway tracks by about five feet to prevent the effects
of the flooding the riverside arena was prone to experience. Although the racing surfaces
were raised, the centre green was not, and photographs from the mid-1930s clearly show a
considerable slope from the edge of the speedway track – now more conventionally placed
inside the greyhound circuit – down to the centre.

An aerial photograph shows the new arena in pristine condition soon after completion, with
a layout very similar to Sheffield's Owlerton Stadium. An impressive main grandstand placed
centrally on the home straight is flanked by two wing stands on the first and fourth bends,
with concrete terracing on which wooden bench seats were placed, allowing advertisements
to promise 'seating in all enclosures'. Open terracing extended around the bends and along
part of the back straight. The new pits were located between the main grandstand and the
fourth bend cover, with a portable ramp built over the greyhound track for the passage of the
bikes and track equipment.

Fred Parker met Supporters' Club members in the early spring of 1933 to update them
on plans for the new season. He introduced the new manager for the controlling company,
White City Ltd, which was to run both speedway and greyhound racing. The man chosen
for the post was William R. Keene, who had been associated with speedway since its birth in
Britain.

Keene had held the position of assistant general manager of London Speedways (Stamford
Bridge and Wimbledon) and in the past had also been attached to Harringay and London
White City. His background also included spells in the entertainment business in the
UK, South Africa, the USA and Canada, his interests embracing theatres, ballrooms and
clubs.

A new stadium, National League status and experienced management was costing the
promoters a considerable sum, and Fred Parker told supporters that the price of a first-class
team was going to be high.

Receipts needed to be at least £250 from each meeting. This was £50 less than the Haslam
promotion had claimed to be the minimum in 1931, but the new enterprise would have the
advantage of more economic joint management for the two sports. It all meant that it would
be impossible to have a sixpenny gate – something which had always been very close to the
heart of the Nottingham fans. Parker was suggesting admission prices of 10*d*, 1*s* 3*d* and 1*s* 8*d*,
plus tax.

Nottingham speedway manager William Keene (left) also managed greyhound racing at the new White City Stadium for owner Fred Parker. Keene managed to make the dogs respectable in Nottingham, as evidenced by the civic guests.

But, in return for increased admission prices, he was promising Nottingham a stronger team than in the past. The new promoter said he had made clear to the sport's authorities that Nottingham must have as many star riders as other teams. The track would not run in the league unless the riders were obtained. It would be hopeless, Parker said, to begin with a losing team.

The National League would start the season with ten entrants. There were eight survivors from 1932 – Stamford Bridge had dropped out while the Chelsea football stadium was rebuilt (never to re-emerge in speedway) but Sheffield was also to reopen, providing Nottingham with a useful local derby.

Fred Parker's views on the need for teams of reasonably equal strength had also been a major preoccupation for the sport's authorities during the close season. For the first time, a measure of rider re-allocation was authorised. The Speedway Control Board issued a list of riders to be retained by each track and also created a small pool of men who were currently out of the UK. The intention was that, as and when they returned, they would be at the disposal of the board for allocation where it was judged they were most needed.

Speedway supporters out of season thrive on the steady release of team news, and the Nottingham fans in the spring of 1933, already looking forward to what promised to be a revival on a much more professional basis than they had known before, showed a keen interest in Parker and Keene's team building.

The Nottingham list was headed by Australian Jack Chapman, a steady performer with Stamford Bridge, who had ridden for Australia at Wembley in the final test of the 1932 series against England. Chapman got a point from his one ride as England won 51-42. He was joined by Ivor Hill from Wimbledon, who had previously enjoyed some success at Harringay.

Left: Jack Chapman was potentially one of the most exciting signings for the new 1933 Nottingham National League side. A steady performer with Stamford Bridge, he had ridden for his native Australia in the final Test of the 1932 series against England.

Above left: The rather severe programme cover for Nottingham's National League season of 1933.

Above right: Would Nottingham's future as a National League track have been assured with the presence in the team of an undisputed top-liner like future World Champion Lionel Van Praag? The decision to allocate Charlie Shelton to Nottingham from Wembley rather than the Aussie was not in the interests of giving the Midland club a side capable of holding its own at the top level of speedway.

Completing an influx from London would be a signing from Wembley. The Control Board ruled that either Australian Lionel Van Praag or Charlie Shelton should move from Wembley to Nottingham. When Van Praag returned from Australia it was, unsurprisingly, decided that it was the Nottingham-based Shelton who should make the switch.

Although the fans were happy to welcome Shelton back to his hometown circuit, the decision was not in Nottingham's favour. Van Praag had been a regular member of the Wembley side in 1932 and would become speedway's first World Champion in 1936. Shelton was more or less surplus to requirements at the Empire Stadium.

Fred Strecker and George Dykes were on board from the 1931 line-up, with local grass-track prospect Fred Tate. The local press was enthusiastic about the Nottingham team, but the better-informed *Speedway News* was not over-impressed with the line-up. 'On past form it is difficult to see a powerful team developing from this group,' said the *News*, adding, fairly patronisingly, that, 'at any rate, few of the men signed on will fail for want of trying.'

Nottingham began the season with new colours, red and yellow, in place of the traditional black and white, and a new nickname, the Wasps, replaced the Olympic tag. Matches in 1933 retained the nine-heat format, but scoring reverted to a 4-2-1 system. Whether or not Nottingham's old habit of losing matches would continue remained to be seen, but the *Speedway News* prediction seemed to be justified as the team lost heavily in its two opening away matches.

At Belle Vue on 13 May the Aces, spearheaded by 12-point maximums from Bill Kitchen and Bob Harrison, won every heat in a 46-16 victory. Fred Tate, riding as reserve, was Nottingham's top scorer. The six men announced earlier as forming the Wasps squad had been augmented by a further signing from London, the New Zealander Charlie Blacklock from Stamford Bridge, whose ability was well known to manager Keene. Blacklock scored a creditable three points at Hyde Road.

Three nights after the Belle Vue struggle, Nottingham appeared at West Ham and slightly improved on their Manchester performance, losing 44-18. It would have been worse only for a heat eight gift to the Wasps, when Tiger Stevenson fell and Tommy Allott was excluded, giving Ivor Hill and Fred Tate an unexpected 6-0.

It was an inauspicious start to the brave new world promised by Fred Parker and William Keene. Nevertheless, the first speedway meeting at the new White City Stadium was launched with enthusiasm by the Lord Mayor of Nottingham, Councillor H. Seely Whitby, on 18 May, well after the starting date in earlier seasons and a week later than originally intended, due to unfinished work at the circuit. The visitors were the attractive Crystal Palace team, with Tom Farndon, Ron Johnson, former Nottingham star Nobby Key, George Newton, Harry Shepherd and Joe Francis.

The Nottingham pairings for Trent Lane's first experience of National League racing were Fred Strecker and George Dykes, Jack Chapman and Charlie Blacklock, Charlie Shelton and Ivor Hill, with Fred Tate at reserve. The Londoners recorded a comfortable 38-24 victory and in the second half Key cleaned up, collecting, as *Speedway News* put it, 'most of the cash and credit'.

There was some consolation for Nottingham in the outstanding performance of Charlie Blacklock on his home debut. Small, stocky and determined, Blacklock was the only Nottingham rider to win a heat against the Palace. His two victories and wholehearted riding – he crashed in his final ride – at least promised a new Trent Lane favourite.

The 1933 National League season, now well under way for Nottingham, was run over thirty-six matches, each of the ten teams racing opponents four times. Although the White City team was again to finish bottom of a league, their performances were considerably better, at least on their home track, than they had been in the Southern League in 1930, and even away from home there was to be nothing quite like the utter humiliation of the 39-7 debacle at Wimbledon in that year.

The White City crowd quickly gained a new hero to add to their established favourites at the start of the 1933 season. New Zealander Charlie Blacklock (riding pillion in this shot) began to score heavily and he was well backed-up by teammate Fred Strecker.

The Nottingham team at the start of the 1933 National League campaign, from left to right: George Dykes, Fred Strecker, Fred Tate, William Keene (manager), Charlie Blacklock, Ivor Hill, Charlie Shelton, Jack Chapman.

The completed 1930 season had seen just two wins and a draw, and the foreshortened 1931 campaign had been a significant improvement upon that. In 1933, Nottingham managed to win a quarter of their league fixtures – nine out of 36, including a first ever away victory, at Clapton.

Nottingham made its way into speedway legend in 1933, not on the strength of a mediocre series of results and another wooden spoon, but rather because of one of the most tempestuous matches in the sport's history and a major showdown with the Control Board. The incidents at Trent Lane in early June 1933 highlighted one of the sport's major problems, and certainly contributed to an innovation which changed speedway for good.

After their poor start to the season, Nottingham raised the hopes of supporters as May progressed. On 24 May, a local derby at Sheffield saw the home side win 35-23, but Charlie Shelton scored a welcome 10 points and Fred Tate contributed his highest score to date of 7.

The next evening saw Sheffield at Trent Lane and Nottingham won a close match 33-30. Blacklock recorded a maximum and Shelton maintained his new found form with eight points. The Steel City side's chances were not helped by a heat two pile-up when Dusty Haigh fell in front of Chapman and Tate, bringing them both down. Haigh was unable to take part in the re-run and scored only two points in the rest of the match.

Wembley on 1 June was a stern test from which the Wasps emerged with little credit, losing 45-16, with only Strecker, who scored 8, enhancing his reputation with the London crowd. With hindsight, the most significant aspect of the meeting was the controversy in heat two, when Charlie Blacklock was excluded after twice being ruled to have tried to jump the gate. The consequences of Nottingham's anger over the inconsistency of referees were soon to become apparent.

Two nights later at Clapton, the Wasps showed little sign that they would ever prove capable of an away victory, losing 48-13 to a Jack Parker and Phil Bishop inspired home side.

The riders had just two days to recover from the physical and mental scars of the two heavy defeats before Wembley were due at the White City on 5 June. Supporters' hopes were boosted by the signing of Les 'Smiler' Wotton from West Ham, and the feeling on the terraces was that a third consecutive home victory might be on the cards.

The match that was to become notorious in speedway history got off to a flying start for Nottingham when Fred Strecker knocked a fifth of a second off his own White City track record, heading home Wembley's Colin Watson and Gordon Byers in 76.4 seconds. But problems, in the shape of unsatisfactory starts, began as early as the next heat.

The trouble reflected the simmering discontent felt throughout speedway that summer about starting procedures. The sport's original rolling starts had been replaced by clutch starts, at first using a flag but later utilising lights. The new method reduced the interminable false starts, which had started to drive fans away from the tracks, but creeping at the start line was rife and speedway appeared to have leapt from the frying pan into the fire.

After a bad start to heat two, Charlie Shelton for Nottingham and Wembley's Ginger Lees were both excluded by the ACU steward, with Wotton showing his worth by beating Lionel Van Praag to add to the Nottingham lead. Although their side was in front, the Nottingham fans nevertheless voiced their discontent at real team racing being replaced by a two-man match race.

The heckling and booing eventually calmed down, but to add to the fans' discontent, by the end of heat seven Wembley had turned the tables and established a 26-22 lead. With two races to go there was, however, still everything to play for. Provincial fans were always anxious to see Wembley, of all teams, beaten, and the spectators were on the edge of their seats.

The situation then deteriorated rapidly as the steward tried to start heat eight in what he believed to be a fair manner. The Nottingham pairing, of Strecker and Jack Chapman, and Wembley's Van Praag all jumped the start, but returned to the tapes expecting to be allowed to continue. Despite the support of the two team managers for a re-run with all four riders, the three were excluded, leaving Wembley's Ginger Lees to coast around on his own, to a chorus of booing, for the four points that would win the match for the visitors.

Former West Ham rider Les Wotton made his White City debut in the notorious match against Wembley which led to a temporary Nottingham closure. Wotton made an immediate impact by beating Lionel Van Praag as Nottingham took an early lead.

The last race was staged quickly, to keep the simmering anger of the crowd in check. Maximum man Wally Kilmister of Wembley won the last heat from Wotton, with the visitors' Harry Whitfield picking up third place, and Wembley had won by 35-24 in circumstances that were far from satisfactory. The interval brought real trouble, with the police needing to intervene to keep the peace as the crowd, in the words of the *Nottingham Evening News*, 'showed its displeasure'.

Nottingham's womenfolk are noted for being strong and independent characters, and that was especially the case in the 1930s, in a city where many of the better-paid jobs, in the cigarette, pharmaceutical and textile factories, were for the fairer sex. So it was not altogether surprising that the spark which set off the trouble came from an incident involving a female Nottingham fan. She asked an unidentified visiting rider for his autograph and was dismayed to find that he had rather ungraciously signed it 'Pudding'. In the decorous words of the local press, the fan made 'a retort' which caused the rider to 'dive over the railing', resulting in 'a free fight'.

After the police and officials had restored order, the second-half programme got under way. Despite the tension in the stadium, among both fans and riders, the ACU official was determined to stick to the letter of the law. Several of the scratch races were disrupted, with at least one race having just one rider left on the track, after exclusions for 'anticipating the green light'.

With racing 'rendered farcical' according to the *Nottingham Evening News*, the Nottingham management announced that the Trent Lane track would be closed and the home match against West Ham, scheduled for just three days later on 8 June, cancelled. Fred Parker told reporters: 'I run the sport for the public, who pay to see races, not to see one man ride around when the rest have been disqualified.' The experienced William Keene was equally emphatic, claiming that, 'on every other track in the country men have been allowed to carry on after making a false start, but at Nottingham they were sent off the track.'

When *Speedway News* reported the incidents, it claimed that Nottingham fans had 'howled that the steward had ruined the match against Wembley' by frequent exclusions. The official at the centre of the controversy was K.S. Topping of Loughborough. He told the press the rules stated clearly that if a man started before the green light showed, he must be disqualified:

> I can't make fish of one and flesh of the other. I have my own opinion as to whether the rule is good or bad, but while it stands I have to abide by what it says. If I had not carried out the rules there would have been a protest by Wembley, which would have been upheld.

The Nottingham management might have been accused of bluffing, something hardly unknown in speedway then or now. Time was very short and, the day before the West Ham match was due to be ridden, the White City promotion was warned by telegram that unless they fulfilled their obligations the track would be forcibly closed by the ACU and racing suspended indefinitely.

Neither side budged an inch. The Speedway Control Board called a special meeting to discuss Nottingham's complaint that a meeting could be ruined for spectators by over-zealous interpretation of the rules on starting. ACU secretary Cecil Smith declared himself 'greatly surprised' at the actions of the Nottingham management and West Ham commented that the sport needed 'firm control'.

Nottingham still refused to back down and the West Ham match was duly cancelled. The dire consequences the Control Board had threatened in its telegram were put into effect on 9 June.

The Trent Lane management was ordered to publicly withdraw any remarks made, 'derogatory to the control of the ACU.' The promoters were fined £25, ordered to pay West Ham £33 15s 10d – a proportion of the gate which had been paid to Nottingham after the early season match at Custom House – and a further ex-gratia payment of £4 was to be made to each of the riders who would have taken part in the cancelled match. The match was awarded 36-0 to West Ham. It was a harsh financial punishment, but wiser counsels had prevailed at Nottingham and Fred Parker decided to pay up.

Nottingham's stubborn stand against authority undoubtedly played its part in convincing the authorities that something concrete had to be done about the starting problem. The Trent Lane incidents had received wide publicity and threatened to damage the reputation of speedway at a time when it had largely lost the 'circus' tag.

The sport was eventually indebted to Crystal Palace chief Fred Mockford and his rider Harry Shepherd, who pressed ahead and soon unveiled a starting gate very similar to those used today. Speedway historians have recently questioned the claim that Mockford and Shepherd invented the starting gate, claiming that the technique had been used in horse racing for some time.

Whatever the facts, the Crystal Palace team introduced the idea to speedway racing. Ironically, in view of the commotion at the Nottingham-Wembley match and the subsequent posterings, the second half of the Palace-Nottingham meeting on 17 June featured the first use of the new gate, which was at first operated manually by the steward from the side of the track, but later electrified and controlled remotely by the official, out of sight of the riders altogether.

In the meantime, Nottingham resumed its fixtures on 15 June, but the temper of the fans cannot have been greatly improved when the Wasps crashed 41-18 to an extremely strong Belle Vue side tracking Varey, Eric Langton, Max Grosskreutz, Frank Charles and Bob Harrison. Again ironically, given the circumstances of the Wembley match, the first heat against Belle Vue produced just one finisher and a 4-0 scoreline to the Aces. Les Wotton suffered engine failure and Fred Strecker and Bob Harrison fell, leaving Frank Varey a clear run. Fred Tate and Charlie Blacklock were Nottingham's only heat winners in a fairly dismal showing.

Nottingham became notorious in 1933 for closing down temporarily in protest against unsatisfactory starting procedures in speedway, which had caused a near riot at the White City during a National League match against Wembley. Crystal Palace star Harry Shepherd (pictured) and his promoter Fred Mockford helped solve the problem by developing the prototype of the starting gate that largely survives until the present day.

The away fixture at Crystal Palace two days later saw a reasonably respectable performance by Nottingham, with the home side winning 41-22. Jack Chapman scored seven points for Nottingham and Charlie Blacklock contributed six.

The Wasps had a break from league racing and a rare taste of success on 20 and 22 June. Nottingham travelled to Plymouth for the first leg of a National Trophy tie and unexpectedly restricted the home side to a narrow 64-62 victory, with Fred Strecker completely dominant, scoring an incredible six-ride 24-point maximum – the best ever individual performance by a Nottingham rider. When Plymouth came to Trent Lane two nights later, Nottingham scored a crushing victory, winning the second leg by an impressive 81-42 margin, for a 145-104 aggregate score over the two legs. Plymouth actually led after three heats, and again after five, but Nottingham then gradually pulled away.

Strecker was again on top form, and this time his efforts were equalled by Charlie Blacklock, both men scoring 20 points from their six rides. Blacklock was pointless in his first ride, but recovered to win his next five races, while Strecker lost to Plymouth's Bill Clibbett in the first heat and nursed his partner Hill home in heat six to give Nottingham a lead they would not subsequently lose. Clibbett did his best to keep Plymouth in the hunt with fourteen points.

The National Trophy heroics were followed by a good performance at Wimbledon, where the Dons were restricted to a 38-24 scoreline. Ivor Hill put his knowledge of Plough Lane to good use, scoring 10 points, helped by Chapman with 5 and Strecker with 4. As on several occasions in away matches in 1933, the Nottingham cause was assisted by misfortunes for the home side. Hill and Strecker gained a 6-0 in the first heat, when Geoff Pymar fell and Huxley, who had been impeded, also came to grief chasing Hill.

Next up for Nottingham were back-to-back league fixtures against both Coventry and Sheffield. When the Brandon men visited Trent Lane on 29 June, star man Dicky Case was absent on Test match duty and the Wasps cashed in, winning 41-21 with a maximum for Fred Strecker. The speedway press reported another chaotic incident at this meeting, which seemed to underline Nottingham's ability to produce the entirely unexpected.

Charlie Blacklock overslid and ran down the slope to the centre green at some speed. The infield area contained a ramp and amazingly Blacklock hit this, travelling through the air while remaining on his machine and eventually re-joining the track! Blacklock was wearing the red helmet cover and the steward put on the red light to signal his disqualification for leaving the track.

After the new White City Stadium had replaced the old Olympic circuit, the level of the greyhound and speedway tracks had been raised considerably to avoid flooding. The slope from the speedway track to the centre green is apparent in this view and illustrates how it was possible for New Zealander Charlie Blacklock to career off the track and down the slope, hitting a ramp and flying through the air, still on his machine.

Coventry's Roy Dook thought the official had stopped the race and, when he slowed down, Blacklock went into the lead. Once again, reality intervened when the steward disqualified the New Zealander.

Two nights later, Nottingham went to Brandon when the scoreline was exactly reversed. Case was back and scored a maximum, and the Wasps best answer was six points from Strecker, who was in the middle of his best run of form of the season.

The team and supporters made the relatively short trip to Sheffield on 5 July. Ernie Evans was the local hero with a 12-point maximum as the home side won 37-26, with Blacklock (8), Chapman (7) and Tate (5) proving the best for Nottingham.

Sheffield came to Trent Lane the next evening and were beaten 39-23, with a starting gate in use at the track for the first time. The Wasps' sting was spearheaded by Ivor Hill's maximum, well supported by Blacklock and Chapman with nine and eight points respectively. Sheffield were without Squib Burton.

Any hopes Nottingham had of further progress in the National Trophy were destroyed by Wembley. The Trent Lane leg of the round two tie was held on 19 July and the Empire Stadium team romped to a 79-44 victory over the eighteen heats. The track was slippery after one of the thunderstorms so common along the Trent Valley in summer time. Ginger Lees scored 22 points and was headed home only by teammate Van Praag in heat two, and Colin Watson (18 points) and Wally Kilmister (16) were also rampant.

Wembley had opened up a 20-point lead after just eight heats. Strecker (11 points) had 2 wins and Blacklock and Tate, with a race win apiece, and Chapman, who totalled 10 points from minor placings, did their best, but it was, overall, a huge disappointment for the home crowd. Nottingham won just four of the 18 heats.

If the Nottingham leg of the tie had been an embarrassment, the Wasps were truly humiliated at the Empire Stadium, losing the match 103-22, with only Blacklock's 7 points (from six rides) representing anything like respectability.

Former Wembley star George Greenwood was allocated by the Control Board to the ailing Nottingham team in the middle of the 1933 season. Greenwood's reluctance to make the switch immediately meant he was not available for the Trentside team's crushing home and away defeats against Wembley in the National Trophy.

Wembley won all 18 heats, 14 of them with the maximum 6 points, for an aggregate 182-66 victory. Four second places – two for Blacklock, one for Strecker and one for Chapman – prevented a complete whitewash.

The Wembley debacle could well have been less of an embarrassment if former Empire Stadium man George Greenwood, allocated to Nottingham by the Control Board at the start of July, had agreed to ride for the Wasps at that date. Greenwood, who had ridden for England in Tests against Australia in 1932, was out of favour at Wembley, showing the all-round strength of the champions. His track knowledge might have added some respectability to the Nottingham showing in the National Trophy match.

Reported to be reluctant to switch to Nottingham, he was not persuaded to make his debut for the Wasps until well into August – a month after his initial allocation. Australian international Dick Wise was also allocated to Nottingham by the Board, but injuries had made him a shadow of the dominating rider of 1930.

Two nights after the Wembley thrashing, Nottingham had to somehow pick themselves up and travel to subsequent champions Belle Vue. Fortunately for the Wasps, Bill Kitchen and Max Grosskreutz were away from Hyde Road on test duty. If they had been present, Nottingham might well have been the victims of a maximum 54-9 defeat. As it was, they restricted the Aces to a 49-14 victory – Bob Harrison again showing his liking for swatting Wasps with a maximum. On this occasion, he shared the honour with Eric Langton. Strecker (5 points) and Blacklock (4) led what little opposition Nottingham put up, which amounted to just three second places.

In the team's two visits to Hyde Road on league business in 1933, Nottingham as a team failed to win a single heat or provide a single individual race winner!

The month of August was to prove something of a rollercoaster at Trent Lane, with five home matches. The Wasps saw off the challenge of both Plymouth and Clapton, then predictably lost to powerful London opposition – first Wimbledon and then Wembley – finishing the month with a narrow and unexpected home defeat at the hands of Coventry.

Fred Strecker equalled his four-lap, clutch-start track record of 76.4 seconds in heat one of the Plymouth match, which Wasps won 40-21, but Blacklock lowered it to 75.8 in a close duel with future Nottingham man Ted Bravery in the next race. Blacklock went on to record a maximum, but Strecker forfeited his chance of being unbeaten in heat eight after he had tangled with Bravery coming out of the gate. Strecker managed to stay on his machine but

Bravery was thrown heavily down the track, and the Nottingham man stayed with him until help arrived. Fortunately, the Plymouth rider was only shaken by the incident.

Fortunes were almost reversed at Trent Lane a week later when, in front of a smallish crowd, Wimbledon triumphed 41-22, with maximums from Vic Huxley and Syd Jackson. Once again, the gulf between the real stars and the journeymen of National League speedway was revealed.

Trent Lane's ups and downs continued with another 41-22 scoreline, this time in Nottingham's favour, as the Wasps faced Clapton. But it was the turn of the heavyweights to triumph again when Wembley visited on 23 August, winning 37-25 with the heat-leader trio of Lees (12 points), Kilmister (8) and Watson (8) proving much too strong. Dykes and Hill were the only Wasps' race winners and those two, with Wotton and Strecker, each managed 5 points. Jack Chapman was hurt in his first ride, when part of his machine pierced his arm, and took no further part in the meeting.

The White City track record was broken on 23 August 1933, but not in the Nottingham versus Wembley league match. The second half that evening featured an international three-way pairs' event, billed to feature England, Australia and New Zealand. In the event, the Kiwi pairing of Wally Kilmister and Charlie Blacklock withdrew, and Les Wotton and Ivor Hill took their place to represent Nottingham.

Harold 'Tiger' Stevenson of West Ham set up a new record time of 75.6 seconds when matched against Australia's Vic Huxley. Nottingham won the pairs event with 10 points, to 5 for England and 3 for Australia.

The final home match in August saw a closer finish, but Coventry took the league points with a 33-30 victory. George Greenwood at last made his home debut but was subdued, scoring just 3 points, and with Chapman missing and Blacklock managing just a couple of third places, Nottingham had no effective reply to the dominance of Dicky Case, who scored a maximum. Strecker was top scorer with 7, supported by Wotton, Hill and Dykes, all with 6 points.

Away from home, the month brought three more defeats, two of which were at Plymouth – on 1 August, when the Wasps collapsed to a 46-16 defeat, and on 29 August, when the 36-23 scoreline in favour of the Devon team represented reasonable respectability for Nottingham. In between, the Wasps were beaten 37-25 at Crystal Palace.

As on several occasions during 1933, the Nottingham total of 16 points achieved during the first visit to Plymouth's Pennycross track was inflated by a gift 6-0 scoreline. Les Wotton won heat five, followed home by Charlie Blacklock, after mishaps involving Frank Goulden and Ted Bravery. Had the race followed the general pattern of the evening and produced a 6-1 or 5-2 for Plymouth, it would have been Nottingham's lowest away total of the season, without the excuse of falling foul of one of the powerful London sides.

The second Plymouth visit was notable for one of the best individual away performances of the season by a Nottingham rider. Les Wotton, who was proving a good addition to the team, scored 10 of the 23 points Nottingham totalled in response to Plymouth's 36. Wotton's achievement on the night was overshadowed by the performance of Plymouth's new German rider, Sebastien Roth, who also scored ten and broke the Pennycross track record. Wotton did at least have the satisfaction of being the only rider to beat Roth.

In between the two long treks to Devon, Fred Strecker and Charlie Blacklock both scored eight points in the 37-25 defeat at Crystal Palace. Yet again, Nottingham were handed a 6-0 in heat four when George Newton and Tom Farndon were excluded and Strecker and his partner George Dykes boosted their earnings. It could be argued, and no doubt was in the dressing rooms and on the terraces, that Nottingham deserved some luck for sticking to the task with an obviously under-strength team.

By the end of August, Nottingham had lost all thirteen of their National League away matches, as well as the two away legs they had raced in the National Trophy. In the league, the narrowest margin of defeat was eleven points, with the best result the two-point deficit in the Trophy at Plymouth. A 44-19 trouncing at Wimbledon opened proceedings for September.

Jack Chapman, back in action, beat Gus Kuhn to give the Wasps their only heat win – this time a legitimate one without any home-team falls or exclusions – and the Australian was the top Nottingham scorer with six points, backed by Hill and Shelton with five.

The Wasps then proceeded to lift the gloom a little for the fans when they won back-to-back matches for only the second time in 1933. The Crystal Palace home match on 7 September was a nail-biting affair. Nottingham took a substantial early lead but the visitors, inspired by former Nottingham man Nobby Key with a paid maximum, scored 6-1s in heats six and seven to go in front 26-23. Strecker won heat eight to reduce the deficit to two points and Wotton narrowly beat Tom Farndon in a thrilling contest in the last race, with Ivor Hill holding out George Newton to clinch the Nottingham victory.

Chapman, returning to the side after his arm injury, fell in the first heat and was out of the team again when the Wasps travelled to Clapton two nights later. His absence hardly suggested that the long unsuccessful run away from home would end, especially given the fact that Nottingham had managed just 13 points on the same track three months earlier with, on paper at least, a stronger side.

Jack Parker was absent from the Clapton side, but the home team must still have anticipated a fairly comfortable victory. Billy Lamont made his first appearance of the season to replace Parker and, after taking some time to settle down, won his third race.

Charlie Blacklock won heat two for Nottingham, and a string of second places for Wasps' riders made the racing respectable. Clapton had established a five-point lead by the end of heat five and must have expected ultimate victory. Things went badly wrong in heat six for the home team when Norman Parker and Vic Collins tangled. Collins was unable to continue and, although Parker remounted, he had to be content with third place behind Ivor Hill and Les Wotton.

With the scores now level, Clapton realised they had a match on their hands. All the luck, moreover, was going to Nottingham. Billy Dallison, who won his other two races, was a non-starter in heat seven and, although Lamont won the race for Clapton, restoring a single-point lead, the three points for Strecker and Shelton kept the visitors in the hunt. Parker increased the Clapton lead to two points by beating George Greenwood and Blacklock in heat eight, but once again the points from the minor positions kept the match alive.

Almost incredibly, the scene was set for a last heat decider – a truly rare event in a Nottingham away match! The Nottingham pairing was the same one that had won the home match against Crystal Palace in the previous heat, and they pulled off another victory. Les Wotton held out a challenge from Wally Lloyd, and Ivor Hill beat Phil Bishop for third place, the 5-2 giving Nottingham a 32-31 victory.

Manager William Keene and the handful of Nottingham fans at Clapton celebrated the rare taste of success. Keene said:

> It is a nerve-racking job to ride in the last heat twice in three days and know that the whole bag of tricks rests on your shoulders and to realise that one mistake will cost the team the match. Les and Ivor deserve a very hearty pat on the back.

Wotton, in fact, got more than a pat on the back. In addition to the cash for the seven points he scored at Clapton – a total he shared with other Nottingham race winners Ivor Hill and Charlie Blacklock – he was presented with a pound note by a supporter and invited to 'have one with me'.

The team and the fans came back down to earth for the visit of Belle Vue on 14 September. Both sides were weakened, with Frank Varey and Eric Langton for the Aces and Les Wotton at Wembley for the *Star* Championship final. Jack Chapman was the other Nottingham qualifier but was ruled out by his injury. Fred Strecker should have gone to Wembley as reserve but, in view of Nottingham's inability to make up a team without him, the organisers allowed Strecker to stand down.

The big difference was that Belle Vue, the eventual champions, were still able to track stars like Max Grosskreutz, Frank Charles, Bill Kitchen and Joe Abbott, illustrating the great gulf between the more powerful National League teams and the weaker sides like Nottingham and Plymouth.

Strecker, obviously showing no resentment at being at Trent Lane rather than the Empire Stadium, beat Charles in heat one and his partner George Dykes took third place from a subdued Grosskreutz to give Nottingham a 5-2 race win. The hopes of the home crowd were raised further in the next race when Blacklock and Greenwood outpaced Gregory and Abbott, giving Nottingham an 11-3 match lead. Blacklock fell while ahead in heat four, but the home side were still ahead after heat six. A 6-1 for Charles and Gregory in heat seven and a 5-2 from Abbott and Charles in heat eight were enough to make the final heat, which Blacklock won from Kitchen and Bronco Dixon – purely academic – and the Aces finally won 34-29.

Blacklock had two wins apart from his fall, Strecker also scored eight and George Greenwood contributed a useful six points. Australian Dick Wise was named as reserve for Nottingham in this match. Adelaide-born Wise, a Test rider in the 1930/31 period, had made his debut for Sheffield in 1930 and subsequently rode for Harringay, Southampton and Stamford Bridge before finding his way to Trent Lane. A rider of undoubted pedigree, his career had certainly lost its impetus at this stage and he struggled to score points.

At Wembley on the same evening, the in-form Les Wotton got the *Star* Championship final off to a sensational start and restored some of Nottingham's reputation in London by beating Dicky Case, Vic Huxley and Tommy Croombs in the fastest time of the night. In his semi-final, Les came second to the eventual Championship winner, Tom Farndon of Crystal Palace.

The Trent Lane side lacked both consistency and luck at this stage of the season. George Greenwood top-scored with ten points in a hard-fought 30-30 draw against West Ham, a week after the Belle Vue match. Wotton won his first race but then his chain broke while he was leading heat four. Arthur Atkinson won heat six, in which Strecker was excluded for crossing the white line and Bluey Wilkinson suffered engine failure whilst in the lead. George Dykes tried to push home for two points, which could have made the difference to the result, but he failed to beat the time limit.

When the Wasps went down to Custom House a few days later, the Hammers won 43-16, but Les Wotton again enhanced his reputation, this time on his former home track, by scoring eight points – half the team total.

Jack Chapman, in and out of the side through injury, returned against Wimbledon at the White City on 28 September. Hill and Wotton put Nottingham into the lead with a 6-1 over Kuhn and Sawford in heat two. Charlie Blacklock claimed a stunning victory in heat three, with George Greenwood snatching third place, giving the Wasps a five-point lead.

The home crowd must have felt that their luck was turning when Charlie Blacklock's engine failed at the end of heat five, but his momentum allowed him to cross the line ahead of Gus Kuhn. It was, however, the end of Nottingham's good fortune. Falls and engine failures in the last four races for the Wasps – Blacklock's hopes of a maximum disappeared when he collided with Geoff Pymar in heat seven – meant four race wins for the Dons and a match victory by 35 points to 27. Vic Huxley was unbeaten for Wimbledon.

There was worse to follow for the home fans in the second half when Les Wotton broke a collarbone. Wotton could not avoid teammate Ivor Hill when he fell, and Les was then struck by Charlie Blacklock's wheel.

The accident ensured that it was a somewhat demoralised Nottingham side that lined up at Coventry on the last day of September, without Wotton and Chapman. Dicky Case missed his first race after being involved in a car accident en route to Brandon, but made no mistake in his other two rides. Stan Greatrex got a maximum and Roy Dook, Cyril Taft and Bill Pitcher also won heats. Nottingham's response was five second places and seven thirds in a miserable 45-17 reverse.

The curtain came down on the home season on 5 October, with supporters at least able to cheer a 40-18 home win over Clapton. The match was a triumph for Charlie Blacklock in what was to prove his final appearance for Nottingham. The New Zealander recorded a 12-point maximum in the league fixture and then won all four of his second-half rides when, with partner George Dykes, he won the Nottingham Pairs championship.

There was a certain amount of relief at the Clapton match that, despite the poor results and the mid-season shenanigans with the ACU and the Control Board, Nottingham had survived the full season.

There were both serious presentations to the riders on the centre green and typical speedway last-night-of-the-season jokes, with a comedy race between 'Oo flung rhubarb', the Chinese champion (alias Fred Strecker), and 'Tishy Mix', the Eskimo flyweight (or Charlie Blacklock).

Les Wotton was noticed in high places with his performance in the *Star* Championship final. Wembley supremo Arthur Elvin (not yet Sir Arthur) awarded Les a special cup to mark his achievement in recording the fastest time of the night at the final, sending it to Nottingham to be awarded to the rider in front of his own fans. Wotton also collected the Nottingham Riders Championship trophy.

A plaque was presented to Jack Chapman – back again from injury – by the Australian Speedway Board of Control for his Test match services. Chapman rode in four of the England-Australia tests in 1933, at Belle Vue, Crystal Palace, West Ham and Wimbledon, and became the only man to figure in official Test matches while a contracted Nottingham rider.

George Greenwood's full international appearances for England were with Wembley in 1932, while Les Wotton was to win his England caps from 1934 onwards, after leaving Nottingham. The other England internationals to appear in Nottingham colours (before being honoured) were Nobby Key and future World Champion and Wembley star Tommy Price, while, for Australia, Billy Lamont and Dick Wise were capped while attached to other clubs.

Nottingham's season ended with yet another pasting in London – 46-17 at Wembley. The suffering Empire Stadium fans saw Nottingham steam-rollered three times in 1933 – including the National Trophy leg – and the Wasps managed just 55 points from the three matches in response to Wembley's 194!

As the fans caught the tramcars and ferry boats back to the city after the Clapton match, the sadness of the end of the season must have been deepened by feelings of pessimism about the future. Would there be another season of league racing at White City?

William Keene admitted in his final set of programme notes that the optimistic management pronouncements at the start of the season had been purely an (understandable) public relations exercise:

> Being at the bottom of the league was almost inevitable. We started with a team which could not hope to win matches. Had we been able to include George Greenwood from the start it would have been quite a different story and I fancy Nottingham would have been at least three rungs up the ladder.

He added that many people had asked him what was going to happen in 1934. Keene said that for his own part he was cautiously optimistic – perhaps again mainly a PR exercise. He told supporters:

> I am unable to say anything definite. As you all know, the support we have had has been very poor indeed. Rather a puzzle to know whether speedway racing is wanted in Nottingham. My own opinion is that we shall run again next year, but I have not the last word in this matter.

When the final league tables and individual rider averages were published, the National League was shown to have two distinct sections. The top group of sides was strong, from champions Belle Vue down to fifth place Clapton – bolstered by brothers Jack and Norman Parker – and sixth place Wembley.

The next three sides, Coventry, Sheffield, and Plymouth, all finished on 22 points and were not that much stronger than Nottingham, who managed 19. But even Coventry, in the shape of the inspirational Dicky Case, and Sheffield, in the form of Squib Burton and Eric Blain, managed to get representatives into the top twenty of the individual averages.

Plymouth's Bill Clibbett was the Devon side's best scorer, coming in at number twenty-three, but the best Nottingham could manage was Charlie Blacklock at number thirty-three.

Blacklock averaged less than six points a match and the Wasps' runner-up, Fred Strecker, was under five points a match.

It was 1930 and 1931 all over again, with the Wasps' heat-leaders able to more than hold their own against the bulk of National League team men, at home in particular. However, they were usually hopelessly outclassed, especially on away tracks, by the star men. No one, over the course of a full season, could return consistently high scores.

It was bad enough that Nottingham lost half their home matches – thus making it unlikely they would hold together a large enough crowd to ensure that league speedway would return. But it is a detailed analysis of the away performances that really shocks, and suggests that a Nottingham absence from the league in 1934 would not disturb fans at the other circuits.

The league table shows that the Wasps lost 17 of their 18 away fixtures and that their points deficit was huge. What the table does not show is that the Nottingham team won only 26 out of the 162 heats raced on away tracks, with the highest success rate being six heat wins in two appearances at Sheffield and the worst being a zero return in two visits to Belle Vue.

On an individual basis, Nottingham riders won just 28 of the 162 league match heats. Les Wotton won 7, Charlie Blacklock 5, Ivor Hill and Fred Strecker 4, Jack Chapman 3, George Greenwood and Charlie Shelton 2, and Fred Tate won 1.

Blacklock averaged just over 5 points a match overall – more than 7 points a match at home but less than 4 points away. Second-rated man Strecker had a similar record.

5

International Interludes

For the majority of Nottingham speedway riders, like their counterparts across the country, the close season brought the necessity to find work, to rebuild motors and frames and, in some cases, to recover from injuries.

For others, it was a time to seek speedway success in sunnier climes. If the English speedway scene was a magnet for Australians and Americans, the tradition of touring parties of Englishmen seeking fame and, more particularly, fortune abroad became established in the early days of the sport.

The first Nottingham rider to race abroad was Joe Gooding, a local who had led an adventurous life long before taking up speedway racing. Towards the end of 1917, aged fourteen and a half, Joe enlisted in the old Establishment Boy Service of the wartime Royal Flying Corps – a grouping designed to form the nucleus of engineer officers for the fledgling air service.

He completed his apprenticeship in what had now become the RAF in 1921 and was posted successively to Egypt, Iraq and India. His first motorcycle, an ex-War Department Douglas, was acquired in Iraq, and when he returned home to Nottingham he got a job as a tester with the Raleigh Cycle Company, which was then introducing motorcycles to its range.

Joe was due to compete in the Isle of Man TT races in 1929, but the start of dirt-track racing at the Olympic Speedway proved a greater attraction.

Gooding really made his name when matched against the great American Sprouts Elder in a heat and then in the final of a handicap challenge at Trent Lane. Elder was impressed and recommended Joe for a place in a party of riders going to South America, where speedway had become established in late 1928.

Joe sailed for Buenos Aires, Argentina, in October 1929, aboard the Royal Mail Ship *Asturias* in a party including the Langton brothers, Eric and Oliver, and Bob Harrison from Belle Vue, Arthur Westwood, Billy Lamont, Dick Wise, Ernie Evans, Frank Goulden, Geoff Kilburn and Tom Wainwright. The party was led by Frank Hunting, brother of the pioneer promoter A.J. Hunting.

After a rip-roaring voyage, during which the riders found it difficult to always conform to the social etiquette demanded, the party linked up with Elder and Frank Varey, who had travelled separately, and prepared to race on the red-brick dust surfaces surrounding football pitches at the two tracks operating in Buenos Aires.

The opening meeting at the Huracan track was set for 26 October, but a few days before, disaster struck for Joe Gooding. Practising on the circuit with teammates, Joe was unable to avoid the fallen Arthur Westwood's machine and he broke his collarbone, breastbone and several ribs in the resulting crash.

Joe was in hospital for three weeks and out of action for a total of nine, missing a good part of the Argentinian season, which included matches between the Huracan track and a team representing River Plate. Once he was fit again, Joe rode for Huracan with Sprouts Elder, Frank Varey, Westwood, Frank Goulden, and Tom Wainwright. Australians Billy Lamont, Ernie Evans and Dicky Wise formed the core of the River Plate side, together with the Langton brothers, Geoff Kilburn and Bob Harrison.

Left: Joe Gooding as a fourteen-and-a-half-year-old member of the Royal Flying Corps during the First World War.

Below: Joe Gooding (centre), pictured with Eric (left) and Oliver Langton (right) at the first practice session of the tour in Buenos Aires. At the next corner there was a pile-up and Gooding broke his breastbone, collarbone and two ribs, and was out of action for some weeks.

On board the Royal Mail ship *Asturias* en route to Argentina in the autumn of 1929. Joe Gooding is second from right in the back row and next to him, on the far right, is future Nottingham promoter Arthur Westwood.

In the early part of 1930 a new track was opened in Montevideo, Uruguay, and Joe, Eric and Oliver Langton, and Bob Harrison moved on. The riders lived out of the city in a small resort, Malvin, and Joe waxed enthusiastic about the lifestyle when recalling his experiences many years later:

What a beautiful coast it was – semi-tropical, with wonderful sands, and the huge Atlantic rollers breaking gently on the shore. It was certainly a great place to spend the winter, and what nights there were under the Southern Cross.

Gooding was greatly impressed with South America as a whole, telling reporters on his return to Nottingham that he did not see a single drunken man or any poverty, that the roads compared with any in England and the shops were 'immensely superior'.

Joe eventually captained the Nottingham team in its Southern League days, a position which won him plenty of open bookings at the London area tracks. He was transferred to Southampton when Nottingham closed and later rode for Lea Bridge. His fellow tourist on the Argentina trip, Arthur Westwood, had opened a couple of tracks in France, and Joe rode there on weekend excursions across the channel.

But, with speedway undergoing one of its periodic recessions in the mid-1930s, Joe decided to rejoin the Royal Air Force, serving until 1947, and was lost to the sport.

Meanwhile, other Nottingham riders caught the bug for international travel. Although the future of speedway at White City was in the melting pot as the 1933 season ended, for at least some of the Trent Lane riders there was an opportunity to forget the uncertainty and the rigours of the English winter.

Nottingham's Aussies, Jack Chapman and Dick Wise, returned 'down under' for the Australian 1933/34 season, and New Zealander Charlie Blacklock also headed for the southern hemisphere. They were joined, on various passenger vessels, by a number of both Australian and English riders taking up engagements at various Australian tracks.

Charlie Blacklock, Fred Strecker and Charlie Shelton pictured before setting out for Australia in the autumn of 1933.

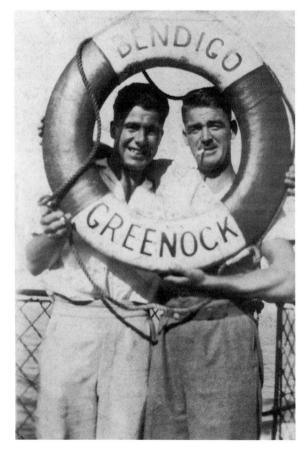

Fred Strecker and Charlie Shelton pose inside an *SS Bendigo* lifebelt on route to Australia in the autumn of 1933.

The Greenock-registered *SS Bendigo* left the shores of the UK in the late autumn of 1933, with passengers that included a lively bunch of English and Australian riders.

On board were Vic Huxley, Chapman, Billy Lamont, Dick Case, Max Grosskreutz, Bill Kitchen and Geoff Pymar. When the ship called at Port Said, four more English riders joined the party – Cliff Parkinson and the Nottingham trio of Fred Strecker, Charlie Shelton and Ivor Hill. Why the four had not joined the ship in the UK, and how they travelled to Egypt, is lost in mists of the seventy years that have elapsed. Perhaps the decision to go abroad was a late one.

The ship paused for a while at Port Said and allowed the speedway group to go sightseeing. A press photograph of the time shows Ivor Hill, Max Grosskreutz, Mrs Grosskreutz, Dicky Case, Mrs Case, Mrs Huxley, Vic Huxley, Fred Strecker and Charlie Shelton sitting around a table on a café terrace, with both Strecker and Shelton resplendent in the traditional Egyptian fez. A rather apprehensive waiter stands behind the party.

The waiter's apprehension was no doubt shared by the captain of the *Bendigo* – a vessel rather appropriately named after the Nottingham-born bare-knuckle prize fighter. The voyage onwards to Australia was a lively one, according to a surviving account written by an anonymous woman passenger – quite possibly drawn from the ranks of the riders' wives.

Today's top speedway riders live a truly global life, reaching their destinations, however far-flung, in a matter of hours in the age of jet travel. The riders of the 1930s enjoyed a more leisurely high seas existence on their travels.

The *SS Bendigo* offered many diversions for a party of fit, boisterous young men, some of whom were on their first journey outside Britain. Dart throwing was one favoured pastime, initially into the smooth, well scrubbed and holy-stoned deck itself, until the ship's alarmed first officer provided a square of board.

Max Grosskreutz had been the inspiration behind the purchase of fireworks during a run ashore in Malta, and these were let off during an on-board dance. It was reported that the ship's captain did not appreciate the humour of the situation and Grosskreutz and Vic Huxley, identified as the ringleaders, found themselves facing a mini court martial!

Deck tennis, bathing in the ship's pool, cards and a fancy dress ball, with Grosskreutz, Dick Wise and Billy Lamont dressed as 'three old salts – Eno's, Epsom and Kruschen', give a good flavour of the times. Some regret was expressed that not all of the riders danced, but Ivor Hill, Charlie Shelton and Jack Chapman kept up the good name of Nottingham in this respect.

Although the meals on board were described as ample, Grosskreutz was said to regularly experience 'a considerable sinking feeling', about 11.30p.m., that could only be allayed by a copious supply of ham sandwiches from the ship's butcher and numerous bottles of beer. 'Many a gay little supper' was held around midnight on the stairs leading to the lower deck, apparently to the horror of the more staid inmates of nearby cabins, who wanted to sleep.

The ship called at several Australian ports where, at each landfall, 'swarms of Australian speedway personalities came on board.' The riders who had made the voyage from Britain eventually split up to fulfil their various engagements – Jack Chapman went to ride in Adelaide, and Max Grosskreutz and Bill Kitchen in Melbourne, while Dicky Case and his wife travelled overland from Sydney to Toowoomba in Queensland, eight days' hard riding on a motorcycle combination, spending Christmas in the bush. Vic Huxley and George Greenwood spent much of the winter in Brisbane – Huxley's home town.

Fred Strecker, Charlie Shelton and Ivor Hill remained in Sydney, where they were contracted to the Empire Speedway Pty, the company owned by Johnnie Hoskins and Frank Arthur, which was promoting at the Speedway Royal (later spelled Royale) at Sydney Showground, and also at the Sports Ground at Newcastle, New South Wales. Huxley and Greenwood were also under contract to the Empire concern, in addition to their Brisbane activities.

Programme

Official State Championship

**For the A.C.U. One Mile State Championship Sash
and "The Johnnie Hoskins Cup"**

THE GRAND PARADE.
LED BY THE TEAM'S MASCOT, IAN HOSKINS.
AGED NINE.

ENGLISH RIDERS:	AUSTRALIAN RIDERS
"TIGER" STEVENSON (Capt.)	CLEM MITCHELL
GEORGE GREENWOOD	(Capt.)
SYD. JACKSON	BILLY LAMONT
CLIFF PARKINSON	BLUEY WILKINSON
MICK MURPHY	DICK CASE
FRED STRECKER	DICK SULWAY
CHARLIE SHELTON	KEN KIRKMAN
	WALLY LITTLE
	JACK SHARPE
	RAY TAYLOR
	IRON MITCHELL

Nottingham men George Greenwood, Fred Strecker and Charlie Shelton competed in the New South Wales official State Championship at the Sydney Speedway Royal, promoted by the legendary Johnnie Hoskins, whose son Ian is listed as the mascot. Other competitors, Cliff Parkinson and Billy Lamont, were later to appear in Nottingham colours.

On Saturday 23 December 1933, Newcastle's Christmas meeting featured a Kangaroos versus London match, run over six heats. The Kangaroos featured Vic Huxley (captain), Billy Lamont, Frank Arthur, Bluey Wilkinson, Clem Mitchell and Dick Sulway. London tracked Tiger Stevenson (captain), George Greenwood, Reg Bounds, Fred Strecker, Geoff Pymar and Charlie Shelton.

At the Sydney Showground a month later, the Kangaroos were matched against the Tigers, with Cliff Parkinson and Syd Jackson added to the English squad. On Saturday 17 February – the last meeting for most of the English riders based at the Showground – the programme featured the official New South Wales Championship for the ACU One Mile State Championship Sash and the Johnnie Hoskins Cup, together with a nine-heat Australia versus England challenge.

The colourful Hoskins was not above a little mild mockery of the flat, East Midlands accents common to home-bred Nottingham riders. He asked his programme readers if they knew what a 'doomper' was, explaining that Shelton and Strecker had been riding surfboards at Bondi Beach when they were picked up by a big wave and 'doomped down so hard they could almost hear St Peter saying "come in".'

Fred Strecker and Charlie Shelton were said to have spent much of their spare time sea-bathing, while Fred was also attracted to the sea angling in the warm waters of Sydney Harbour. An article published at the time said Charlie Shelton had been 'much intrigued' by the local 'milk bars' and was planning to introduce 'those insidious milkshakes' to his speedway pals at home. The contrast to Nottingham in winter could hardly have been greater.

Most of the England-bound riders returned to Europe on the *SS Hobson's Bay*, with Tiger Stevenson deciding to return to the UK via the United States. When the Nottingham-attached riders did return, it was to find that their track had closed again.

6

Pirates on the Trent?

William Keene's 'cautious optimism' in the autumn of 1933 about the future of speedway at Nottingham had proved to have no foundation. White City was by no means the only circuit to throw in the towel, and there were licence transfers as well as closures before the 1934 season began.

Just six of the ten 1933 National League tracks continued – Belle Vue, Plymouth, Wembley, West Ham, Wimbledon and Lea Bridge – the latter reverting to its original name after operating as Clapton. The Crystal Palace promotion was transferred to a new South London venue, at New Cross, and Harringay and Birmingham Hall Green reopened to make a league of nine teams. During the course of the season, the Control Board withdrew the Lea Bridge licence, but Walthamstow stepped in to take over the fixtures.

The riders from the closed tracks at Nottingham, Sheffield and Coventry were dispersed among the operating National League sides. Les Wotton, Fred Strecker, Jack Chapman, Charlie Blacklock and Fred Tate went to Hall Green, while George Greenwood returned to Wembley.

For many of the lesser lights of the 1933 Nottingham team, as in 1932, rides were hard to come by, despite the number of non-league circuits operating. Even for the established names, there was no guarantee of a team place, and many of Fred Strecker and Fred Tate's appearances in Birmingham colours came in the Reserve League that also operated in 1934.

There were also the inevitable transfers during the course of the season, which saw Charlie Blacklock, originally allocated to Hall Green, line up for Harringay.

Nottingham is listed in some quarters as having operated in 1934 on an open licence. Some meetings did take place at Trent Lane, but there is reason to doubt whether or not they were actually licensed by the Speedway Board of Control and the ACU.

Five meetings at the White City Stadium have actually been traced, which were run in August and September 1934 as a series of 'inter-county events', with Nottinghamshire meeting Warwickshire, Staffordshire, Sussex, County Durham and South London.

The meetings were promoted by the Nottingham Motor Sports Club, and the honorary secretary was listed as A.F. Piper, an official of the old Nottingham Supporters' Club at the time of closure.

The programmes published for the meetings are very basic, with no articles or notes, and the list of officials contains none of the names of the men who officiated during the 1933 National League season. There is certainly no mention of the track having a Control Board or ACU permit.

The riders listed in the programmes are unrecognisable, with the exception of three men. Rocky Burnham and Buster Brown had been on the fringe of the Nottingham team ever since speedway was introduced to the city. Neither was likely to find team rides anywhere in 1934, so riding in what may well have been unlicensed meetings was not a major risk. Brown was to be killed in an air raid on Nottingham in the Second World War, while Burnham played a part in the development of post-war rider Lionel Watling, who gained First Division experience with Birmingham and Norwich, in addition to riding in the lower divisions for Tamworth, Long Eaton and Leicester. The third recognisable name was that of Archie Shelton, the younger brother of Charlie.

NOTTM. "MOTOR-SPORTS" CLUB
(ORGANISERS)

White City Speedway
TRENT LANE, NOTTINGHAM.

VOL. ONE.   **No. 5.**

Officials :
Clerk of the Course : H. THOMPSON
Starter : H. FELLOWS
Timekeeper : L. JARVIS
Lap Scorer : S. E. TREECE
Doctor : Dr. FOLEY
St. John's Ambulance Brigade.

Should it be necessary to abandon the meeting through any cause prior to the sixth race in the programme, tickets for a subsequent meeting will be issued at the exits. In no circumstances will any money be returned.
Betting is absolutely prohibited at all meetings held at Nottingham Speedway
The Promoters reserve the right to refuse admission.

TRACK 380 YARDS.

4 LAP RECORD CLUTCH START, 75 3/5secs.
TIGER STEVENSON, 26 AUGUST, 1933.
1 LAP RECORD FLYING START, 18 2/5 secs.
1 LAP RECORD CLUTCH START 20 4/5 secs.
BILL WYKES, 29 AUGUST, 1934.

WEDNESDAY, 12th SEPTEMBER, at 8 p.m.
OFFICIAL PROGRAMME—THREEPENCE.

Hon. Secretary : A. F. PIPER, 164 Wilford Grove, Nottingham.   *Phone 85341*

GREYHOUND RACE MEETINGS
are held at the WHITE CITY every Monday, Tuesday, Thursday, Friday and Saturday at 7.45 p.m.

Best Dogs,   Popular Prices of Admission.   Best Racing

A programme cover from one of the 'pirate' meetings held at the White City Stadium, Nottingham, in 1934.

Rocky Burnham, who usually struggled to find a team place at Trent Lane, was one of the few Nottingham riders to compete in the 1934 'pirate' meetings under his own name.

George Dykes competed in the 1934 unlicensed
events under the pseudonym of J. Trent. George was
also riding during this period under a different name
at the equally unlicensed track at Norwich.

Some copies of the rare programmes for the 1934 meetings have pencilled notes alongside
the 'official' names of the listed riders. In the edition, published for the Nottingham versus
County Durham match on Wednesday 12 September, it is suggested by the unknown
writer that 'D Pink' is in fact Fred Tate, 'A Johnson' is Fred Strecker, the fairly unimaginative
pseudonym of 'J Trent' covers the identity of George Dykes, and 'B Roberts (captain)' is Ivor
Hill. Charlie Shelton and Harold Brailsford may also have taken part in the meetings.

Nottingham lost to Warwickshire 26-28 in the nine-heat contest, beat Staffordshire 34-20,
Sussex 28-26, Durham 34-20 and lost to South London 26-28. The meeting against South
London on 19 September was the last for which any evidence can be traced, although the
programme advertised an unspecified attraction the following week.

The match against Staffordshire was a re-run of a meeting abandoned after six heats because
of bad weather, when Nottinghamshire were leading 22-11. In the re-run meeting, Roberts
(Hill) scored a nine-point maximum, and he recorded a further eight points in the match against
Durham. Johnson, or Strecker, had eight points against Durham and four against Staffordshire,
while Trent (Dykes) had eight against Staffordshire and six against Durham.

Heat times varied between 76.1 seconds, recorded by a Durham rider listed as 'D McPhail',
and 83 seconds. These were more or less in line with average race times in National League
racing in 1933, when the track record for a four-lap, clutch-start race, of 75.3, was set by Tiger
Stevenson of West Ham.

The times add weight to the argument that the 1934 White City matches were not being
contested by teams of unknown novices.

The meetings included sidecar racing and car racing, with a record shown in the
19 September programme of 22 seconds for a one-lap, flying-start circuit by a car (whether it
was a midget car or some other type of four-wheeled vehicle is unknown).

The programme also listed a one-lap, flying-start record of 18.2 seconds and a one-lap clutch
start of 20.4 seconds for a speedway machine ridden by one Bill Wykes of Staffordshire.

In contrast to the way the earlier Trent Lane meetings in the Southern and National Leagues
were covered by the local press, with columns of match reports, previews and comment, the
1934 meetings resembled, in space and style, the way the newspapers would cover grass-track
events locally.

It is difficult to be conclusive, but the evidence for the 1934 activities suggests that pirates
did indeed launch the Jolly Roger on the banks of the River Trent.

7

Provincial Revival

Speedway, nationally, hit a pre-war numerical low in 1935. The one division operating – the National League – was reduced from the nine teams of 1934 to just seven.

Birmingham Hall Green, Plymouth and Lea Bridge/Walthamstow withdrew, leaving six London clubs in the form of Wembley, Wimbledon, West Ham, New Cross, Harringay and newcomers Hackney Wick.

The Londoners were, nevertheless, all easily out-raced by the seventh member of the league, the hugely glamorous and successful Belle Vue Aces. The northerners repeated their 1934 triple crown of success in the National League, National Trophy and the ACU Cup.

There were no open meetings at Nottingham in 1935, and the year opened with sad news for the remaining speedway fans on Trentside. Charlie Blacklock, whose form in Nottingham's torrid National League campaign of 1933 had often proved a rare bright spot in a difficult season, had been killed racing in Australia.

Blacklock had fitted in well with the local Nottingham riders and was a particular friend of Fred Strecker. He was a protégé of Roger Frogley, who discovered him during a winter trip down under. Riding in Sydney in January 1935, where the English test team was also currently appearing, he was involved in a spectacular crash and received fatal injuries when his own machine fell on top of him.

Speedway News, in its obituary notice, described Blacklock's riding as 'earnest', adding that it did not always secure the success that reaps great financial reward. It was a fairly grudging, if perhaps realistic, assessment, but Nottingham fans would remember the five straight victories he won in their 1933 National Trophy demolition of Plymouth at the White City – all the more remarkable in view of the fact that Charlie had fallen heavily in the first of his six rides, clipping the back wheel of the rider in front and being somersaulted into the fence.

The supporters initially believed he had been seriously hurt, but he recovered and, in his next race, beat Plymouth top scorer Bill Clibbett and then went through the card, including the final of the second-half scratch races.

The one glimpse of better times ahead for Nottingham in 1935 was provided by the success enjoyed by several provincial tracks running on open licences, particularly at Cardiff, Plymouth and Southampton, which were to provide the basis of a welcome expansion for the sport a year later.

When 1936 dawned, it brought with it news of the formation of a National Provincial League – essentially a second division for the National League – including a Nottingham team. The new White City venture was to be promoted by the Cardiff management, which had profited from large crowds the previous season. Dick Southouse was to be the speedway manager at Trent Lane and, after a poll among supporters, the 1933 nickname of the Wasps was retained, with colours of orange and black replacing red and yellow.

Nottingham's original colours for the Southern League debut in 1930 had been black vertical stripes, and in the early days the team was known as the Olympic. The national speedway press occasionally referred to Nottingham as the 'Lacemen', but this was probably a generic reference to the city's main trade, rather than an official name, and it was never used by the local press.

Southampton, Bristol, Liverpool, Plymouth and sister track Cardiff also lined up for the Provincial League, which had been carefully thought out by the promoters.

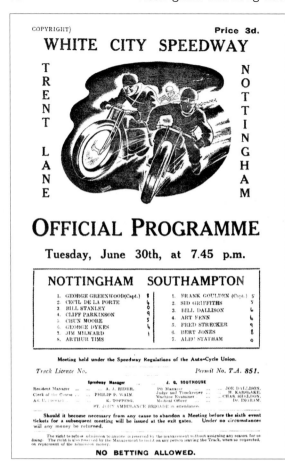

The programme issued by the original 1936 management unusually featured the two competing sides on the front cover. Trent Lane favourite Fred Strecker rode for Southampton that season.

In the supplementary National Provincial Trophy, West Ham entered a second team, known as the Hawks, racing their home matches at Southampton.

Speedway News for 1 April 1936 spelled out the basis on which the new league would operate. Each promotion was required to deposit 100 guineas as a guarantee. A gate of 3,000 would constitute 'a paying proposition'. Each management was allowed to sign not more than nine riders, who were to receive a weekly payment of fifty shillings maintenance money each and were to be guaranteed one home and one away meeting per week.

There was to be no start money in the league, but points money would be paid at the rate of ten shillings a point. In the supplementary Provincial Trophy competition there would be ten shillings a start and ten shillings a point. A Provincial League high flyer would be able to earn, in theory, £25 a week.

It was all good news for the large number of riders across the country – one estimate said as many as 150 – who had found no competitive outlet other than second halves and rides on open licence (or unlicensed) tracks in 1934 and 1935.

Nottingham were to ride on Tuesday evenings and *Speedway News* said the White City track, always one of the best outside London, had been maintained in excellent condition and was ready for racing.

The Trent Lane fans welcomed the sport back to Nottingham on 14 April 1936. They responded well to the revival, with a crowd of around 7,000 reported by the local press. The *Nottingham Evening News* had helped to boost the chances of a good turn-out when it featured pictures of captain George Dykes practising at the White City.

The local media gave a warm welcome to Nottingham's 1936 return to the track and previewed the season by showing George Dykes practising at the White City.

Reports of the opening meeting said organisation had been perfect, with the electric starting gate, improved upon since its initial introduction in 1933, eliminating irritating false starts. Liverpool Stanley slightly spoiled the general euphoria by winning the Trophy match 38-34, but in general the crowd went home happy. George Dykes set the fastest time of the night, 77.5 seconds, in the opening race, leading from the front a Nottingham team composed of some fairly unfamiliar names, including Norman Trimnell, former Plymouth rider Bill Stanley, Bob Henderson, George O'Brien – apparently on a one-night loan from Cardiff – and Les Fulham.

Opening their programme in the Provincial League on 21 April, Nottingham defeated Cardiff 38-34. The visitors won seven of the twelve heats, but engine trouble, and the fact that in one or two races they were only able to field a single rider, eventually cost them the match.

Ted Bravery was unbeaten in his four rides for Cardiff and George O'Brien – seen in the Nottingham colours a week before – had three wins. Nottingham had added Chun Moore on loan from Belle Vue and Wembley man Jim Millward to the side, and Moore top-scored with two wins and two second places. Captain George Dykes was suffering from flu and went home to bed after his first ride.

Four consecutive defeats – two at home and two away – followed for Nottingham. At Southampton, in a league match on 23 April, the Saints were only 6.5 points away from a total whitewash, winning by 53.5 points to Nottingham's 17.5. Bristol were league visitors on 28 April and won 43-33.

Nottingham performed creditably at Liverpool's Stanley Stadium on Monday 4 May, holding the home side to a 35-34 scoreline in the Trophy. Hopes must have been high for the return the following evening, but Liverpool rode the White City circuit well to win 41-30 – their second success on Trentside in less than a month.

Against the Merseyside team, Nottingham reversed the position of their earlier home win against Cardiff. Nottingham riders won seven of the twelve heats, but three 5-1s for Liverpool, and plenty of the minor placings when a Nottingham man crossed the line first, ensured a comfortable Liverpool victory. Bill Stanley finished with 11 points for Nottingham in his best display for the club, and Chun Moore scored 8, with 10 points from Jack Hargreaves the top Liverpool score.

The gloomiest aspect of the evening was the crowd of only 2,000 – just two thirds of the figure needed to make a profit. The team was relatively weak and contained virtually no familiar names apart from George Dykes. In the early part of the 1936 season, former Nottingham favourites were still attempting to make an impact in the National League.

George Greenwood, returning after a long period on the sidelines through injury, was announced in the probable Wembley line-up as second reserve. Fred Strecker and Les Wotton were at Harringay and both appeared for the North London team in a National League match at Hackney. Strecker was in and out of the Harringay side and found greater success as the season progressed in the Provincial League at Southampton. Fred Tate lined up at Hackney Wick.

Two future Nottingham promoters were also in the news. Arthur Westwood was reported to be presenting speedway to Parisian crowds at the Stade Buffalo, in partnership with Fred Whitehead of Hackney. The White City crowd, disappointed with the way the Nottingham revival was going, had little idea that Whitehead was within weeks of taking over the promotion and bringing the Trentside track a large and unexpected measure of speedway success.

Nottingham's eventual 1936 good fortune stemmed from the demise of Cardiff. The White City team should have raced away in Wales on 10 June and entertained Cardiff on 16 June. The matches never took place. The large crowds enjoyed by the Welsh team for open licence meetings in 1935 dwindled away when the league team began to struggle.

Speedway News for 13 June bemoaned the loss of the Welsh track:

> It is tragic about Cardiff. Just at a time when we thought speedway was growing, a track suddenly shuts up. It's the same old story of trying to run in double harness. The same company operated Nottingham as well and it just didn't work. Bigger promoters found out years ago that it doesn't do to run two or more tracks under the same management.

It is an argument that has raged for almost as long as speedway has been in existence. The history of the sport is littered with claims by supporters that their own circuit was being neglected in favour of a sister track. Promoters have a history of switching riders between tracks at short notice, particularly when one club appeared to be a better financial bet than another. The irony is that Nottingham were saved in 1936 through a takeover by Hackney!

The original promoting company did not immediately dispose of their Nottingham interest after the Cardiff withdrawal. When Southampton, including Fred Strecker, came to the White City on 30 June 1936 in a Trophy fixture, Dick Southouse was still in charge.

Some team strengthening had taken place, with the return of George Greenwood, struggling for a place at Wembley, and the signing of Cliff Parkinson from the Empire Stadium team. Also briefly associated with Nottingham at this stage, on loan, was the Wembley junior and future World Champion Tommy Price.

Right: Even before the change of management midway through 1936, Nottingham's team had been strengthened by the signing of Cliff Parkinson from Wembley.

Below: With speedway, particularly in the Provincial League, struggling for crowds in the early part of 1936, some promoters saw midget car racing as at least part of the answer to declining interest in solo speedway. As this picture shows, a car was tested at Nottingham in 1936, although there is no evidence of a full meeting.

Opposite: The Nottingham management in 1936 advertised 'seats in all enclosures' – unusual for a provincial track, but justified, as evidenced by this 1936 shot by fan Dick Smart.

OFFICIAL PROGRAMME 3D

WHITE CITY SPEEDWAY

| CHALLENGE MATCH NOTTINGHAM v. BELLE VUE | TRENT LANE, NOTTINGHAM | FIRST SEASON 24th Meeting Tuesday Evening SEPTEMBER 29th, 1936 |

This Meeting is held under the Rules of the Auto-Cycle Union.

Track Licence No. 322   Permit No. T.A. 877

A.C.U. Steward & Starter: Machine Examiner: Judge & Timekeeper:
C. R. TOPPING,   D. STUART.   H. KARSLAKE.
Medical Officer in attendance: Clerk of the Course:
Dr. INGRAM.   F. WHITEHEAD.

The Staff of St. John Ambulance is in attendance.

OUR WEEKLY SPEEDWAY BROADCAST

Like all good things, the speedway season of 1936 at Nottingham must come to an end, and to-night is our final meeting.

The management, which took over in the middle of July of this year, take this opportunity of thanking everyone for their support. Nottingham people rallied magnificently to our efforts, and our association with the sporting activities of the town have given us very great pleasure.

The Speedway Supporters' Club will of course continue its activities during the winter, and anyone who has not yet become a member can do so by obtaining a form from the kiosk in the car park, or by getting in touch with the Secretary, Mr. A. J. Piper, 164 Wilford Grove, Nottingham.

Speedway seasons come and speedway seasons go, but never in the history of the sport has there been such a successful one as in the present year.

The National Provincial League has undoubtedly been the cause of this great boom, and it is interesting to observe that Bristol has been the high spot of the season's activities. Even in the present month of September, they have been breaking all records with their crowds, and on Tuesday last had the record of 18,000 paid attendance.

The future of the Provincial League seems

assured, and that being the case you will see us here again next season.

A review of the season's fixtures is not practicable, because as you know we did not take over until the middle of July. All that we can comment on is that it seems very unfortunate for Nottingham that we did not take over right from the commencement of the season. Had we done so there is no possible doubt both in our minds and in those of the people who have been watching the progress of Nottingham Speedway, that we would have been the champions of the National Provincial League this season. As it is, we finished a very good third, but two points behind the League leaders.

Since we took over, Nottingham have only lost two Provincial League matches, and both of these were away—one at Southampton when we lost to the champions, and the other to Bristol, the runners-up.

Before leaving the prospects for next season, let us say here and now that we do hope the Auto-Cycle Union will take a firm hand regarding the eligibility of riders to take part in Provincial League competitions.

Flagrant abuse of the rules and agreements entered into—by Bristol in particular by including such men as Morton and Collins who are regular members of the Wimbledon

— 1 —

When Hackney chief Fred Whitehead took over the Nottingham promotion midway through 1936, he not only considerably strengthened the team but improved communication with the fans through the introduction of a completely new and very informative programme.

The Southampton match was full of controversy. After a close tussle, George Greenwood and Jim Millward lined up against Southampton's Frank Goulden and Strecker for the last heat, needing a maximum to give Nottingham victory. As Strecker and Goulden jumped away from the start, Greenwood was seen by the crowd to protest that they had touched the tapes before they rose.

Greenwood and Millward rode off the track and parked their machines by the starting gate in protest. The Southampton men completed the four laps in 94 seconds – some 19 slower than the track record – and took a 5-0 to win the match 39-31. In an earlier race, George Dykes had been excluded for breaking the tapes, hence the anger of the Nottingham riders. To add to the confusion, the tannoy system had broken down!

July 1936 was a turning point, not only for Nottingham but also for the Provincial League as a whole. Cardiff's withdrawal, and now the takeover of Nottingham by Fred Whitehead (officially announced early in the month), had thrown the lower division into turmoil.

Although the terms and conditions laid down at the start of the season had promised riders one home and one away meeting a week, things almost ground to a halt in late June and early July. The fixture book showed a long list of matches for the period but, after the Southampton Trophy match at Nottingham on 30 June, only three further fixtures were fulfilled up until 13 July. To further complicate matters, Johnnie Hoskins was reported to be threatening to withdraw West Ham Hawks from the Trophy, in protest against the Control Board's attitude on overseas riders.

On 14 June, current Provincial League leaders Bristol came to Nottingham White City for a league match. The West Country side had already beaten Nottingham twice at Trent Lane. On this occasion, however, it was a very different Nottingham side they had to face. In addition to George Greenwood, Tommy Price and Cliff Parkinson from Wembley, new owner Fred Whitehead had drafted in Stan Dell and Phil 'Tiger' Hart, and Ted Bravery had moved in from defunct Cardiff.

Manuel Trujillo, a Los Angeles-based American rider of
Hispanic origin, caused a sensation at Nottingham in
the summer of 1936 by unexpectedly breaking the track
record by a substantial margin. His time remains, to this
day, the fastest ever recorded at the White City.

When the White City side paraded against Bristol, only Chun Moore remained from the
team that had lost to Southampton a fortnight before. Nottingham overwhelmed Bristol by
53 points to 19, and Tommy Price set a new track record of 74.8 seconds in winning heat
one, knocking nearly a second off Tiger Stevenson's 1933 time. Greenwood had 10 paid 12,
Parkinson and Moore scored 9, Dell 8, Price 7, Hart 6, and Bravery 4, in one of the most solid
displays of team scoring the Nottingham fans had ever seen. Nottingham riders won every
heat – seven by 5-1 – and Bristol had little answer.

At this point in the season, the Provincial League tracks, shocked by the closure of Cardiff
and struggling for popularity, were handed a tremendous lifeline in the form of the All
American team headed by Putt Mossman. The visitors proved a major attraction and some
sources have credited the survival of the league to their activities. Nottingham entertained the
Americans twice at White City, drawing 36-36 on 21 July and losing 32-38 on 25 August. An
incident occurred during the second meeting which puzzles speedway historians to this day.

The American touring team included some high quality riders – notably Jack Milne, who
was to win the World Championship title at Wembley in 1937 as a New Cross rider, and his
younger brother Cordy, a Hackney team man who finished third in the same event. Also in the
team at Nottingham White City on that August evening was a twenty-two-year-old Hispanic
American called Manuel Trujillo, who was to write himself into the Trent Lane history book
in no uncertain manner.

There was little hint of anything unusual in the challenge match between Nottingham and
the Americans. The Stars and Stripes triumphed by 38-32 in front of a big Trent Lane crowd.
The biggest thrills for the spectators came in the two duels between Nottingham's George
Greenwood and Jack Milne. The American took the honours in the first clash but Greenwood
got his revenge later in the match.

Greenwood and Jack Milne both finished the match with 11 points. Ted Bravery scored 8
for Nottingham and for the Americans Pete Colman (9 points) and Sam Arena (8) gave the
best backing to the elder Milne. Manuel Trujillo had his moment in the limelight, winning
heat eleven with the fairly routine time of 77.6 seconds. His performance gave no indication
to the fans of what was to follow after the interval.

Bo Lisman was a member of the American touring team which rode at the Provincial League tracks in 1936.

The second half of the programme consisted mainly of the heats and the final of the Anglo-American scratch race. Cordy Milne won one of the heats, in the slow time of 81.1 seconds, but Trujillo astounded everyone in the stadium, including, no doubt, himself and his teammates, by scorching around the Trent Lane circuit in an almost unbelievable time of 72.5 seconds – more than two seconds faster than the track record established earlier by Tommy Price.

What happened to Trujillo in that scratch race heat? He obviously drew some inspiration from his own performance as he went on to win the final of the event, although in the less shattering time of 75 seconds. Reporting the meeting that evening for the *Nottingham Journal* and the *Evening News* was speedway correspondent A.J. Turner, who was a sports journalist in the city for many years. Turner described Trujillo's record-breaking ride in the following terms: 'Trujillo was flat out and therefore on the boards the whole time. He never turned the taps off until the finish of a smashing ride.'

Flat out Trujillo certainly was – and probably not completely out of choice. Joe Orchard and his younger brother Alan, from the Bakersfield area of Nottingham, not too far from Trent Lane, were regular supporters at the White City. Joe, now eighty-five and living in Westcliff-on-Sea in Essex, believes that Trujillo's throttle jammed at the start of the race, leaving the American rider with the choice of attempting to lay down his machine – a dangerous option with three other riders behind him – or hanging on for dear life over four laps.

Another Trent Lane story – that Trujillo lost control after crossing the finish line and ended up going through the wire safety fence, up the terracing and over a fence onto an adjoining football pitch – cannot be verified. Whatever the circumstances, he was out on the track again a couple of races later to lift the second-half trophy.

After the Second World War, Manuel Trujillo rode in Dublin for the all-American Shelbourne Tigers team, staged by Wimbledon promoter Ronnie Greene. Trujillo died in Los Angeles in 2006 at the age of ninety-two. His Nottingham track record will remain on the record books for ever.

It says something for the quality of second-half events in the 1930s that the Nottingham track record was twice beaten in the scratch races after the interval. These, staged following the end of a league or cup match, were usually considered, at least in later years, as simply a means of filling out the programme and giving the riders some extra money.

Former Nottingham rider Fred Tate, seen here with his fiancé, and complete with eye patch and arm in a sling, was badly injured at Wimbledon in a World Championship qualifier. He was forced to retire, but was offered a job within the Nottingham management by promoter Fred Whitehead. Tate was also involved on the management side at Long Eaton in the early 1950s.

There was to be a return to Nottingham in an off-track capacity, and in sad circumstances, for former favourite Fred Tate. In the Wimbledon qualifying round for the new World Championship, the Hackney man was the surprise packet of the night, scoring 11 points to win the round ahead of Dicky Case, Morian Hansen and George Newton. New Cross star Ron Johnson – the favourite to win the meeting – had withdrawn with a rib injury sustained in the second Test against Australia a few nights before, which the Aussies had won 56-49.

Tate's triumph quickly turned to tragedy. The second half of the Wimbledon meeting that evening featured a challenge match between the Dons and a combined New Cross/Hackney side. In heat seven of the match Tate appeared to touch Case as they went into a bend together. Both came down directly in front of Geoff Pymar, who had no chance of avoiding them.

Fred Tate suffered multiple injuries and was rushed to hospital. During his convalescence, Fred Whitehead announced that Tate was to be appointed track manager at Nottingham once he fully recovered.

After the crushing victory over Bristol, Nottingham went on to score some overwhelming home victories in Provincial League, Provincial Trophy, and challenge matches. *Speedway News* at the end of July 1936 said the 'new' Nottingham seemed to have one ambition: 'that is to win a match by the highest possible score'!

Liverpool, twice winners at White City in the early weeks of the 1936 season, in both the Provincial League and the Trophy, felt the full force of the new look team on 28 July. Nottingham won 55-17 over the twelve heats – a margin of two more points than that recorded over Bristol.

Speedway News described the match as, 'not racing at all – it's simply a slaughter.' The Trent Lane faithful, seeing a strong Nottingham team display consistency for the first time ever, seemed to have no complaints. Nottingham won nine heats by 5-1 and missed another maximum heat win only when Chun Moore fell on the last bend when lying second to Cliff Parkinson.

When Fred Whitehead took over the
Nottingham promotion midway through
1936, he quickly scrapped the black
and gold colours and 'Wasps' nickname.
Nottingham reverted to black and white,
but this time in the form of Hackney-
style hoops. George Dykes, who played
a major part in the Trentside team's
crushing victory over Liverpool, models
the Nottingham race jacket in the Trent
Lane pits.

George Greenwood recorded a 12-point maximum, including one race win after he
had suffered a flat tyre during the first lap! Ted Bravery got a paid maximum, Stan Dell got
10 points, Cliff Parkinson 9, George Dykes 7, and Chun Moore 5, in the biggest win ever
recorded by a Nottingham team.

Eric Blain was Liverpool's best man, with six points, and the press reported that Tommy
Price (not the future World Champion, but his northern namesake), tipped by many as the top-
notcher in the PL, was a big disappointment, scoring just four points. The Nottinghamshire
and England fast-bowler Harold Larwood, the Notts miner of 'bodyline' fame, presented a
second-half trophy to Stan Dell.

At this stage, Nottingham were being seriously fancied for the Provincial League
championship. They recorded a seventh successive league victory on 2 August by winning
37-35 at basement club Plymouth, despite a 12-point maximum for the home side by Billy
Lamont. Cliff Parkinson with 10, Bravery with 9 and Greenwood with 8 were the leading
Nottingham scorers.

The Plymouth result took Nottingham level on match points at the head of the Provincial
League table with Bristol. A huge test for the resurgent White City team came a few days later,
when they visited the Knowle Stadium to face the West Country side on their own small and
tricky circuit.

Speedway News reported that, while Nottingham rode well, they seemed to have taken on
something of an 'inferiority complex'. Bristol won 43-29 and Eric Collins broke the track
record in the opening heat.

George Greenwood was beaten twice – by Collins in that first race and then again by Wal
Morton in the last heat. Tiger Hart supported Greenwood and scored nine points, but Bravery,
Dykes, and Wembley loanee Price were below par.

After the match, Bristol led the table by two points from Liverpool, with Nottingham third.
Southampton – the eventual champions – were in fourth place, but had raced three fewer

George Greenwood, who returned to
Nottingham after the takeover by Fred
Whitehead, won the initial Provincial
Riders Championship trophy. The final
and conclusive round of the competition
was staged at White City.

matches. Plymouth, with only one win to that point, were rock bottom. In the final analysis, Nottingham won three of their four remaining matches to finish on 18 points. Bristol won two of their remaining three matches, but Southampton had been using their matches in hand to steadily catch up.

The exciting climax to the Provincial League season came at Bannister Court, Southampton on 24 September. The Saints beat Bristol 41.5 points to 29.5, to equal the Bulldogs' 20 league points. Southampton's superior race points difference was enough to also give them the title. Nottingham's 18-point total gave them third spot, but again this was achieved on the strength of superior race points over fourth-placed Liverpool.

In the Provincial Trophy, with the majority of the matches raced mid-season, Nottingham did not show up so well. Southampton won the Trophy to record a season's double, with Bristol again second. Liverpool were third, Plymouth fourth, and Nottingham fifth, with West Ham Hawks, who did complete the season despite Johnnie Hoskins' earlier threats, taking the wooden spoon.

The White City supporters were left to rue the fact that the takeover by Fred Whitehead had come with a significant part of the season already behind them, before the team was so spectacularly strengthened.

The Nottingham fans had a major consolation when George Greenwood won the inaugural Provincial League individual championship. Rounds were staged at each of the surviving Provincial League tracks, and after the events at Bristol, Plymouth, Liverpool and Southampton, George Greenwood led the field with 44 points – one ahead of Tommy Price (of Liverpool) – with Frank Goulden of Southampton in third place with 40 points.

With the final round being contested on his home circuit, Greenwood was the hot favourite for the title and, during the course of an exciting and close evening's racing, watched by a good crowd, he did indeed lift the title – with a certain amount of help from his fellow Nottingham riders in the line-up.

Phil 'Tiger' Hart damaged the chances of Tommy Price by beating him in heat two, and Stan Dell and Ted Bravery weighed in next, beating Frank Goulden into third place. Goulden was last home in heat five, and his chance had gone. Greenwood had won his first two races, beating Price in the sixth heat. But it was not all over yet, as the former Wembley man dropped his only point of the meeting in heat twelve. Goulden, having said goodbye to his own victory hopes, pulled something special out of the bag to head Greenwood home.

Heat seventeen was the crucial contest. Prior to that, Price had won his last two rides and Greenwood had won his fourth ride. In his fifth outing, a win would see George win the evening's meeting by a point and the overall Provincial League title by two points. A second place would see him finish level with Price on the night, but still lift the title by a single point.

Greenwood's chances of securing the necessary points were probably not hindered by two of his opponents in his last ride being teammates Ted Bravery – out of the running for a rostrum place – and George Dykes – reserve on the night. *Speedway News* reported, without any obvious trace of irony, that Greenwood 'made no mistake and ran home an easy winner.'

Overall, he totalled 59 points out of the 75 possible from the five rounds, with Price on 57. Billy Dallison of Southampton was third with 50 points, Frank Goulden fourth with 47 and Nottingham's Ted Bravery fifth with 43.

The trophy for the winner was presented by Major Vernon Brooke, chairman of the Speedway Control Board. The riders took the microphone after the presentation ceremony, with Greenwood telling the fans he was proud to have won on his home track. Price congratulated the winner, saying that one slip or engine failure for George would have meant that the trophy would have been his.

Billy Dallison capped all the earlier remarks when he made the logical point that if all the other riders had suffered engine trouble, or fallen off, he would have been sure to have been the champion.

Speedway News only gave two cheers for the Greenwood victory, saying:

We suppose everyone will be delighted that George Greenwood has won. For years he was a popular and match-winning member of the Wembley team. It was only through injury that he lost form so badly and had to seek a place in the Provincial League.

We welcomed the Provincial League as a recruiting ground for new talent and we thought it would be a good thing to include a few experienced riders to set a standard which newcomers must reach as soon as possible. But winning matches seems to have become an end in itself. The Provincial League Championship was instituted to give young riders a chance to compete under championship conditions. But again the original idea has been completely lost sight of and the first eight riders in the final placings have all ridden for at least six years.

It seems a bit naive of the *News* to complain about the importance of winning matches. It is generally accepted that a side has to be capable of at least winning the majority of its home matches if it wants to keep the turnstiles clicking healthily.

The concept of lower divisions being merely training grounds for talent is, largely, unworkable. Much the same arguments were used by some speedway administrators and commentators in the early 1960s, when a new Provincial League came to the rescue of the ailing National League, which had been reduced to seven tracks. When former First Division men and full internationals like Graham Warren and Eric Boothroyd rode in the new PL, there were plenty of complaints – although not from the fans at Wolverhampton and Middlesbrough.

There were many disputes during the course of 1936, with Nottingham leading the protestors when Bristol included Wal Morton and Eric Collins, who were getting regular National League rides with Wimbledon. Fred Strecker also had rides for both National League

Harringay and PL Southampton. The author of the Nottingham programme notes felt this sort of thing would 'kill the sport' and he urged the ACU to take action for 1937:

> We suggest that, next season, when a rider becomes attached to a Provincial League team, he must ride for that team permanently throughout the whole season and cannot go back to the National League until the start of the next season. That would stop National League clubs from lending out their better class men to tracks with the win-at-any-price spirit, which is becoming more and more prevalent.

Nottingham had, in fact, been prepared to make an issue of the situation when they faced Southampton in the last league match of the season at the White City on 22 September. The Saints were still trailing Bristol by two points in the league table and were desperate for a win. They at first indicated that they would use the experienced Dicky Smythe in their team, until Nottingham said they would make an official protest to the Control Board in the case of an away win. As the compiler of the Trent Lane programme notes said:

> Nottingham proved their superiority over the league champions in no uncertain fashion [Nottingham won 47-24], which only goes to prove that on collateral form Nottingham are the champion team. To prove our words, we are prepared to engage either Southampton or Bristol in a home and away fixture over eighteen heats, for any local charity.

By the time the programme notes were published at Nottingham's last meeting – a challenge match against Belle Vue on 29 September – the crucial decider had taken place at

The stadium facilities and track arrangements at Nottingham White City as the 1936 season drew to a close were, without a doubt, good enough for the National League. But, as promoter Fred Whitehead pointed out in his final programme notes, the facilities were not matched by crowd levels.

Bannister Court and the Saints, despite their defeat at Trent Lane, were champions. Nothing further was heard of any charity fixture.

The challenge fixture against Belle Vue ended in a comfortable victory for Nottingham, by 46 points to 26. Belle Vue were without Max Grosskreutz, riding for Australia against a team rather ambitiously labelled The World, at West Ham, but Frank Varey, Eric Langton, Bob Harrison, Bill Kitchen, Wally Hull, Acorn Dobson and Oliver Langton at reserve provided attractive if, on the night, not particularly formidable opposition.

Whatever the circumstances, Nottingham said a happier farewell to a speedway season than at any time since 1929. Fred Whitehead had introduced a much improved programme format to Nottingham when he took over the track, with plenty of information for the fans, and by the end of the season Fred Tate was also contributing editorial matter.

The management thanked supporters for having 'rallied magnificently to our efforts since our takeover'. Whitehead added:

> It seems very unfortunate for Nottingham that we did not take over right from the start of the season. Had we done so, there is no possible doubt both in our minds and those of the people who have been watching the progress of Nottingham Speedway that we would have been champions of the Provincial League.

After the Whitehead takeover, Nottingham lost just two league matches, at Southampton and Bristol. The 1936 season, Mr Whitehead said, had not only been a success for Nottingham but also for the sport as a whole. Most tracks had enjoyed large crowds well into September, with Bristol recording a record paid attendance of some 18,000 people.

Welcoming Belle Vue, he said many followers of speedway were looking at the match as an indication of Nottingham going into the National League for 1937. Whitehead was adamant that this would not happen:

> Let us state here and now that whatever the result tonight, we shall definitely not enter the National League next season.
>
> First class riders are costing from £500 to £1,500 – and even at the latter price they cannot always be bought. To reinforce the Nottingham team would require an expenditure of some £6,000 in men alone, apart from equipment, workshops etc.
>
> So far the Nottingham public has only just shown sufficient interest to support a Provincial League team. We hope that the support will increase by a considerable extent next year, and if it does we will seriously consider the promotion of Nottingham to higher circles in the speedway world.

8

Provincial Success

What was to prove the last full season of speedway racing at Trent Lane, Nottingham, was also without a doubt the most successful from the point of view of results. Hackney Wick chief Fred Whitehead, who had rescued Nottingham from potential closure midway through the 1936 season, his right hand man Fred Evans, and former White City rider Fred Tate formed an effective management triumvirate.

Four of the five 1936 Provincial League sides emerged for the 1937 season, with only Plymouth, always vulnerable in league speedway because of their geographical location, reverting to open licence meetings. Birmingham Hall Green and Leicester Stadium reopened and Norwich, which had run without an ACU licence since 1931, became legitimate and swelled the ranks of the Provincial starters to seven.

Hall Green was a late substitute for Portsmouth. Right up until the start of the season, multi-venue promoter Arthur Westwood had hoped to enter the South Coast track. Fixture cards for the Provincial League, including Portsmouth, had already been printed and were stacked in the corridors of the Speedway Control Board headquarters in Pall Mall. When it became clear that Portsmouth (and mouth-watering local derbys with Southampton) were not going to materialise, the fixtures were altered in favour of Hall Green.

The season offered the Provincial League itself, with each side again racing four times against each opponent, the Provincial Trophy, with the league sides meeting twice, the Coronation Cup, run between the PL teams on a knockout basis, and the *Daily Mail* National Trophy. In the latter competition, PL teams contested the first two rounds, sending one team forward to meet the seven National League sides in the quarter finals.

Nottingham opened the season earlier than had usually been the case on Trentside, with a two-legged Easter challenge against the revived Leicester. The first leg was at a bitterly cold and snowy Blackbird Road on Good Friday evening, 26 March 1937. Leicester Stadium was competing as a team for the first time since withdrawing from the Southern League after eight matches in 1931 (when the fixtures were taken over by Coventry). Leicester were short of riders and the team had to be made up with loan men from Liverpool. Former Leicester star Squib Burton performed the opening ceremony, but the small and chilled crowd was disappointed by Nottingham's eight-point victory.

The return came on Easter Tuesday evening at the White City, when Nottingham were again the winners, this time by ten points. Fred Strecker was back at Trent Lane, partnering Frank Hodgson, under contract to Nottingham's parent track, Hackney, and a product of the Dagenham training track. The ever-reliable George Dykes, who top-scored with eleven points, former West Ham man Tommy Allott, Fred Tuck, signed from Plymouth, ex-Wimbledon rider Sam Marsland and Australian Jack Hyland completed the Nottingham line-up.

Hackney Wick themselves were the next visitors to the White City, on 6 April, in what was described as a 'try-out' for the linked teams before the start of league racing. Strecker and Dykes were the only Nottingham men to win heats as Hackney won by 32 points to 21. The Londoners included Stan Dell, who had been at Trent Lane for part of 1936, Dick Wise, a Nottingham reserve in 1933, American Cordy Milne and Dane Morian Hansen.

The 1937 season was Nottingham's most successful from a results point of view and, although crowd levels varied, there were usually enough people to create a good atmosphere. Photographer and fan Dick Smart captured the definitive action shot from the White City on an evening in 1937. The exhaust fumes of four machines can be seen as Australian pioneer 'Cyclone' Billy Lamont sweeps into the first bend in front of a well-filled grandstand.

Fred Strecker is the name most frequently associated with speedway in Nottingham, but when he wore the club's colours in the challenge matches against Leicester and Hackney, it was in fact the first time he had raced for his home-town team since 1933.

Speedway's transfer maze was almost as complicated in 1937 as it is today, with riders being contracted to one management, but then being loaned out or otherwise moved between tracks. In 1936, Fred had been listed as a Harringay rider, loaned to Southampton in the Provincial League. In the winter of 1936/37, he was transferred from Harringay to Hackney but was immediately put on loan to East London promoter Fred Whitehead's Nottingham interest.

Immediately after appearing for Nottingham in the two early season challenges, Fred was off again, back to Hackney, having been recalled in complicated circumstances. The East London team had been forced to release a foreign rider. Wembley manager Alec Jackson, with a large number of men under contract at the Empire Stadium, offered Fred Whitehead the chance to sign Billy Lamont. Whitehead jumped at the chance to sign the spectacular Australian, but allocated him to Nottingham, preferring to keep Strecker at Hackney.

The Nottingham fans were none too pleased with the loss of local hero Strecker. True to form, a section of the Trent Lane crowd were already complaining about the make-up of the team and the quality of the racing before the new season was a month old.

The Strecker problem was eventually solved when he was permanently transferred from Hackney to Nottingham for a fee of £50 – presumably just a paper transaction, as he was contracted to Fred Whitehead in any case. In the end, the Nottingham fans did rather well, as Lamont, still a force to be reckoned with, spent more or less a full season at the White City, although he also rode some National League matches for Hackney.

Fred Whitehead declared his determination, evidenced by the permanent transfer of Strecker, to build a truly Nottingham team. But with only four matches raced – the two winning challenges against Leicester, the Hackney match and a perfectly respectable performance in holding Bristol to a 48-36 scoreline at Knowle in the first leg of the *Daily Mail* National Trophy – some so-called Nottingham fans were unhappy with the team, unhappy with admission prices and, unbelievably, talking about boycotting the track.

Whitehead went on the offensive in the columns of the *Nottingham Evening News*. He said he was 'bitterly disappointed with the poor sportsmanship already shown by some of the Nottingham speedway public.' Before a single competitive match had been run at home, some

Promoter Fred Whitehead voiced his determination to give Nottingham a successful Provincial League team for 1937 and this line-up, blending youth and experience, displayed the potential. From left to right: Billy Lamont, Frank Hodgson, George Dykes, Fred Tuck, Sam Marsland, Tommy Bateman and Fred Strecker.

followers were already condemning the team, and one letter suggesting a spectator boycott had attracted seventy signatures. Whitehead concluded:

> This sort of thing does not actually worry me, because it suggests there is interest in speedway racing. But the thing that does give me cause of anxiety is the fact that this interest is conditional on Nottingham having a team which always wins. This state of affairs is deplorable. Nottingham people appear to just hate losing and take a beating in a very bad manner.

Fred Whitehead then indulged in some very plain speaking indeed. He emphasised that he was not promoting speedway at Nottingham for the love of the sport, but to make money:

> I took over at Nottingham after the first company had failed in the middle of last season, and immediately gave Nottingham fans a winning team, which was nearly the equal of the National League sides.
>   Did the Nottingham public support me? Not a bit of it. Actually, in the twelve meetings I ran at Nottingham, never losing a home match, I lost a total of £155 without counting my own labour and valuable time. In 1937 I have entered upon a definite policy of making Nottingham a self-supporting team, and whether supporters like it or not, that policy will continue.

Whitehead told the *Nottingham Journal* that admission charges at the White City compared favourably with tracks elsewhere. The minimum cost of running a meeting at Nottingham, on a season's average, was £300, and to get that amount of money through the gate, after tax,

Left: The 'Three Freds'. Nottingham management duo Fred Whitehead (left) and Fred Evans (centre) are pictured with New Cross promoter Fred Mockford.

Opposite: Speedway in the late 1930s was beginning to take on an appearance that, in many respects, would last until the 1960s. The foot-forward style of racing, less spectacular than the old-time leg-trailing, was well established by this time as the riders hit the first bend at the White City.

meant an attendance of at least 5,000 people (compared to the 3,000 which had been quoted at the start of the Provincial League venture). He said:

> My attendances so far this season [for two challenge matches and an open meeting] have been 3,500, 2,900, and 2,200. How in the name of goodness do speedway supporters expect me to reduce the charges for admission when such paltry support is forthcoming?

The question of making or losing money would not matter as far as his promotion of speedway at Nottingham in 1937 was concerned:

> I will give Nottingham one complete season of speedway with a reasonably good team, and don't get annoyed if it is beaten occasionally, as all teams are. At the end of the season it will be up to the Nottingham public to decide whether or not they really want speedway. I am not begging for patronage, as it has been my custom to win through on sheer merit.

The figures quoted for the actual attendances at White City for the first three matches in 1937 are at odds with the estimates made in press reports, which often doubled the 'official' statistics from the promoter. It illustrates the huge problem faced by those reporting speedway, from historians to present-day reporters.

It is fairly clear, at this point in speedway's development, that while Belle Vue and the London National League teams (with the exception of Hackney) were flourishing, Provincial League speedway was, generally speaking, another matter. Cardiff and Plymouth found the going too tough in 1936. Leicester and Liverpool failed to survive the 1937 season.

Fred Whitehead was as good as his word when he said he would give Nottingham a full season of speedway. In terms of providing a 'reasonable' team, he greatly exceeded his modest promise, bringing two trophies to a previously success-starved track.

Real competitive action began at Trent Lane when the already faltering Leicester side arrived for a league match on 27 April, to be crushed by 65-19 – a huge 46-point margin. George Dykes, Fred Tuck, Tommy Allott, Sam Marsland, Steve Langton and Bill Stanley lined up for Nottingham, with Frank Hodgson and Don Hemingway as the two reserves. Leicester tracked player-coach Norman Trimnell – a Nottingham rider in the early part of 1936 – and included two riders who were later to feature in the affairs of Long Eaton.

Paddy Mills (real name Horace Burke) was a Leicester man who achieved considerable post-war success with Norwich Stars when they were managed by Fred Evans. He later moved into management himself with Southern Area Leaguers Brafield, but left the Northamptonshire circuit after a disagreement with the promoters, and ran Long Eaton as an unlicensed track.

Wilf Plant, a Melton Mowbray garage proprietor who had been attached to Wimbledon, also rode a few matches for Nottingham in 1938. He went on to ride in the wartime meetings at Belle Vue, was the leading light for Middlesbrough in the immediate post-war years, and finished up with Long Eaton in 1952.

Leicester provided very little opposition in the White City curtain-raiser. With the Nottingham riders consistently outgating their opponents, the early heats were largely a formality. Only heat eight offered any real spectacle, as Mills and Nottingham's Bill Stanley jousted for second place, with the home rider getting his nose in front just a few yards from the finish line.

The following evening Nottingham provided the opposition in Birmingham as Hall Green reopened. Nottingham won their second match in two days by a large score – 57-26 on this occasion. In front of an estimated 10,000 spectators, Nottingham secured 5-1s in half of the fourteen heats – the new format for the Provincial League – and, in all, provided twelve heat winners. Sam Marsland had his best match in Nottingham colours, recording a 12-point maximum, and there were 11 points apiece for Fred Tuck and Frank Hodgson.

Bristol came to Trent Lane on 4 May for the second leg of the *Daily Mail* National Trophy tie, and Nottingham almost pulled back the 12-point deficit. The home side won 46-37 on the night, losing by just three points (85-82) on aggregate. The displays in the first leg at Bristol and the victory at Hall Green gave an indication that Nottingham could not only win home matches but could also compete effectively away from the White City. The ability to restrict opponents to reasonably narrow margins away from home was to prove crucial later in the season in the Coronation Cup.

There was a setback when Liverpool won 53-31 at White City on 18 May in a league match, but Nottingham were back to winning ways with an away win at Norwich on 22 May (49-28) and a 51-31 home victory over Hall Green on 25 May – again both in the league.

Two more exciting matches with Bristol followed, bringing victory for the Bulldogs at Knowle (49-31) and for Nottingham at Trent Lane (42-40). A narrow 40-42 defeat at the hands of Liverpool at Stanley Stadium was followed by a 60-24 home win for Nottingham against Norwich, as a spell of seven Provincial League matches in less than three weeks came to an end on 8 June.

There was some relief from the pressure of league racing when Nottingham beat Hackney 43-40 in a home challenge match, but the Liverpool hoodoo continued as the Merseysiders won 56-50 at Stanley. It was Liverpool's third win over Nottingham, with only a third of the season completed.

A real purple patch then followed as Nottingham raced three Provincial Trophy matches in the last week of June 1937 and scored more than 70 points in each one. Birmingham were despatched 75-32 at Trent Lane and Norwich were beaten 72-36 at The Firs. The win that sealed the hat-trick of overwhelming victories was all the more welcome, as the previously dominant Liverpool team were defeated 73-32 at the White City.

The overwhelming victory at Norwich represented Nottingham's highest-ever score away from Trentside. By this stage of the season Nottingham had already recorded two comfortable wins against Norwich – 49-28 in Norfolk and 60-24 at Trent Lane. Since the earlier victory at The Firs, Nottingham had been considerably strengthened by the return of Ted Bravery, a Trent Lane success in 1936. George Greenwood was another welcome addition to the squad, having found the National League heavy going at Hackney. Someone had to move the other way, and Frank Hodgson found himself at Waterden Road.

The Nottingham line-up at The Firs, featuring Greenwood, Bravery, Strecker, Dykes, Allott, Tuck, Marsland and Lamont, was a formidable combination for the Provincial League. It held together remarkably well for the rest of the 1937 season, apart from a longish spell on the injury list for George Dykes. The regular line-up was augmented as necessary by Don Hemingway and Lincolnshire grass-tracker Tommy Bateman, Australian Jack Hyland having moved on since the early weeks of 1937.

At this halfway point in the season, Nottingham were in third spot behind Southampton and Bristol in what had sadly become a six-team league. Leicester had withdrawn as early as 15 May after experiencing poor results and even poorer crowds, which fell to as low as 500.

As it had in 1936, the Provincial League wobbled mid-season. After the Leicester collapse, Liverpool were the next team to face closure, with Stanley Stadium attendances dipping. Thankfully, Belle Vue again came to the rescue by taking over the Liverpool fixtures. The Speedway Control Board stepped in after receiving a warning that the entire league was in danger of going bust and Fred Whitehead and Ronnie Greene of Bristol were reportedly, 'given a free hand to set the Provincial house in order.'

After losing 60-47 away to Bristol in the Provincial Trophy, Nottingham had their first 1937 meeting with Southampton. The Saints were beaten 59-48 in a Trophy match.

The second half of the 1937 season was to prove the highest point, in terms of results, in the Nottingham speedway story. Following the victory over Southampton, Nottingham won their final ten home matches. There was to be only one more away success (61-46, at Birmingham in the Trophy) and that meant there was to be no league title for the White City men. But hard riding by the Nottingham team in the away legs of Coronation Cup ties was enough to secure comfortable aggregate victories and the first ever silverware for the team and the fans.

Tuesday 13 July saw Trent Lane stage the first of the 1937 series of English Provincial Riders versus Australia international matches. The Trent Lane contest proved to be the closest of the series, with the Australian team, consisting entirely of men with experience at official Test level, winning 55-53.

The Aussies tracked Lionel Van Praag, winner of the inaugural 1936 World Championship, and Bill Rogers, Dicky Case and Vic Duggan, Eric Collins and Ron Johnson, with former Wasp Dick Wise and Nottingham's Billy Lamont as the reserves. The English Provincial Riders team featured George Greenwood (captain) and Fred Strecker from Nottingham, Bill Dallison and Frank Goulden from Southampton, Harry Shepherd of Bristol and Tommy Price of Belle Vue/Liverpool, with George Dykes of Nottingham and Les Bowden of Hall Green as the reserves.

In front of a crowd reported by the local press as approaching 15,000, the match was as exciting as the scoreline suggests, with the scores level at 27-27 at the halfway stage of the eighteen-heat match. England took a two-point lead in heat twelve and, to the delight of the

The Nottingham team was constantly fine-tuned throughout the 1937 season. This shot, posed in a way that would not have seemed out of place in the 1960s, contained two riders who had not featured in the earlier team line-up, while Billy Lamont was absent injured at this stage of the season. From left to right: Frank Hodgson, Fred Tuck (giving a V-sign to the photographer!), George Dykes (on machine), Fred Strecker, Tommy Allott, Sam Marsland, Ted Bravery. George Greenwood also featured in the team in 1937.

crowd, it was George Dykes who led partner Harry Shepherd home in front of Billy Lamont for a 5-1. Although Van Praag and Case won the next two heats, the English team filled the second and third places to retain the lead. Strecker won heat fifteen from Lamont and Collins, and the Trent Lane supporters began to anticipate an England victory.

Heat sixteen reversed the fortunes of the match. Bowden overslid when challenging Van Praag for the lead and Shepherd had to lay his machine down to avoid his partner. Bowden remounted for the third-place point. Australia edged ahead with a 4-2 in the penultimate heat seventeen, Greenwood finishing just a wheel behind Case, with Duggan in third spot.

The scene was set for a final-heat decider, with England needing a 5-1 to force a draw. Dallison was a clear winner but Collins managed to hold off Frank Goulden to clinch victory for the Aussies.

Australia owed much to the individual brilliance of Van Praag – considered a possible Nottingham signing at the start of 1933 – who scored a six-ride, 18-point maximum. Case scored 13, Rogers and Collins 7 apiece, Duggan 6 and Lamont 3, while a subdued Ron Johnson had just a single point. England were solid – Dallison finishing with 14 points, Strecker 9, Greenwood 8, Goulden 8, Shepherd 7 and Dykes 5, while Bowden and Price had a point apiece.

The Australians won all four of the subsequent matches in the series – 79-29 at Bristol, 60-48 at Belle Vue, 64-43 at Southampton and 56-51 at Birmingham. George Greenwood was the aggregate top-scorer for the outclassed English side, with a creditable total of fifty points.

Billy Lamont's career had dipped since the early days of speedway, but the 'Cyclone' was still a huge attraction for the crowds. Young Nottingham fan Alan Orchard and his friends took up their Trent Lane race-night position on the first bend terracing and were thrilled by the fence-scraping activities for which the veteran Australian had always been known and which, at one track, were reputed to have included actually riding up on the fence itself, wall-of-death style, for a brief but heart-stopping few moments!

Seventy years later, Alan recalled:

> Lamont was a great thrill-maker, particularly for the younger fans, who really enjoyed the whole spectacle of speedway racing on a 1930s style deep cinder track. We got absolutely covered in cinders when Billy, after seeming to be going on the inside, suddenly came out wide and brushed the safety fence. But it was worth it and very thrilling.

Back in club action, Nottingham suffered a setback to their hopes of success in the Provincial Trophy, crashing to a 69-38 defeat at Bannister Court against Southampton. Ted Bravery (12), Fred Strecker (11) and George Greenwood (7) kept the score respectable but without the injured George Dykes, Nottingham were weak at second string and reserve, with Tuck, Bateman, Lamont, Marsland and Hemingway only registering eight points between them.

Four days after the South Coast trip, the Nottingham riders suffered a blow to their morale with the death of Trent Lane second-halfer Archie Shelton, the younger brother of former Nottingham and Wembley rider Charlie Shelton. Now aged twenty-two, Archie had started racing at the age of seventeen. He had tried his luck at Leicester too, and featured in a challenge match line-up during the brief revival at the Leicester Super track in 1936. At Nottingham, he was having difficulty breaking into the team.

A member of the Tornado Motorcycle Club like his brother Charlie, Fred Strecker, George Dykes and other Nottingham riders, Archie had been involved over the years in some spectacular crashes while racing, and had also suffered severe injuries in a road accident.

On Saturday 17 July 1937, he rode in a meeting on the non-league circuit at Bell End, Holbeach, in South Lincolnshire. After returning for a brief rest at the family home in West Bridgford, Nottingham, he set off with his mother and two sisters in the early hours of the next morning to fulfil a booking at the Rye House Sunday training track.

Whilst warming up his machine in the pits at the Hoddesdon, Hertfordshire, circuit, he complained of terrible pains in the head, collapsed, and was taken unconscious to Hertford Hospital, dying later that day of a brain haemorrhage caused by a fracture of the skull in an earlier incident. No inquest was judged to be necessary.

The funeral took place at Wilford Hill, Nottingham, attended by White City track manager Fred Tate, who a year earlier had been judged to be only two hours from death after his horrendous crash at Wimbledon. Floral tributes were sent by the Nottingham management, the riders and the Supporters' Club. Charlie Shelton had retired from racing at this stage, and was acting as mechanic to George Dykes.

The team put the tragedy behind them for the important home leg of the Coronation Cup semi-final against Bristol. The White City team had been given a walk-over in the quarter final when Leicester closed down. A 55-29 victory gave real hope of qualification for the final, and this proved to be the case. The Trentsiders fought like tigers at Knowle in the return, holding Bristol to a 47-37 scoreline.

Sandwiched in between home league victories, over Norwich on 27 July and Southampton on 3 August, came success for George Greenwood and Fred Strecker in the Provincial Riders' Best Pairs Championship at Norwich on 31 July. After the fifteen heats of the meeting had been completed, the Nottingham pair were level on 20 points with Les Bowden and Steve Langton of Birmingham. Greenwood at this stage had 14 points from his five rides, while Bowden had the maximum 15 points and had established a new Firs track record.

In the run-off, Bowden led out of the gate but was pushed all the way by the Nottingham star, who simply refused to give in. Eventually the pressure paid off, Bowden was forced into a mistake and fell, leaving Greenwood to coast home. Fred Strecker had supported him with six points.

The success enjoyed by Nottingham in 1937 was marred by the tragic death of Archie Shelton, younger brother of Charlie, who collapsed from a brain haemorrhage while warming up his machine at Rye House. Shelton is pictured fourth from the left in this group shot of riders at Wembley.

Birmingham won a Provincial League match at Hall Green by 44-39 on 4 August. Six days later, Nottingham faced Southampton at White City in the first leg of the Coronation Cup final. Again, the home side were dominant on the Trent Lane circuit, running up a 61-23 victory and a comfortable lead to defend at Banister Court.

The following evening on the South Coast the lead proved to be ample. Southampton managed a 47-36 home win, but the aggregate score of 97-70 mirrored Nottingham's superiority over two legs. The actual Coronation Cup, Nottingham's first national trophy, was soon after presented to George Greenwood and his fiancé, Miss Ivy Elliston, who were to marry at the end of the season.

The trophy was handed over to George and Ivy at the Nottingham Palais de Dance, a favourite haunt of the riders over the years. Southampton had provided the opposition at Trent Lane earlier in the evening and accompanied the Nottingham boys to the Palais, where George was persuaded to fill the cup with champagne for general consumption.

At this point, the Provincial League championship was still theoretically winnable by Nottingham, the Coronation Cup was in the bag and there was a real hope of lifting the Provincial Trophy. Norwich were beaten 69-39 at home in the Trophy on 17 August and Bristol were swept aside by 68-40 at White City in the same competition a week later, effectively delivering the honour to Nottingham.

In the final Provincial Trophy table, Nottingham had 14 points from the 10 matches, Bristol were second with 13 and Southampton third with 12 points. Fred Strecker won the Oscroft Trophy, presented by the Nottingham motor firm, for being the highest White City points scorer in the Provincial Trophy competition.

Southampton ended Nottingham's league title hopes with a narrow 44-40 win at Bannister Court. But this was certainly one of the Trentsiders' finest displays of the season and, as *Speedway News* reported, the White City men certainly 'scared the Saints'.

The scores were level pegging as the match neared its conclusion, but Nottingham's hopes dipped in heat nine when Fred Strecker, who had taken a second place and a win in his first two rides, crashed out of the race and out of the meeting. Southampton's 5-1 in the penultimate heat won them the match, rendering academic the 5-1 for Nottingham in the final heat recorded by Bravery and Bateman.

From this point until the end of the season Nottingham were unbeatable at the White City Stadium, recording victories over Liverpool (now transferred to Hyde Road, Manchester and known as Belle Vue Merseysiders), Bristol, Southampton and Birmingham. Away from home the form was less convincing, with defeats at Bristol, Southampton, Norwich – who had strengthened their team since Nottingham's runaway victory earlier in the year – and at Hyde Road against the Merseysiders.

Their inability to win on the road in the league – their last victory had been at Norwich in June – cost Nottingham any hope of the title. Bristol won the league with 30 points from their 20 matches, Southampton were second with 26 points, and Nottingham third with 22.

The final Trent Lane meeting of 1937 saw Nottingham at home to Birmingham, completing a comfortable 50-33 win. Fred Strecker top-scored with 11 points, Ted Bravery and George Greenwood had 9 each, Tommy Allott 8, and George Dykes (recovered from the broken bones in his foot that kept him out of several vital matches) netted 5. Reserves Fred Tuck and Sam Marsland scored 3 and 1 respectively. It was the final appearance of the most well balanced and successful side in Nottingham's history.

The second half of the meeting, really giving the fans value for their money, saw a nine-heat challenge match against National League Harringay, which Nottingham also won, by 23-13. Greenwood scored a maximum 9, Strecker 6, Allott 5 and Bravery 3 points. Alec Statham was best for Harringay with five points, while the visitors also included ex-Nottingham man Les Wotton.

Good value indeed, but had the Nottingham fans really appreciated it? The answer seemed to be no. The programme notes for the final meeting had much to celebrate. The winners of the *Daily Mirror* Provincial Trophy and the Coronation Cup were hailed as the 'record-breaking team of the year'. But, although the *Daily Mirror* Trophy was presented to Nottingham skipper George Greenwood at the end of the final meeting, there was a darker edge to the proceedings.

Fred Whitehead had complained earlier in the season that attendances over the first three meetings had failed to average 3,000. After the perceived early season weaknesses in the team had been resolved by the introduction of newcomers of a high quality, there had been few subsequent complaints about rider strength.

However, despite the on-track success, the evidence is that the fans failed to turn out in sufficient numbers. The reported attendance of 15,000 at the English Provincial Riders versus Australia match – probably a media exaggeration – was balanced by a reported crowd of only 1,500 for the home leg of the Coronation Cup semi-final against Bristol. Even in the 1930s, supporters preferred league racing to the subsidiary competitions.

Speedway News had reported a 'vastly improved attendance' for the home leg of the Coronation Cup final against Southampton and the *Nottingham Evening News* claimed a 'record crowd for a league match' for the final Provincial League meeting against Birmingham. Presumably, given the claims for crowds in the early years, the newspaper meant a record for the 1937 season.

Whatever the true figures, they were clearly not enough to remove some of the doubts in Fred Whitehead's mind regarding the attitude of the Nottingham sporting public to speedway racing. In what were to prove the final programme notes of the Hackney management team, the writer paid tribute to the successes of the 1937 season, but added a note of warning:

> Although the team has been a sporting success, it cannot be said that the venture of speedway promotion at Nottingham has been a financial success, and the management very much regret having to state this undeniable fact. We do however, thank most sincerely those two or three thousand regular attenders who have turned up at the White City to give their support, and we hope they are well satisfied with the season's show.
>
> …
>
> Regarding next year, our activities are closely bound up with the fate of the Provincial League. Should it be a strong league, with plenty of clubs in the Midlands represented, then Nottingham will continue; otherwise, our position will have to be seriously reviewed.
>
> …
>
> Finally, there is one thing in which the management glory and that is the fact that in spite of the many abusive and rank unsportsmanlike letters they received in the early part of the season, they take great pleasure in recalling that they have kept their word to the Nottingham speedway public by presenting good shows and a winning team, second to none.

9

No Abiding City – 1938

Fred Whitehead's hopes for a strong second tier of speedway in 1938, with plenty of Midland clubs, were not fully realised, although Sheffield's entry did bring the promise of a useful local derby for Nottingham. Predictably, Whitehead cashed in his interest in Nottingham. At the same time, to further reduce his costs, he downgraded Hackney Wick to the lower division.

Whitehead had kept his word to the Nottingham public by presenting good racing and by putting together a winning team throughout 1937. Now he handed the rights to promote at the White City Stadium to Arthur Westwood who, said the *Speedway News*, had 'made such a big success' of Birmingham Hall Green the previous season.

Westwood – originally associated with Wolverhampton in 1929, where he had contested a match race against Fred Strecker – had soon shown a liking for the management side of speedway and promoted open meetings at Monmore Green. His riding career took in stints at Wimbledon, Southampton and Clapton, and he travelled to Argentina in the party that included Nottingham's Joe Gooding.

He retired in the mid-1930s to concentrate on promotion, and as the 1938 season dawned he was in control of no fewer than four tracks. Three of these – Hall Green, Nottingham and Sheffield – were entered for what had now been renamed the Second Division of the National League and he also intended to run meetings on an open licence basis at Leeds.

Westwood's multi-track interests reputedly earned him the name 'the Woolworth of the speedways'. His empire has certainly proved complicated for subsequent generations of speedway historians. The letterheading for Birmingham Speedway (Hall Green) in 1938 proclaimed that it was operated by Portsmouth Speedways Ltd, while the Nottingham programme for that season stated that the track was operated by Sheffield Speedways Ltd.

In January 1938, Arthur Westwood attempted to take advantage of some form of management consistency at Trent Lane by offering employment to Fred Evans, who had been Fred Whitehead's assistant at Nottingham in 1937 (and at parent track Hackney). A copy of the offer letter from Westwood survives. Fred Evans, who was later to serve as an army officer in the Second World War, was to be employed as general manager or secretary, 'as the directors may think fit', to Birmingham, Nottingham and Sheffield speedways, starting on 14 March 1938 at a salary of £9 a week. Evans would be retained on the Westwood payroll during the close season, but at a reduced rate of £3 a week.

Presumably Evans eventually rejected the offer, as he continued to be active at Hackney and there is no programme or media mention of him holding any position at Trent Lane in 1938.

Fred Whitehead had been no slouch when it came to publicity and he had also possessed a definite mind of his own when dealing with the sport's authorities. But his approach was a measured one and his personality very unlike the flamboyant Westwood. Once 'Westy' had taken control of a track, the press advertising and programme covers generally proclaimed that the venue was 'presented by Arthur Westwood'.

His weekly programme notes at Trent Lane were headed by a photograph of a smiling and dapper Westwood, and were preceded by the heading, 'Can yer 'ere me muvver' – a catchphrase made popular by one of the leading comedians of the day. The highly personal touch adopted by the promoter seemed to strike a bright note as the 1938 season began, but Westwood's relationship with the Nottingham sporting public was soon to turn decidedly sour.

Whitehead had brought success to Nottingham by building a squad which combined the skill and experience of George Greenwood, Billy Lamont, Fred Strecker, George Dykes, Tommy Allott and others with the more youthful promise of Lincolnshire grass-tracker Tommy Bateman, as well as Fred Tuck and Sam Marsland. Other experienced men, like Steve Langton and Phil 'Tiger' Hart, had seen the Nottingham side through spells when regular team men were injured and altogether there had been few weaknesses.

A shiver went down the spines of the more knowledgeable Nottingham supporters when it was announced that the new Sheffield side, to be captained by Eric Blain, would be recruited from 'the fairly large collection of talent associated with Birmingham and Nottingham'.

The 1938 season promised to be one of stability for speedway as a whole, with no fewer than nine sides declared as starters for the restructured second division. Birmingham Hall Green, Norwich, Nottingham and Southampton carried on from 1937. Bristol moved up to the National League, swapping places with Hackney and, although Liverpool/Belle Vue Merseysiders dropped out, three tracks reopened: Sheffield, Lea Bridge and Newcastle. West Ham again operated a second team – the Hawks – but this time in the league itself, rather than just the Trophy, as had been the case in 1936.

Division Two matches in 1938 were to be supplemented with the English Speedway Trophy – Nottingham being placed in the Northern Section with a Belle Vue second team, Sheffield, Newcastle and West Ham Hawks.

Nottingham started the new campaign with a challenge match against a Wembley reserve side and included five of the eight riders who had been on parade for the final match of 1937 – Greenwood, Strecker, Dykes, Bravery and Tuck. Missing from the line-up were Tommy Allott, who had moved to Sheffield, Sam Marsland, and Tommy Bateman. The latter had been a particular favourite of Fred Whitehead, who had taken the opportunity to sign him for Hackney.

In place of the missing trio from 1937 were Charlie Challis and the inexperienced Trent Lane juniors Ted English and Harold Brailsford. Billy Lamont, absent through injury at the end of 1937, had also moved to Sheffield.

Nottingham recorded a comfortable 49-33 victory against a Wembley side that included Les Bowden, Colin Watson, Malcolm Craven and Eric Gregory. Greenwood, with a maximum 12 points, and Bravery, with 10, headed the Nottingham score-chart, while Les Bowden and Colin Watson scored 7 apiece for the visitors.

Right: Arthur Westwood made a bad start with the ultra-critical Nottingham fans by transferring Tommy Allott (pictured here) and Billy Lamont to another of his many promotional interests, Sheffield, and by also excluding Sam Marsland from his initial squad.

Opposite: White City floodlit at the start of the 1938 season. Sadly, the lights were soon to go out for good on speedway racing on Trentside.

Altogether, it was a satisfying start for Nottingham. The local press reported that 'fairylights, fireworks and four thousand spectators' welcomed the new season at Trent Lane. In the following week's programme, Arthur Westwood was extremely upbeat about the prospects for the season. No one, he said, had given the White City men much hope against a Wembley team which included four men who had ridden for the First Division side. 'As it was, we cleaned them up in a very convincing manner and if we continue to ride as we did last week, we shall want a lot of beating,' he said.

More ominously for the Nottingham fans, Westwood's programme notes also confirmed that every track, 'had to lose one or two of their riders in order to make up the complement of teams required for the second division.' The always controversial issue of pooling – particularly contentious when riders were switched between teams operating under the same management – had raised its head.

The worst fears of the fans were being realised. When Nottingham lined up for the English Speedway Trophy match against a Belle Vue second team on 19 May, it was revealed that Ted Bravery had followed Allott and Lamont north to Sheffield. Nottingham had now effectively lost three riders of heat leader standard. The place of Bravery, an experienced rider and an effective points scorer, was taken by junior Bill Burns. On a track criticised by the riders – George Dykes said it was, 'like riding on marbles, without any grip' – Nottingham were heavily beaten by 47-32. To make matters worse, both Strecker and Dykes suffered engine seizures.

George Dykes looks none too happy as he waits in the Trent Lane pits for his next ride. After the second match of the season at the White City, Dykes described the track surface as: 'like riding on marbles, without any grip.'

The local press said the condition of the track surface was reflected in the riding of Fred Strecker. He rode well to collect his first win of the season, but, according to the *Evening News*, was, 'obviously always riding with exceptional caution'.

Ernie Price top-scored for Belle Vue with 12 points and Oliver Hart contributed eight. George Greenwood was Nottingham's top man, dropping a single point to Price in heat one – the only race to see anything like a normal timing at 78.8. The state of the track was made clear by an extraordinary time for one heat of 89.4.

Westwood nailed his colours firmly to the mast in the programme for the Belle Vue match, greeting the Trent Lane faithful with another catchphrase, 'Watcher folks', and calling for the creation of 'one big happy family' at the White City. All his promotional efforts, he said, would be no good without the support of the fans. He claimed, perhaps rashly, that Nottingham had a side as strong as any in the second division, and said he would do his best to put them 'right on top'.

The Trent Lane honeymoon period for Arthur Westwood had proved exceptionally brief. The Belle Vue result, which would have been unthinkable with the strength of the 1937 team, coupled with the state of a track usually regarded as well kept and fair, led to instant repercussions and, with hindsight, probably doomed the promotion to its eventual failure. The Trent Lane fans, never slow to voice criticism, now prompted *Evening News*-featured sports columnist H.D. Grain to question the sportsmanship of the Nottingham public.

Westwood had clearly made a better impression on the media than on the fans. Grain wrote that the promoter had 'bravely' faced a demonstration by angry fans after the match. Grain said:

> Afterwards, in his private office, in the presence of ACU officials, captain George Greenwood and a few friends, Westwood commented even more determinedly than ever: 'I'll win through yet. I'll get another rider by next week if I have to buy up half of London.'

Arthur Westwood's rallying call to make management and supporters at Nottingham 'one big happy family' largely went unheeded by the fans. In addition to their wrath at losing key riders to other tracks, the supporters and others criticised Westwood for advertising visiting teams as 'Wembley' and 'Belle Vue' when they were in fact the second strings of the two National League outfits.

Grain added in his column that he had told Westwood that in Nottingham he had 'a very strange and critical public' to deal with: 'It is an indisputable fact that in Nottingham, whether it is football, cricket or anything else, you can only win the public over to your side if you have a winning team.'

The *Evening News*, showing rare concern for the point of view of the promoter, reported that there had been difficulty in getting the right amount of cinders for the reconstruction of the track (hardly a major job when Trent Lane had been raced on successfully in 1937). Moreover, the drawbridge leading from the pits over the greyhound circuit would not carry more than four tons, preventing the use of a really heavy roller on the track.

The press previews of the next home fixture, against West Ham Hawks, again in the English Speedway Trophy, revealed that the poor result against Belle Vue and the track problems had been particularly unfortunate as the crowd had been up on the first night's reported attendance of 4,000.

Westwood fought back gamely, reporting that the mechanical problems suffered by Nottingham riders had been addressed by the purchase of two new machines for use as track spares, while the team's other machines had had their engines stripped and tuned.

The preview also revealed that the amount of cinders used on the track, 'to meet ACU requirements', had in fact been excessive. For the West Ham match, 100 tons of the dressing had been removed, thousands of gallons of water had been poured on to aid binding, and two heavy rollers had been at work on the surface.

On track, the debutant against Belle Vue, Burns, who had failed to score, was replaced by another young hopeful, Ken Glover, who had shown up well in the second half. The result of the behind-the-scenes work paid instant dividends, Nottingham beating the Hawks 53-31, with a maximum for George Greenwood. The 'King of Crash', Phil Bishop, top-scored for West Ham with nine.

Nottingham fans, disgruntled by the loss of Allott, Lamont and Bravery to Sheffield, received a small amount of consolation when former Wimbledon man Sam Marsland came back into the picture after an outcry in the media. Unfortunately, by the time he returned, the skids were under the promotion.

Nottingham travelled to another Westwood interest, Sheffield, on 28 April, strengthened by the return of Sam Marsland. George Greenwood continued the superb form which had seen him drop only one point in three successive Trophy matches and he dominated Owlerton with a 12-point maximum. Fred Tuck provided most of the support for Greenwood, with nine points, but Sheffield's solid scoring throughout the order brought them a 46-35 victory.

The Owlerton solidarity came from top-scorer Stan Williams (9) and, turning the knife in the wound, from the former Nottingham trio of Bravery (9), Lamont (8) and Allott (8). For Nottingham, the remaining six riders scored only 14 points between them, with Marsland managing just a single point on his return to the side.

On 3 May, Sheffield came to the White City and recorded a fairly crushing victory, with a similar 47-35 scoreline. Ted Bravery and Tommy Allott again rubbed it in for the home crowd, each scoring 11 points, and Billy Lamont made it a 'Nottingham 1937' rout by adding 8 points, including two heat wins.

George Greenwood was late arriving after a car breakdown en route from his London base and was beaten into third place in his first ride by Lamont and Williams. He also finished behind Tommy Allott in a later heat, to finish with a comparatively low nine-point total. To make the situation worse, the attendance, for a local derby, was said to be 'disappointing'.

The White City outfit's performances on track continued to vary. Newcastle, visiting Trent Lane for the first time on 9 May, were no match for the home side, losing 55-27. Fred Tuck turned in his best-ever performance for Nottingham, scoring a 12-point maximum, and Fred Strecker and George Greenwood scored 9 apiece. Greenwood, whose equipment was always immaculate, suffered a rare engine failure, while the back-to-form Strecker collided with Newcastle's Maurice Stobart in his last ride but escaped with shock and bruises after being somersaulted through the air.

Newcastle won only three of the fourteen heats. George Pepper – later to be killed in action as a Second World War fighter pilot – and Stobart top-scored with seven points each. The fans at Trent Lane were dwindling in numbers, and those who remained were increasingly vocal against Arthur Westwood. Results were far from disastrous and the problems with the track surface had been overcome. But the winning team of 1937 had built up expectations, and the loss of Bravery, Allott and Lamont to Sheffield really rankled on the terraces.

Wilf Plant made his debut for Nottingham in the home leg of the 1938 National Trophy tie against Hackney. Plant was the only rider to have appeared for both White City (1938) and Long Eaton (1951/52). Nottingham won the two-legged tie on aggregate, but the match was declared void when the Trent Lane side withdrew from league racing.

The first part of 'the match that never was' between Nottingham and Hackney at Trent Lane took place on 16 May. The East Londoners were the visitors in the first leg of the 1938 National Trophy knockout competition, run over eighteen heats. George Greenwood, still a rider of the very highest quality at Second Division level, led Nottingham to an unexpected victory over the eventual divisional champions. The former Wembley man won all his six rides to record an 18-point maximum, and good contributions from Strecker (12) and Tuck (10) brought Nottingham a 60-48 victory on the night and a 12-point lead to take to East London for the second leg.

Hackney owed most to former Nottingham rider Frank Hodgson and the newcomer Archie Windmill, who each scored 11. Trent Lane discovery Tommy Bateman was also in the Hackney side, along with post-war Eastbourne promoter Charlie Dugard. The match was also notable for the debut in Nottingham colours of former Wimbledon rider Wilf Plant.

Windmill – president of the World Speedway Riders Association in 2001 and still a great enthusiast for the sport – has happy memories of Nottingham in the late 1930s:

> It had a uniform shape and usually a good surface, and gave everyone a fair chance. Often when you went away to a different track you had no idea what it was going to be like and it took a couple of races to settle down. There was no mucking about when you went to Nottingham.

The mid-to-late thirties saw a gradual switch from leg-trailing to the foot-forward style of riding which, after the Second World War, was almost universal. 'At the time of the changeover, Nottingham was a track where you could use either style successfully,' Archie recalls. 'It was more difficult on the really big circuits like West Ham, where your leg really started to ache if you rode foot forward over what was a lap distance of nearly a quarter of a mile.'

The Nottingham fans and media did not give the Trent Lane men much hope for the second leg at Waterden Road, but Arthur Westwood's men held Hackney to a scoreline of 59-48 and an aggregate victory by two points.

The prestige of beating the powerful Hackney side and progressing to the next round of the national knock out competition should have firmly removed the memories of the Belle Vue debacle earlier in the season. Nottingham, whilst not reaching the heights of the previous season, had a competent squad, capable of winning most home matches. They possessed, in George Greenwood, probably the top rider in the Second Division and retained local favourites Strecker and Dykes.

The feelings against promoter Westwood ran deep, however, and even the victory over Hackney, so hard fought on the track, was to disappear from the record books courtesy of a committee decision.

On 24 May, four days after the aggregate triumph at Hackney, Trent Lane staged an eliminating round of the 1938 World Championship. There was a particularly warm welcome from the fans for Ted Bravery, married that morning to his Plymouth bride – who watched the racing from the grandstand restaurant.

Phil 'Tiger' Hart of Birmingham, briefly a Nottingham rider in the Provincial League, won the round with 14 points from George Greenwood's 12. Cliff Parkinson, another one-time Nottingham rider, and Tommy Allott scored 11, George Dykes ten and Bravery 9, with the top six positions occupied by current or former White City men.

Press reports of the meeting the next day were completely overshadowed by the news, perhaps not wholly unexpected, that competitive racing was to end at Nottingham White City.

The track's death pangs were to be drawn out over what must have been an agonising time for the small but enthusiastic band of hardcore supporters. Arthur Westwood had been warning of the likely outcome of declining attendances for some time, particularly at a meeting for supporters held in a local hotel. When the press revealed that he had finally decided to cut his losses, at least as far as league and trophy racing were concerned, there was a gap of a week between the announcement and the final meeting.

The substantive announcements were not even made directly by the promoter. The local media, and subsequently the fans, first learnt of the withdrawal of the Nottingham team from Division Two and the National Trophy direct from the Auto Cycle Union, the overall governing body. The ACU statement read:

> Owing to the cessation shortly of official speedway racing at the Nottingham track, and the transference of the team to open at Leeds, the Auto Cycle Union has decided to cancel the result of the National Trophy match Nottingham versus Hackney Wick. Nottingham's place in this competition will be taken by Leeds, and Leeds will now play Hackney Wick in the first round.

The programme cover for the final White City Stadium meeting on 31 May 1938. Promoter Arthur Westwood again had no hesitation in billing the match as being against 'Belle Vue' rather than the Manchester club's reserves.

The English Speedway Trophy match Nottingham versus Belle Vue Reserves scheduled for June 14 at Nottingham will take place at that track on May 31, when Nottingham will also meet West Ham Reserves, and thus end the Nottingham fixtures.

Arthur Westwood's response when asked if the official statement was correct was uncharacteristically brief: 'It must be if the ACU say so,' he told reporters.

Speaking to the *Evening News* speedway correspondent A.J. Turner, Westwood expanded a little on the situation. The promoter's losses on the six matches prior to the World Championship round had been just over £77. The poorly supported World Championship meeting had lost him another £60 in just one night. 'I am not a millionaire. I have had to work hard for my money and I can't afford to carry on losing like that,' Westwood said. He denied that he was forsaking Nottingham altogether and said he would continue to run open licence meetings – he actually used the strange term 'circus meetings' – if the crowd at the last competitive meeting warranted a non-league continuation. The promoter added:

> I have put more work and money into Nottingham than any of my other tracks. Nottingham has a good team, evidenced by the fact that they beat Hackney Wick in the National Trophy, but it has not been appreciated except by the loyal few.

Pulling out of official speedway at Trent Lane after completing the English Speedway Trophy fixtures meant Westwood avoided losing his pre-season guarantee of £500 to the ACU. That would have been forfeited had Nottingham withdrawn after riding a single Second Division match. Under these circumstances, the neutral observer could hardly criticise Westwood for getting out while the deficit was still reasonably small.

The final meeting at Trent Lane, with Belle Vue Reserves as visitors, went ahead as planned, with the Manchester team beating an obviously demoralised Nottingham 48-34. West Ham were unable to raise a team for what should have been an English Speedway Trophy double-header and therefore conceded the points.

Because of the Hawks' withdrawal, the last speedway action at Nottingham took the form of a second-half scratch encounter with Nottingham riding against a combined Belle Vue/Birmingham side.

Nottingham's last ever team in competitive speedway, for the main match against Belle Vue, consisted of George Greenwood and Harold Brailsford, Fred Tuck and Sam Marsland, the evergreen pairing of Fred Strecker and George Dykes, and Wilf Plant and Ted English as the reserves.

The line-up for Nottingham's last-ever match at the White City Stadium, in the English Speedway Trophy against a Belle Vue second team. The Nottingham team was a mere shadow of its 1937 strength, hence the premature closure.

ENGLISH SPEEDWAY TROPHY MATCH

NOTTINGHAM

VERSUS

BELLE VUE

NOTTINGHAM (Black & White)	BELLE VUE (Red, & Black Ace of Clubs)
GEO. GREENWOOD, Capt.	TOMMY PRICE, Capt.
HAROLD BRAILSFORD	OLIVER HART
FRED TUCK	ERNIE PRICE
SAM MARSLAND	ALAN BUTLER
FRED STRECKER	JACK HARGREAVES
GEO. DYKES	HAROLD JACKSON
Reserves :—	Reserves :—
WILF PLANT	JACK GORDON
TED ENGLISH	LEN EYRE

For the second-half event against Belle Vue/Birmingham, the pairings were Greenwood and Plant, Tuck and Marsland, Strecker and Dykes, with Don Hemingway as reserve. Fittingly, Strecker and Dykes were programmed as the Nottingham pairing in the last heat of the match, the last ever race at the White City Stadium.

The chances of any further speedway at Nottingham disappeared on a night of what was described as 'dismal weather', with less than 1,000 people in the stadium and another considerable financial loss for the promoter.

Crowds had been just about adequate for the two seasons of Provincial League speedway in 1936 and 1937. The first two meetings under Arthur Westwood in 1938 reportedly attracted up to 4,000 spectators on each occasion – a level sufficient to make the sport pay at Second Division level.

Just what happened to send the figure down to below 1,000? The wholly unsatisfactory 19 April match against Belle Vue, with the riders apparently going through the motions and recording the lowest times ever for the circuit on a bumpy track, and the home defeat by a Sheffield team largely made up of men who had contributed hugely to Nottingham's successes the previous season were, without fear of contradiction, major factors.

It is also difficult to avoid the conclusion that the hard-to-please Nottingham supporters disliked Arthur Westwood's fairly confrontational management style almost as much as they resented the way he had transferred their favourites to Sheffield.

Many speedway tracks over the years have closed suddenly mid-season or have failed to resurface for a new season. Nottingham staged a final meeting after the death sentence had been pronounced and the licence, in effect, had been transferred to Leeds.

Arthur Westwood had an almost unprecedented opportunity to put across his side of the story, in his own words, without any media editing. In his final programme notes, for the 31 May Belle Vue match, he took full advantage and did not mince his words.

The catchphrases and bravado style already familiar to the fans were in evidence. His farewell to Trent Lane was a curious mixture of regret, realism, hard financial statistics and open criticism of the failure of the Nottingham public to respond to his efforts.

The regret was expressed together with his 'heartfelt thanks' to those who had supported him. 'No words can express the disappointment that I feel in having to close down the track. I hate to be associated with a failure and all my efforts have been in vain,' he said.

The financial statistics made dismal reading at the time and, if accurate – as one assumes they are – made ample justification for his decision. Even today, the figures make interesting reading as an insight into speedway's pre-war finances.

Comparisons, said Westwood, were odious, but gates at his Birmingham Hall Green track were averaging between 8,000 and 9,000 a meeting, and at Sheffield the previous week the World Championship qualifying round had attracted 15,716 people:

> For the qualifying round at Nottingham, where the racing was just as good as at Sheffield, only 2,700 people turned up. You must realise as well as I do that, although speedway racing is the greatest sport of the age, to me as a promoter it is a business proposition. I am leaving you with a clear conscience. I have done my best to do a job of work, but the venture has failed. Now, who is to blame?

Elsewhere in his notes Westwood suggested that Nottingham fans should attend the opening meeting at Leeds (some eighty miles away) and spoke of the possibility of chartering a train. He said:

> I am proud of the riders. I am taking them to Leeds with full confidence that they will give a grand show and do a fine job of work. I am sorry to rub it in, but I must take the boys where they will be appreciated.

Fine words again. For the record, Leeds completed the 1938 season of Second Division fixtures, finishing bottom of the table with just two wins and 4 points to show from sixteen matches. The Lions, as they were known, also raced the rescheduled two-leg National Trophy tie against Hackney, as decreed by the ACU, losing 122-92 on aggregate. Records show an aggregate attendance at Leeds in 1938 of around 61,000, suggesting that gates were little higher than they had been at Nottingham.

The same figures support Westwood's contention that his other tracks were much more successful at the turnstiles. Sheffield attracted an aggregate of 202,000 people in 1938, whilst 147,000 paid for admission at Hall Green.

As Nottingham had completed their English Speedway Trophy fixtures before withdrawal, the team's record was retained in the final table. Nottingham finished third of the five teams in the Northern Section, with four wins from eight fixtures, including the points conceded by West Ham.

At the end of the season, Arthur Westwood's promoting licences were reported to be withdrawn. The 1938 World Champion Bluey Wilkinson took over the reins at Sheffield, and Leeds and Birmingham Hall Green failed to surface for 1939. Westwood's final active fling in speedway was promoting at Tamworth in 1947 and 1948, although he continued to be a regular spectator at tracks for much longer and was president of the Veterans' Association in 1976.

Most of the Nottingham riders went with Westwood to Leeds for the remainder of the 1938 season. When the Fullerton Park track failed to reopen for 1939, and Bluey Wilkinson built a new team at Sheffield, many of Westwood's contracted men from both Leeds and Sheffield, including Ted Bravery, Tommy Allott, Fred Tuck, George Dykes and Fred Strecker, moved on to Stoke.

Nottingham White City Stadium in its final form, following the end of speedway. The 380-yard speedway track has been concreted over in this view and was used to parade the greyhounds at wet meetings. The proximity of the River Trent (top right) can be seen.

When Stoke closed mid-season, the riders dispersed again to various homes, with Strecker and Dykes finishing the season – and, effectively, their speedway careers – at Norwich. Other former Nottingham Provincial League men active in 1939 included George Greenwood and Wilf Plant at Middlesbrough, Billy Lamont at Newcastle, and Frank Hodgson, Phil 'Tiger' Hart and Stan Dell at Hackney Wick.

Of the men who had appeared in Nottingham's colours in top-level racing, in the Southern League in 1930 and 1931 and in the National League in 1933, Les Wotton and Jack Chapman were at Harringay in 1939, Cliff Parkinson was at Wembley, and Nobby Key was at Wimbledon.

Many of the Nottingham riders went on to enjoy further speedway success in the post-Second World War period and at the start of the boom season of 1949, with three divisions in operation for the first time ever, Tommy Price (Wembley), Fred Tuck (Bradford) and Les Wotton (New Cross) were riding in the First Division, whilst Second Division-based ex-Trent Lane men Phil Hart and Stan Dell were at Birmingham, Frank Hodgson and Wilf Plant were at Middlesbrough, Ted Bravery and Charlie Challis were at Norwich, and Tommy Allott and Tommy Bateman were at Sheffield.

Nottingham's influence lingered, albeit in a small and indirect way, in the world of speedway racing.

10

Nottingham – An Epilogue

Greyhound racing survived the war years and continued at Nottingham White City until 1970, when the stadium owners were granted planning consent to close and demolish the track and build warehouses and industrial units on the site.

Although the city fathers had vehemently opposed greyhound racing in the 1920s, the proposal to close the White City drew criticism from some elected members, one of whom described the stadium as 'an oasis in the middle of an industrial area'. The White City management, although admitting that there had been increased totalisator takings at the track in the months before the planning application was submitted, said it was unlikely that the stadium could be made into a going concern, as attendances had been falling over a number of years.

The final greyhound meeting was staged on Saturday 12 September 1970. The crowd of around 1,500 – double the normal attendance – were handed a black-edged 'In Memoriam' card as they approached the turnstiles, mourning the loss of the stadium as a sporting venue after nearly forty years.

Quite why Nottingham White City had failed to resurface as a speedway venue during the sport's golden age of the late forties and early fifties is something of a mystery, but is usually explained by the reluctance of the greyhound company to accommodate the bikes again. Ironically, given the immediate destination of the Nottingham team after the 1938 closure, only two of what can be called England's major cities failed to stage speedway after the Second World War – Nottingham and Leeds.

Although in some cases the tracks have now vanished, Birmingham, Manchester, Sheffield, Liverpool, Bradford, Newcastle, Hull and Southampton – numerically the largest provincial centres – all staged speedway.

The White City track was concreted over, allowing the greyhounds to be paraded on a firm surface on wet nights but virtually ruling out speedway. Efforts were made to reintroduce the sport in England's eighth most populous city. Reg Fearman, who promoted at Long Eaton with his partners from 1963-1967, says that many people 'knocked on the door' at Trent Lane. Frank Hughes, who promoted stock car racing at Long Eaton and Skegness together with his brother Neville, a well-known stox driver in the fifties and early sixties, also confirms that he looked at White City. Their efforts came to nothing.

Planning archives reveal that an application for a speedway circuit was made to Nottingham City Council in the late 1940s for a site close to the southern ring road and the Clifton Bridge. This application was rejected. The speedway press reported at the same time that Control Board officials had been visiting prospective new venues, including Nottingham, although this might have meant an inspection of the Station Road, Long Eaton circuit.

In later years, a new greyhound track was built not far from the site of White City, in the car park of Nottingham Racecourse, and a well-known current promoter is reported to have considered the possibility of introducing the sport at the venue. The name of Nottingham did resurface in speedway for two seasons. When Dan McCormick revived Long Eaton in 1979, after one of the track's temporary closures, he used the name Nottingham Outlaws in a bid to attract more support for Station Road from the city, taking a wild west rather than a Sherwood Forest theme. The move was not particularly successful.

The greyhounds are paraded for the last time on the former White City speedway track on the last night of dog racing in September 1970.

Nottingham's only post-Second World War speedway. The grass track, sanded on the bends, was situated off University Boulevard, next to the Beeston Sidings railway yard, visible in the background. Here, Belle Vue star Louis Lawson, second from the right, leaps out of the gate. Lawson's Aces teammate Dent Oliver also rode in the meeting, staged for charity.

Programmes for the meetings held in 1947 at the Nottingham Highfields track gave no indication of the venue or the year, but former world number three Louis Lawson, who rode in the meetings, provided the answers.

At the end of 2005, evidence was discovered that there had been speedway, of a kind, in Nottingham in the post-war era. A programme came to light, headed 'Speedway', produced for a meeting in the summer of 1947 but without any indication of the actual venue. The promoting club, and the fact that all the advertisements were for Nottingham companies, suggested that the track must have been somewhere in or around the city.

Organised by Nottingham Cheetahs Motor Cycle and Light Car Club, the meeting featured a team labelled Nottingham – including the young Belle Vue team men Dent Oliver and locally-born Louis Lawson – versus The Rest, who included Middlesbrough riders Wilf Plant and Geoff Godwin.

The mystery was soon explained, with Lawson, who has lived in Nottinghamshire for all of his eighty-five years, providing the answers. Louis remembered riding at the track, which was situated at Highfields, off University Boulevard, Nottingham, on a site now partially occupied by a science park. Further enquiries established that the track was a 'sanded oval circuit'.

Speedway history involves a great deal of fascinating detective work. Louis Lawson's memories and his description of the venue set bells ringing. A previously unidentified photograph of riders leaving the starting gate on a grass track, with a substantial crowd in the background, standing behind a metal barrier, has a backdrop of a line of poplar trees, behind which stand wagons in a railway goods yard. An examination of present day Highfields reveals the line of trees still intact. Behind the trees are the rusting tracks of a goods yard!

It is still unclear how many meetings were held at the Highfields track. The first that can be traced was on Monday 30 June 1947, with a second held three weeks later on Monday 21 July. Press coverage of the meetings was sparse – newspapers were still badly affected by post-war paper rationing and there was little space for sport.

Wilf Plant won a Silver Helmet contest on 30 June, while Louis Lawson lifted the Club Cup on 21 July, following the Nottingham versus the Rest match. At the same meeting, Wilf

Louis Lawson started out in grass-track events promoted by White City speedway favourites Fred Strecker and George Dykes at Bonser's Farm, to the north of the city of Nottingham. Lawson is seen on his first grass machine in the late 1930s.

Nottingham-born Louis Lawson, world number three in 1949, was a teenage spectator at White City but never rode on the track. Here, riding for his only club, Belle Vue, he heads Birmingham's Graham Warren at Perry Barr.

Louis Lawson (right) on the rostrum at Wembley, with winner Tommy Price of Wembley, who rode on loan for Nottingham in 1936, and runner–up Jack Parker (left).

Plant set a new track record time of 62 seconds, which suggests that the circuit was a fairly small one. Crowds at the venue were estimated at reaching 'several hundreds'.

Advertisements in the undated programme which has come to light include one for the motorcycle shop run by Birmingham, Leicester and Long Eaton rider Lionel Watling. The second half of the meeting featured a scratch race including a 'Leo' Watling – probably Lionel.

The meeting officials included C. Shelton as pit manager – probably the pre-war Wembley pioneer and Nottingham Olympic rider Charlie Shelton. Shelton and fellow Nottingham men Fred Strecker and George Dykes were always closely involved in promotion in the area and were among the Nottingham riders who staged an indeterminate number of meetings at Long Eaton in 1930.

The Nottinghamshire speedway flag was certainly kept flying during the late 1940s by Louis Lawson, who had first ridden a motorcycle in the fields near his Gunthorpe home and competed in grass-track meetings organised by the Nottingham Tornado Motorcycle Club at Bonser's Farm, to the north of the city, in the late 1930s.

After gaining a great deal of grass-track experience in the Bristol area when he was stationed there during the Second World War, Louis was spotted by Frank Varey and given rides at Sheffield and Belle Vue. He bought Bluey Wilkinson's machine, which had been left during the war years in the workshops at Sheffield's Owlerton Stadium, and broke into the Belle Vue side when speedway started up again in earnest.

When the World Championship was revived in 1949, Lawson took third place in front of 93,000 people at Wembley Stadium. The first post-war title was won by Tommy Price, the Wembley and England star who had ridden briefly on loan for Nottingham during the

A modern-day shot of Louis Lawson at his Nottinghamshire home on the bike he rode in the 1949 world final at Wembley.

Provincial League days. Price became the first Englishman to win the World Championship and, with Jack Parker of Belle Vue as runner-up, it was an unprecedented clean sweep for England.

One would certainly need to be an optimist to predict the eventual return of speedway to the city of Nottingham in the twenty-first century. Planning and noise regulations alone are making the introduction or reintroduction of speedway to urban areas a difficult task, although the Birmingham revival scheduled for Perry Barr in 2007 is encouraging.

11

The Archers in a Golden Era

When the Second World War called a premature halt to the 1939 speedway season, the sport had established itself as a serious activity in Britain. Although the number of tracks was nowhere near the figure of the initial boom a decade or so before, those that did offer regular league speedway were, for the most part, well established, well organised and well attended.

Sport in general was encouraged during the war years as a means of providing recreation for those members of the armed forces fortunate enough to be either stationed in the UK or on leave, and for the millions of home-front workers putting in long hours in munitions factories or keeping the railways and other essential services running.

After the initial suspension of activities, professional football organised itself into mostly regional competitions. Guest players were introduced, which meant that men stationed in a city as PT instructors were encouraged to turn out for the local side. Speedway was not so fortunate. Journeys had to be necessary and petrol was strictly rationed. The sport was mainly kept alive by Manchester's Belle Vue where, from 23 September 1939 to 20 October 1945, the Hyde Road track staged weekly meetings during the appropriate months of the year.

No fewer than 170 senior meetings and six all-novice events, watched by more than 2 million spectators, were run by the indefatigable Miss Alice Hart, the Belle Vue speedway manager. Programmes proudly boasted that 'no petrol whatsoever' was used, grading the track between races was abandoned to save fuel and, of course, all meetings were run in the daylight hours.

Many pre-war Nottingham riders were active at wartime Belle Vue, gaining an honoured place on the Hyde Road roll of honour. Fred Tuck, Les Wotton, Wilf Plant, Tommy Allott, Tommy Price, Ted Bravery, Tommy Bateman, Stan Dell, Phil 'Tiger' Hart and Dicky Wise all competed at one time or another and Tuck, riding with West Ham's Eric Chitty, won the All England Best Pairs in 1943.

Southampton and West Ham had each run a single meeting in 1940 and, towards the end of hostilities in 1945, New Cross reopened for a short season, reportedly having to lock 10,000 disappointed fans out of the first fixture.

This enthusiasm was the forerunner of what was to follow. When speedway returned on a proper league basis in 1946, more than 6.5 million people flocked through the turnstiles at the dozen tracks which had managed to open and it was reported that 57,000 watched West Ham's opening friendly against Wembley.

Despite the difficulties caused by continuing rationing, and by a government which regarded weekday sport as a threat to industrial productivity and imposed a stinging entertainment tax, speedway expanded rapidly in the late 1940s. In the West Midlands, Birmingham, Coventry, Stoke, Cradley Heath and Tamworth were up and running by the time the 1948 season got underway, but the East Midlands was slower to get off the mark – perhaps not altogether surprising, given that both Nottingham and Leicester had struggled to attract the crowds in the 1930s.

In addition to the grass and sand-track speedway at Nottingham's Highfields in 1947, a Leicester team raced in three away challenge matches in 1948. Former Nottingham rider Charlie Challis appeared in all three, and another White City favourite, George Dykes, rode in one match.

Former Nottingham men Charlie Challis and George Dykes reappeared briefly when Leicester returned to the speedway scene in 1948. Challis captained the new Hunters team in its three away challenge matches that year and is pictured on the machine. Dykes is third from the right, while on his right is future Long Eaton promoter Ron Wilson.

Grass-track racing continued in the Nottingham and Derby area in the post-Second World War era and helped to produce speedway riders. In this shot at Bonser's Farm, Nottingham, the sixteen-year-old Lionel Watling, later to ride for First Division Birmingham, Tamworth, Long Eaton and Leicester, gets some tuition from former Nottingham man Rocky Burnham (in plus fours) and his father.

Leicester reappeared at the Blackbird Road Stadium in 1949 as members of the Third Division. The Hunters' first match that year was a challenge, away to Rayleigh, and the team included the two former Nottingham men. Unfortunately, George Dykes was injured and made no further appearances, while Challis also quickly faded from view.

During that year, with the door apparently closed to speedway by the management at Nottingham White City, the focus turned to Station Road, Long Eaton, where the roar of speedway machines had not been heard for nearly two decades.

Greyhound racing had also survived the war and Long Eaton Stadium had, for some time, been part of a consortium controlled by Leicester Stadium, which also included the dog tracks at Hull and Doncaster. One of the directors of the controlling company was the pioneer Leicester dirt-track rider Arthur Sherlock, who had ridden at Station Road in 1929.

Sherlock believed that speedway could make the struggling Derbyshire venue a paying proposition again. For, by 1949, Long Eaton Stadium was struggling, with the dog racing reportedly losing £150 a week.

A major fire in March 1948 had destroyed most of the grandstand accommodation and the clubroom, and had badly damaged the greyhound kennels and other facilities, killing eleven dogs. The alarm had been raised by passers-by who noticed smoke coming from the kennel area. Together with the firefighters, members of the public did their best to try and liberate the fire-maddened animals, some of which bit their rescuers.

When Sherlock and his associate, former Leicester Tigers rugby star Stan Saunders, approached the Long Eaton Urban District Council, the initial response was encouraging. As in Nottingham, greyhound racing had never been well thought of by council or church leaders – more influential in those days than now – and Sherlock and Saunders were not alone in thinking that motorbikes were potentially a better bet than greyhounds.

Several of the local councillors were clearly influenced by the possibility that a successful speedway team might mean the end of greyhound racing at Station Road. The consensus of opinion was that the yapping of the dogs was a nuisance and that motorbikes could be the lesser of the two evils!

The council agreed that no fewer than six of its elected members, together with the sanitary inspector, should accept an invitation from Sherlock and Saunders to attend a Friday evening meeting at Blackbird Road and report back.

The councillors were duly impressed, reporting that the main objections from local residents at Leicester revolved around the outward facing tannoy system, which would be amended at Station Road. Councillor W.H. Martin said he had been amazed to find that the noise from the bikes was not as bad as he had thought it would be.

He told the special meeting of the council, held to consider the speedway application, that he had been delighted to see, 'such a respectable crowd, so enthusiastic and with no gambling allowed.' He did not think a cleaner sport had ever been seen.

Most of the once extensive spectator facilities at Long Eaton Stadium were destroyed by an outbreak of fire in 1948 before speedway returned to the venue.

The fifteen members of the council, who were also influenced by the offer of Sherlock and Saunders to make the centre green at the Stadium available for a new town football club, gave their unanimous backing to speedway. By early July the *Long Eaton Advertiser* reported that the new track was ready, with 1,700 tons of cinders laid on the foundations of the 1929 circuit. The new strip would be surfaced with three inches of fine ash. The riders were to have centrally-heated dressing rooms with hot and cold showers and the pits were to be in full view of the spectators.

The *Advertiser* said attention had also been paid to the fairly rudimentary surviving spectator facilities. Plans were in hand for a new stand and a start had been made on the new social club. The capacity of the Stadium was believed to be around 15,000, but the planned programme of reconstruction would eventually lead to a capacity of 50,000, in what would become 'a Wembley of the Midlands'.

The team would be known as the Archers and, although it was too late to join the Third Division for 1949, the side would ride challenge matches with a view to league membership in 1950. All that remained was final approval from the Speedway Control Board.

That body seemed less impressed than the members and officers of Long Eaton Urban District Council. A month later, the *Advertiser* reported a 'speedway bombshell' in the shape of a refusal by the Board to grant a racing licence. Arthur Sherlock told the newspaper that some £10,000 had already been spent on the new track and other facilities, and a Control Board official who had inspected the work had been satisfied with what he had seen.

Mr John Batson – press liaison officer for the Control Board – said it was not policy to give reasons for decisions. Some three months later, the Control Board relented and granted a provisional licence for challenge matches for 1950. It was not, however, the end of problems for the Stadium management, who were hit by another, if less serious, outbreak of fire in mid-January 1950.

The floor of the surviving stand, part of the roof, the totalisator facilities and the judges box and greyhound control panel were damaged, but the new clubroom was not structurally affected, although stock valued at £1,000 was spoilt by heat, smoke and water.

By mid-April, the *Nottingham Evening News* was able to publish a picture of the finishing touches being applied to the 370-yard track and associated facilities. The earlier intention to use cinders topped with ash had been revoked, and the *News* reported that red shale had now been laid.

There had been speculation that Long Eaton would go straight into Third Division racing, taking the place of Rayleigh, but the doubts about the future of the Essex track had been put to rest.

Hard facts about the new promotion and its team building activities began to emerge in the local press. What had finally persuaded the Control Board to grant a licence is not altogether clear, but both Arthur Sherlock and Stan Saunders appeared to have vanished (at least publicly) from the equation. The track was to be managed and the speedway licence held by Bob Peett, speedway manager at Leicester in 1949, who had also been associated with Harringay.

Long Eaton Speedway Ltd had four named directors – S.H. (Stan) Lish, the managing director, Bob Peett, W.A. Galloway and D.J. Boyer.

Speedway Control Board chairman Lt Colonel Vernon Brooke inspected the circuit on Wednesday 17 May and the first meeting was set for the following Thursday, 25 May.

Starting up a full month or more after most tracks had opened for the 1950 season meant that team building, even for challenge matches, had not been easy. The management had staged trials at Station Road behind closed doors and, as a result, had signed a mixture of veterans, loaned riders from other clubs, and young hopefuls who had failed to find a track during the opening month of the season.

The press reported that the job of captaining the Archers had been given to Don Gray, on loan from First Division New Cross, where he had made a handful of team appearances the previous season. He was joined at Station Road by two other Old Kent Road juniors, Eric Minall (18) and Fred Siggins, who at just seventeen and a half was to be the baby of the side.

Right: Few of the riders signed by Long Eaton for the initial season of challenge matches had much experience of league speedway. One exception was Eric Mason, formerly with Halifax and Hull. He was to prove a valuable acquisition, with the ability to score heavily, particularly at Station Road.

Below: The original Archers squad lines up in front of the grandstand at Station Road at the start of the 1950 season. From left to right, back row: Bob Peett (speedway manager), Bill Humphries, Eric Minall, Russell Davey, Bob Ibbotson, Fred Siggins, Eric Mason, Stan Lish (promoter). Front row: Johnny Higham, Frank Malouf, Pedlar Palmer, George Butler.

Bradford-born Eric Mason had ridden at Halifax and Hull, and Wimbledon asset George Butler had gained experience at Poole in 1948 and Hastings in 1949. Bob Ibbotson from Melton Mowbray had, in the past, ridden at Leicester and Fleetwood; Johnny Higham was a Yorkshireman with some experience at Wombwell, who had shown up well in the private trials; and Russell Davey from Norwich was described as being a protégé of former Yarmouth skipper Syd Hipperson, who lined up for 1950 with Leicester.

Two days before the actual meeting, Bob Peett staged a full-scale dress rehearsal at Station Road, with free admission. The track staff marched out to the sound of a post horn, the National Anthem was played and the riders contracted to the Archers were introduced to a crowd of around 3,000, who were waiting for the first of three exhibition laps scheduled for the rehearsal.

Peett was not satisfied with the smoothness of the presentation and sent everyone back to their marks to start again! Only when he was completely happy did the racing begin, featuring, for the first time on a speedway track, the race jacket design of a green archer on a yellow background.

The first opposition for the Archers, on 25 May, was provided by a composite side named the Third Division Stars – remarkable for the inclusion of no less than five riders who were to be associated with Long Eaton at a later stage.

Nottingham-born Lionel Watling of Tamworth captained the visitors and was joined by his teammates Eric Boothroyd and Ivor Davies, plus Johnny Carpenter, Ron Wilson and Pedlar Palmer from Leicester, and Pat Flanaghan and Doug Papworth of Aldershot.

Ernest Palmer was to be transferred from Blackbird Road to Long Eaton very soon after the initial meeting; Watling was to ride for the Archers on loan later in 1950 and again in 1952; Flanaghan made odd appearances in the Archers' colours; Boothroyd was a star at Station Road in the Provincial League team of 1964; and Ron Wilson was to become co-promoter with Reg Fearman in the mid-1960s, when his son Ray became one of the Derbyshire track's finest-ever products.

The *Derby Evening Telegraph*, which was to give extensive coverage to speedway, reported that rain on the night kept the crowd down to about 3,000, far less than the 10,000 to 15,000 expected. There was no fairytale beginning on the track either, with the *Telegraph* reporting that the Archers had been 'out-ridden and out-manoeuvred'.

The Third Division Stars registered a 52-31 victory, led superbly by Watling, who scored a 12-point maximum and recorded the fastest time of the night at 73.3 seconds. Don Gray did all that had been expected of him by the home fans, dropping just one point to Watling, and Eric Minall with 7 points and Eric Mason with 6 also impressed. Butler (2 points), perhaps the most experienced man in the Archers team, overslid in his first race and was excluded. He was thrown heavily in a later heat when his chain snapped, causing the rear wheel to lock.

Fred Siggins also had a disappointing debut, scoring a single point and experiencing a fall and engine failure. Ibbotson, with 2 points, and Higham, with 1, completed the scoring for the Archers, with Russell Davey failing to score.

Syd Hipperson of Leicester won Station Road's second meeting, an individual trophy event, in front of what was described as an improved attendance, and he equalled Lionel Watling's fastest time of 73.3 seconds in the process.

The first bona fide team to visit Long Eaton in 1950 was Rayleigh. Don Gray had been recalled to New Cross, but the Archers had found a good replacement in Ernest 'Pedlar' Palmer, transferred from Leicester following his good showing – 5 points from two rides – for the Third Division Stars in the opening meeting.

Palmer was a Sheffield-born former army despatch rider and bomb disposal man who had experience at Wombwell before joining Leicester for the Hunters' inaugural season. Like many riders, his opportunities had been restricted by the Second World War, and he was already thirty years old in 1950, but the Long Eaton management had no hesitation in handing him the captaincy vacated by Gray.

He led the Archers to a 52-31 victory over Rayleigh, scoring 10 points himself, and recorded his first maximum for the club a week later when Aldershot were beaten 49-35. Eric Minall also scored a maximum against the Shots, and Australian veteran Frank Malouf – formerly with Fleetwood – made his debut in this match as the management sought to strengthen the side with experience.

Palmer was again the mainstay as the next two matches were lost, against Tamworth and Liverpool. For the match against the Chads, Long Eaton brought in former Hanley skipper Dave Anderson, who had been out of the sport injured.

Lionel Watling had been included in the Tamworth team at Station Road but both the rider, who had a business in Nottingham, and the Archers management were anxious to see him perform at Station Road whenever possible. He was included in the side against Swindon,

Above left: Although New Cross loanee Don Gray acted as captain for Long Eaton's first match, he was recalled to South London after that one single appearance and the job went to Ernest 'Pedlar' Palmer, pictured here, a wartime despatch rider and bomb disposal man, signed from Leicester.

Above right: Australian Frank Malouf from New South Wales was already approaching the veteran stage, at least in terms of age, in the early 1950s. Nevertheless, Malouf, seen here in the Station Road pits, continued to ride in Australia until the early 1960s.

who were currently lying second in the Third Division, and his 12-point maximum helped Long Eaton to a 52-32 victory.

Frank Malouf and Fred Siggins scored 11 points each in the Archers' most satisfying display to date. In the second half of the meeting, George Dykes attempted another comeback, riding in a match race against Mick Mitchell. The Swindon captain won what was described as 'a slow race' and, sadly, no more was heard of a return to racing for the former Nottingham White City man.

The regular challenge matches at Station Road were giving the fans an appetite for the real thing, and rumours began to circulate that Tamworth, struggling to attract a paying crowd in Division Three, would close down and allow Long Eaton to take over their league fixtures.

Unlike many speedway rumours, this one held a fair amount of truth. Bob Peett confirmed that he had been approached by Les Marshall, the Birmingham promoter, who also controlled Tamworth. Mr Marshall had asked if, in the event of Tamworth pulling out, Long Eaton would take the vacant Third Division place, subject to Control Board approval.

Peett and his fellow directors accepted the proposal and agreed terms for some of the Tamworth riders, but the Control Board persuaded Les Marshall to carry on until the end of the 1950 season.

When the Tammies arrived at Station Road on 13 July to give the home side a chance to take revenge for the earlier defeat, there was a major gap in the Staffordshire team's line-up. Lionel Watling was riding for Long Eaton – something perhaps only possible in speedway and, despite the fact that it was only a challenge match, something of a slap in the face for Tamworth fans making the short trip down the A453.

Left: Lionel Watling was a Tamworth rider in Division Three in 1950, but when the Tammies came to Station Road for a second challenge match, he was included in the Long Eaton team.

Below: Skipper Ernest Palmer (left) and Eric Mason set off on a pre-match parade in 1950, with the solid starting grid visible in this shot.

The long and the short of it. Bob Ibbotson (left), later a Scarborough fishing-boat skipper, and Ernest Palmer in 1950.

The Archers' line-up of George Butler and Pedlar Palmer, Watling and Minall, Siggins and Malouf, with Bill Humphries, signed from Birmingham, and Bob Ibbotson as reserves, looked capable of acquitting itself well in the Third Division and was, if anything, stronger than the team which was to eventually take its place in league racing at the start of 1951.

The Tamworth team looked makeshift in comparison and Long Eaton recorded a 53-30 victory, led by Malouf with 10 points, Watling with 9, and Palmer and Siggins with 8 points apiece. The Tammies, however, had the rider of the night, with Ivor 'Digger' Davies dropping just 1 point, being beaten by Frank Malouf in the final heat.

Inconsistent form, which often depended on whether or not Watling was available to ride for the Archers, continued into August. Bank Holiday Monday, then at the start of the month, brought Division Two's Sheffield to Station Road. Visiting captain Len Williams set the pace in the first heat, clipping two-fifths of a second off Lionel Watling's track record to set a new fastest time of 73 seconds dead. Williams beat Pedlar Palmer to the line, inflicting the home skipper's only defeat of the match.

Long Eaton, surprisingly, took an early lead, with a 5-1 from Eric Minall and Eric Mason in heat two, but Sheffield levelled matters in the next race and then steadily drew ahead for an eventual 49-35 victory.

Eric Minall caused a stir when he was unable to slow down after crossing the finish line for his second heat win of the night and hit the fence on the first bend! He was unhurt and able to take part in his next scheduled heat. Len Williams also won his second race but then faded and the Burton-on-Trent-based Peter Orpwood was top scorer for Sheffield with nine points.

The bank holiday visit of Sheffield had drawn a reported crowd in the region of 12,000 and, according to the local press, even this was well exceeded on 15 August, when the Leicester Hunters came to Station Road. Leicester were nicknamed 'the team of captains' with no fewer than seven members of the Blackbird Road squad having held the captaincy with one team or another.

Above: Second Division Sheffield attracted a large crowd to Station Road for an August Bank Holiday Monday 1950 challenge match. Peter Orpwood (inside) and Jack Chignall of the Tars, as Sheffield were known at the time, have the advantage, but Ernest Palmer (second from right) is about to come through to take the lead. Bob Ibbotson is on the outside.

Left: Promising Jim Taylor went back to Australia after the 1950 season and never returned.

Five of them were in the line-up at Station Road: Cyril Page (Leicester), Harwood Pike (Wombwell), Mick Mitchell (Swindon), Joe Bowkis (Poole), and Les Beaumont (Cradley Heath). Future Long Eaton promoter Ron Wilson completed the Hunters' line-up, with Australian discovery Lionel Benson and Johnny Carpenter at reserve. Long Eaton gave a debut to another Australian, Jim Taylor, who had impressed in a second-half debut the previous week.

In one of the closest and most exciting matches yet seen at Station Road, the two sides were never more than two points apart over the first nine heats, with first Leicester and then Long Eaton securing and then losing a narrow advantage. The riders went to the tapes for heat ten with the scores level on 27-27, but Harwood Pike and Lionel Benson outrode Mason and Minall for a 5-1.

Malouf and Humphries brought it back to level pegging when they beat Mitchell and Bowkis in the next race to bring the scores to 33-33, with heavy rain now starting to fall. In heat twelve, Long Eaton lost Siggins, who hit the fence on the home straight, opposite the timekeeper's box, and crashed heavily on the concrete starting grid. In the re-run, Carpenter and Beaumont scored a 4-2 over Bob Ibbotson to give the visitors a two-point lead.

With two races to go, the streaming rain was thinning out the crowd in a stadium largely without cover. Debutant Aussie Jim Taylor became an instant hero in heat thirteen when he held off the Hunters' duo of Carpenter and Benson to set up a last-heat decider.

The Archers needed a 5-1 to win the match and a 4-2 for a draw, and things got off to the best possible start when Palmer and Malouf shot out of the gate in front of Pike and Ron Wilson. First Palmer fell and was out of the race, and then Malouf also overslid. The Australian remounted, only to fall again as he chased the Leicester duo, and in the end the two visiting riders coasted over the line for a 5-0 heat win and a 45-38 victory in the match.

Harwood Pike top-scored for Leicester with ten points and Ron Wilson scored nine, but the real aces for the Hunters were reserves Lionel Benson and Johnny Carpenter, who each notched eight points, making up for disappointing displays from Page, Mitchell, Bowkis and Beaumont. Minall and Malouf with eight and Palmer with seven were the best of the Archers.

Fred Siggins broke an ankle when he crashed on the concrete starting grid and wrote off the frame of his machine. Siggins had become a huge favourite with the Station Road crowd and supporters rallied round to buy him a new frame.

Two dances were held on the same evening by the Supporters' Club, leading to claims, in some quarters, of a split in the organisation. The main event, held at the Blue Ball Hotel in Risley, was attended by Anne Shelton, one of the most popular singers of the immediate post-war period and a rival for Vera Lynn's title of 'Forces' Sweetheart'.

She was welcomed to the event by Ernest 'Pedlar' Palmer, the Archers' captain, and presented with a bouquet by Mrs Palmer. After singing four songs, accompanied by her personal pianist, she signed autographs and pictures as well as the plaster cast on Siggins' ankle.

Results-wise, the Archers continued to win the majority of the challenge matches at Station Road, gaining revenge for an earlier defeat by beating Liverpool 46-37. Eric Minall lowered the track record to 72.3 seconds in a 50-34 win over Swindon.

There was another big Station Road crowd for the deciding match in a series of three contests between Young England and Young Australia. The teams were made up of riders from Midland sides and the description 'Young' stretched the imagination a little, given the inclusion of the two captains for the night, the thirty-year-old Ernest Palmer for England and the veteran Frank Malouf for Australia.

England tracked Palmer, Eric Minall, Fred Siggins and Eric Mason from the home club, Cyril Page, Harwood Pike, and Ron Wilson from Leicester, and Lionel Watling from Tamworth. Australia featured Malouf and Jim Taylor from Long Eaton, Lionel Benson from Leicester, Bill Harris and Lindsey Mitchell from Hanley, Frank Young from Cradley Heath, Cecil Hookham from Tamworth and Bluey Langtry, described as being attached to the Belfast open licence promotion.

England took an immediate lead, when Pike and Palmer scored a first heat 5-1 over Malouf and Taylor, and held it until the Stoke Division Two pairing of Harris and Mitchell levelled things in heat five. The Aussies went ahead for the first time in the following race and the scores continued to fluctuate. Watling and Palmer gave England a four-point lead when they recorded a 5-1 in heat nine, but Malouf and Taylor turned the tables in the next race to make the interval score 30-30.

After the restart, the lead once again continued to change hands and, after heat thirteen, the score was again level, for the seventh time so far in the match, at 39-39. It seemed that nothing could separate the two well-matched sides for long, as England's reserves Wilson and Mason restored the four-point lead with a 5-1, only to see Harris and Taylor show a clean pair of heels to Minall and Siggins.

At the end of the 1950 season Station Road staged a Young England versus Young Australia challenge match. Here, Lionel Watling is presented during the parade. Next to him, Leicester Hunters man and future Long Eaton promoter Ron Wilson looks apprehensive.

Heat sixteen was the most eventful of the night. Malouf was excluded when he failed to beat the two-minute warning siren. Frank Young took his place and then collided with Watling going into the first bend. Young landed on his feet and took part in the re-run, but Watling, who appeared to land on his head, was carried off unconscious with blood streaming down his face.

Cyril Page won the re-run for England with the heat points shared, but Lionel Benson and Bill Harris gave Australia a four-point lead in the penultimate race. England needed a 5-1 to level the match but, although Malouf dropped out with an engine failure, Benson headed Page and Pike home to give the Aussies a 56-52 victory. Benson was the rider of the night, dropping only 1 point from his six rides.

The full scorers were, for England: Palmer (9), Pike (9), Page (9), Watling (8), Minall (7), Wilson (6), Mason (3) and Siggins (1). For Australia: Benson (17), Harris (12), Mitchell (9), Taylor (7), Malouf (5), Young (5), Langtry (1) and Hookham (0).

Watling, who was tipped to sign for the Archers on a full-time basis for 1951, was found to have facial lacerations.

The inaugural season came to a close at Station Road with a defeat for the home side at the hands of a scratch team dubbed The Rest, who won by 48 points to 36. Joe Bowkis (9), Cyril Page (8) and Lionel Benson (8) headed the score chart for the winning team while Eric Mason (8), Minall (7) and Watling (7) were best for the Archers on a night when Pedlar Palmer broke yet another pair of spectacles!

The general feeling was that the twenty-three meetings held at Station Road during 1950 had established the venue as being worthy of league recognition for the following season. Sixteen of the meetings were challenge matches pitting the Archers against Third Division opposition, and the home side won nine and lost seven, scoring 728 points against 613.

One of the finest fifties action shots at Station Road. A determined 'Pedlar' Palmer comes inside Bob Jones of Swindon on the first bend, with Bob Ibbotson lying third, in this *Derby Evening Telegraph* picture from 29 June 1950.

Ernest Palmer (far right) is presented with the 1950 Supporters' Trophy at an end-of-season dance in the Pavilion Hotel, adjacent to the Stadium.

No fewer than 303 of those points came from two men. Ernest Palmer rode in all 16 matches against Third Division clubs, and scored 148 points, with two maximums. Frank Malouf missed just the opening match against Rayleigh, and top-scored with 155 points, including four maximums.

Palmer and Malouf would provide two of the three heat leaders needed for Third Division racing in 1951, and the odds were heavily on Lionel Watling – who had scored 278 points for Tamworth in league matches – being the third.

With Jim Taylor – the find of the season – and Eric Mason, as well as the possibility of another year at Station Road for the New Cross loanees Minall and Siggins, and competition at reserve between Bill Humphries, Bob Ibbotson and newcomer Johnnie Jones, the Archers management did not appear to have too many team worries for the future.

12

League Status at Last

Long Eaton's debut in league speedway racing came twenty-two years after a team was apparently entered into the 1929 English Dirt-Track League, never to actually race a match. The first taste of proper competitive action for the Station Road supporters came at a time when speedway was still expanding, despite the fact that the actual number of paid admissions to tracks in 1950 – nearly 10.5 million – was down on the 12 million admissions in 1949. One reason put forward for the decline, by a still optimistic speedway press, was the bad weather often experienced around the country in 1950.

The 1951 season began with thirty-eight licensed tracks, including non-league newcomers Ipswich. The continuing burden of high entertainment tax was a drawback, with speedway paying 1s 1d per half crown admission, compared to the 3d paid by soccer on the same admission price. The Labour government of Clement Attlee, struggling with post-war reconstruction, was desperate for revenue, yet wary of upsetting the huge numbers of soccer fans.

Despite this, there was a high degree of optimism in March 1951. There had been some changes to the management structure at Station Road. Bob Peett, the 1950 director and speedway manager who was originally granted the licence to stage the sport at the Derbyshire venue, had been appointed general manager of Long Eaton Stadium. Long Eaton Speedway managing director Stan Lish at first also took on the duties of clerk of the course and team manager, with his nephew Ken Lish (whose real surname was Bandy) as speedway manager and occasional performer in second-half junior races. Soon after the start of the season, however, Stan Lish's brother, Charles, a pre-war rider with Norwich and, as such, a teammate of ex-Nottingham favourites Fred Strecker and George Dykes, took over as clerk of the course and team manager.

Long Eaton were scheduled to start the second full season at Station Road with what appeared to be a highly attractive challenge match against a Swedish touring side. Respected Midland speedway journalist Barney Bamford told his *Speedway News* readers that the Swedes were being underestimated by the sport's administrators. He believed the tourists – effectively a full Swedish national side – were good enough to face Division Two opposition at least, although his views, he complained, had been ridiculed by the authorities. The headline on his article read: 'Heaven help the Third Division'. Bamford was right to claim that the Swedes were way above Third Division class, and Long Eaton were the first side to be steamrollered.

When the teams paraded at Station Road on the evening of Easter Monday, 26 March 1951, the Archers, compared to the visitors, looked to be only a moderate side. Ernest 'Pedlar' Palmer would again captain the Long Eaton team and Australian veteran Frank Malouf, with Eric Mason, Fred Siggins, Russell Davey, Bob Ibbotson and Bill Humphries, had been retained from the 1950 non-league side, together with the promising Johnnie Jones.

The downside was that three highly significant names were missing from the side that had worn the Archers colours in the last home match of the previous season. Track record-holder Eric Minall was absent, said to be awaiting his call-up for National Service, and Jim Taylor, the young Australian who had showed so much promise the previous year, had decided to remain down under for 1951. The Nottingham-based Lionel Watling, a star with Tamworth in 1950 and also very successful when he guested for the Archers, had been tipped to move

Top: The Long Eaton squad which competed in the National League Third Division in 1951. From left to right, back row: Ken Lish (management and sometime second-halfer), Percy Brine, Frank Malouf, Peter Moore, Bill Humphries, Jack Winstanley, Charles Lish (team manager), Archie Wainwright (mechanic). Front row: Eric Minall, Eric Mason, 'Pedlar' Palmer, Johnnie Jones (crouching).

Above: Archers' Eric Mason (second from left) and skipper Ernest Palmer accept a team flag from the Supporters' Club at the start of the challenge match against the Swedish tourists that launched the 1951 season. Promoter Stan Lish supervises.

Left: The Long Eaton programme for 1951 acknowledged that support came from both Nottingham and Derby.

permanently to Station Road when the Fazeley track closed down. Instead, he was recalled to his First Division parent track, Birmingham.

The visiting team featured Olle Nygren – a twenty-one-year-old who was, later in the season, to ride successfully for First Division Harringay – plus the Carlsson brothers, Bertil and Eskil, Sune Karlsson, ex-Wall of Death rider Stig Pramberg and Gunnar Helqvist. Archers' skipper Ernest Palmer received a new team flag, donated by the Derby branch of the Supporters' Club, before the racing got under way. That was the final time that evening that the spotlight was to be on Long Eaton. The Swedes, as predicted by Barney Bamford, were far too good for Third Division opposition, winning by 57 points to 26.

Although Palmer won the first heat from the Carlsson brothers, the skipper's success raised false hopes. The Swedes won nine of the fourteen heats, with four drawn. The Archers' only race success came in heat ten, when Malouf headed home Eskil Carlsson for a 3-2, with neither of the other two riders finishing. Palmer scored 8 points and Malouf 7 to give the score some respectability. Sune Karlsson and Olle Nygren scored 12-point maximums for the visitors and Nygren beat Eric Minall's existing track record of 72.3 seconds, lowering it to 70.8. Nygren's record was to stand for twelve years.

There was more pain to come for the Archers over the next few days. Swindon came to Station Road on the Thursday evening following the Swedish match and won the first leg of a *Daily Mail* National Trophy match by 58 points to 49. Long Eaton showed only one change from the team that had crashed to the Swedes and, although on the night the new rider's contribution was modest, in the long term his arrival was to prove highly significant.

The new man, who had featured in the second half of the programme against the Swedish tourists, was another young Australian, Peter Moore from Melbourne, whose first season in English speedway, with St Austell in 1950, had given little indication of the force he was to eventually become.

The Trophy match was run over eighteen heats and Long Eaton were kept in the match until close to the end by the brilliance of Frank Malouf, who scored 17 points from his six rides, losing only to Swindon top scorer Danny Malone in heat eight. Malouf got his revenge in heat sixteen, but throughout the match the Robins scored solidly down the order. Malouf's main support came from Bob Ibbotson, with 8 points, and Palmer, with seven, but it was not enough. Two nights later the Archers went to Blunsdon for the second leg, which Swindon won by 71 points to 37.

Young Australian Peter Moore, with St Austell in 1950, made his Archers debut in a National Trophy match against Swindon and developed rapidly at Station Road in 1951.

The Swedes came back to haunt Station Road again on 5 April, when Sune Carlsson and Lennart Carlstrom won an All Stars Best Pairs competition, with a joint total of 21 points. On the night, Frank Malouf was again the most successful individual, scoring 12 points.

Ernest Palmer suffered a cut eye in the Best Pairs – a frequent injury for the captain, who rode in spectacles – and missed the opening away match in the Festival of Britain Trophy at The Weir Stadium, Rayleigh. The home side cantered away to win 82-38, with the only significant contributions for the Archers coming from newcomer Ted Gibson (8), Bill Humphries (6) and Peter Moore (5).

Gibson, who appeared in one or two Festival of Britain Trophy matches for the Archers but had disappeared by the time the Third Division fixtures began, was a rider of modest ability, but one of the sport's many characters who later became noted (and to some degree notorious) when he tried to revive speedway racing in Spain. A former grass-tracker whose racing experience went back to the early 1930s, he rode speedway post-war for Tamworth and Plymouth, and raced in South Africa in the English winters of 1948/49 and 1949/50, before being given a chance at Station Road.

Gibson's Spanish adventures came to a head in 1953, when an English touring party he organised had to borrow money from the British Consul in Barcelona after the initiative had begun to lose money. When the party, who had travelled in a converted coach, machines and all, managed to reach Dover, Gibson reportedly disappeared, leaving his own bike behind. This was later sold and the proceeds divided between the almost destitute riders.

Four 1951 matches for the Archers had brought four heavy defeats for a side quite obviously below strength. Fortunately for the suffering Station Road fans, the next visitors were newcomers Wolverhampton, making their post-war debut as a team. The Wolverhampton management decided to operate with a team of novices at Monmore Green.

Results all season were fairly disastrous, although the track built up and, astonishingly, retained a loyal following of around 5,000 fans. In their challenge match debut at Station Road, the men in gold and black were beaten by 58 points to 24. Frank Malouf and the fast-emerging Peter Moore each scored 11 points.

The Festival of Britain Trophy, in honour of the event held on London's South Bank to celebrate Britain's post-war recovery, was proving to be a disaster all-round for the Archers, who lost 63-57 to Rayleigh at home. Another challenge match, this time providing the opposition for Wolverhampton's first post-war meeting at Monmore Green, gave the team a rare away victory by 48-35, with a first ever 12-point maximum for Peter Moore.

But real disaster was to strike just under a week later when Long Eaton travelled to Penarth Road, Cardiff, to meet the Welsh newcomers in a Festival Trophy match. Fred Siggins, trying to get past the two team-riding Cardiff men in heat six, fell and Bob Ibbotson, close behind his partner, failed to avoid the fallen rider. His machine hit Siggins and caterpaulted Ibbotson into the air. Both riders were taken to hospital and Long Eaton, again using Ted Gibson to fill a hole in the team, eventually lost 83-36. Johnnie Jones top-scored with eight, while Peter Moore continued to progress in difficult circumstances and scored seven.

Manager Ken Lish travelled to Cardiff on the Sunday after the match to visit the injured riders, who were detained in different hospitals in the Welsh capital. Ibbotson sustained a fractured skull and a broken collarbone and was destined to stay in hospital for several weeks. The immediate hero had been Long Eaton team mechanic Archie Wainwright, who had driven all night to the Midlands to collect Ibbotson's wife and take her to her husband's side.

Fred Siggins, only eighteen years old, had suffered a broken thigh and ankle and was also facing the prospect of many weeks out of action. Siggins was a rider who never stopped trying, whatever the opposition. As he was being brought into the Cardiff ambulance room on a stretcher, he told the Archers' new team manager Charlie Lish, 'I am sorry, Charlie, but I did try!'

On the night of the Cardiff meeting – also Long Eaton's traditional Thursday race night – a side labelled as Long Eaton Juniors had taken on Aldershot Juniors at Station Road. The 'Juniors' label was a misnomer as far as Aldershot were concerned, as the team was their Third Division line-up minus top men Basil Harris and Trevor Redmond. Aldershot won 53-31, with Russell Davey, out of the main team line-up, top-scoring for Long Eaton with 7 points from three rides. Support came from junior Ray Binfield from Earls Barton in Northamptonshire, who won two heats.

Right: Injury-prone teenage loanee from New Cross Fred Siggins broke his ankle and smashed a frame in 1950. At Cardiff in 1951, he broke a thigh and an ankle in the crash that ended his partner Bob Ibbotson's speedway career.

Opposite: Crowds were healthy at Station Road in 1951, evidenced by the packed ranks of supporters on the fourth bend in this start-line action shot from a Long Eaton versus Rayleigh clash. The line-up is, from left to right: Jack Unstead (Rayleigh), Johnnie Jones (Long Eaton), Jules Benson (Rayleigh), Jack Winstanley (Long Eaton).

To try and boost the gate with the main Archers away from home, the management had booked Nottinghamshire man Louis Lawson, one of Belle Vue's top men and third in the 1949 World Championship, to ride a best-of-three match race series against fellow England international Cyril Brine of Wimbledon. Lawson won the series in what was to be his only riding appearance at Station Road. He was, however, a familiar face in the pits, and renewed his acquaintance with Long Eaton during the sixties revival.

The already-weak Archers were now facing a team crisis. Birmingham promoter Les Marshall telephoned the Lish family to offer his condolences and the services of another young Australian, Cecil Hookham, a second-halfer at Perry Barr who was struggling to come good.

Hookham went straight into the team when Swindon visited for a Festival Trophy match on 3 May. The visitors won 68-52, making good use of their reserve strength – particularly essential in the Trophy matches, which were contested by ten-man teams over twenty heats. Pedlar Palmer was back to something like his 1950 form, top-scoring with 13 points, and Peter Moore finished with 12. There was no dream debut for Hookham, who registered only two points, and Long Eaton were also forced to track juniors Johnny Robinson and Johnny Hanson, who both failed to score.

Long Eaton, in fact, won only one of their six matches in the central zone of the Festival of Britain Trophy. They beat Cardiff 62-58 on 10 May, but it was not enough to prevent them finishing bottom of the zonal table. This was the Archers' first win in an official competitive fixture, some seven weeks after the start of their season. Malouf, Palmer and Winstanley each scored 10 points and Peter Moore had 8 in three rides before withdrawing from the meeting with influenza. Mick Holland top-scored for the visitors with 15 points.

After a 58-26 defeat away at Rayleigh in their first ever Third Division match, the Archers took another break from competitive matches to contest a strange Whit Monday challenge match against comparatively near neighbours Sheffield. Strange because the Second Division team, as the local press reported, was in the process of disbanding, and several riders had already joined other sides.

Leicester Hunters men Cyril Page and Harwood Pike, together with Cecil Hookham, Bill Humphries and Johnny Robinson from the Archers squad, joined Owlerton skipper Len

Left: Long Eaton paid New Cross £150 for Eric Minall's contract in 1951. During 1950, Minall had been on loan from the Rangers.

Opposite: The spectacular leg-trailer Percy Brine was signed in the early part of 1951 to try to strengthen the team, but an eye injury ended his career.

Williams in perhaps the oddest team ever to wear the Sheffield colours. Long Eaton won the match 48-36, but Williams was the outstanding rider, notching a maximum.

The outstanding feature of the evening for Archers' fans was the return to the side of Eric Minall, despite his comeback being marred by engine trouble. Although Minall had indeed received his call-up papers for National Service, he had failed the medical! Long Eaton paid a transfer fee of £150 to New Cross chief Fred Mockford to buy the teenager's contract outright.

Minall took his place in the eight-man line-up for Station Road's first-ever league match three days later, on 13 May, against Exeter. The match was thrilling enough, with spills and good quality racing, but Long Eaton were denied a winning debut, Exeter taking the points with a 44-39 victory.

Long Eaton had also won their fight with the Control Board for the right to sign former Liverpool veteran Percy Brine. He slowly established himself in one of the reserve slots and was to provide the most memorable individual performance of the Exeter match. Leg-trailer Brine and Peter Moore were chasing the fast-gating Exeter pairing of Bob Roger and Ken Walsh when Moore collided with his teammate, bringing them both down. Despite his shaking, Brine rode superbly in the re-run and was only just beaten to second place.

The *Long Eaton Advertiser* reporter was deeply impressed. Brine's form, he said, had improved tremendously and he was a certainty for a full team place. 'He is never beaten until the flag comes down or he falls off,' was the verdict. The Exeter match proved to be something of a turning point for the Archers, at least at home, and the team went on to win the next eight Third Division matches at Station Road. Away from Derbyshire, it was to be a very different story.

Poole arrived at Station Road on 24 May, lacking the inspirational Ken Middleditch. Even so, it took a 5-1 in the last heat from Peter Moore and Ernest Palmer to send the Pirates packing. Wolverhampton were the next visitors in another challenge match, and Frank Malouf and Jack Winstanley, each with 11 points, led the Archers to a 56-26 victory.

Long Eaton's riders now set off on their first Third Division 'western tour', riding at Exeter one night and St Austell the next. Like many other teams over many years, the Archers found the narrow and steeply-banked, near quarter-mile County Ground, with its fearsome solid steel safety fence, to be an intimidating speedway venue. Exeter completely whitewashed the visitors, 65-18, with Eric Minall the only Archer to win a heat on his way to 6 points.

Lancashire farmer Jack Winstanley – a former teammate of Archers' skipper Ernest Palmer at Leicester – was a reliable points scorer in the Third Division in 1951. Winstanley continued to ride on and off until 1968.

The riders picked themselves up and carried on down into Cornwall. At the Cornish Stadium they managed to score twice as many points as the previous evening, keeping the St Austell margin of victory to a respectable 52-32. The verdict from the home fans was that Long Eaton, with Minall again top-scoring with 7, supported by 6 apiece from Winstanley and Jones, and 5 from Peter Moore, 'were not outclassed'.

Another away trip took Long Eaton to Poole, on 11 June, and another drubbing, 68-16, at the hands of the home side. *Speedway News* said Poole were so superior that the match 'deteriorated into a farce.' It would have been a complete whitewash if Tony Lewis had not experienced engine failure in heat one, allowing Winstanley and Palmer to follow Middleditch home for a 3-3.

A 52-32 victory over Cardiff at Station Road, with solid scoring down the order was, predictably, immediately followed by another thrashing, as Cardiff took revenge in a 59-25 victory at Penarth Road. The pattern was to be repeated for the rest of 1951, with a couple more home defeats helping to ensure that the Archers' final league position would be a lowly one.

Speedway relies almost entirely on reasonably well-balanced teams, if matches are to be at all interesting. Even the most rabid fan will tire of constant 5-1 heat wins, with the opposition trailing badly, and matches that become meaningless after a few heats. The Station Road crowd were largely spared this negative experience and, in all but a few home matches, the result was in doubt until quite late on in the proceedings.

Eric Mason got a first ever maximum when St Austell were beaten 54-30 at Station Road, and Peter Moore got 11 paid 12 against his old club. Then Wolverhampton were swamped by 60-24, with Winstanley becoming the latest Archer to record a first maximum. Johnnie Jones, his partner, unbeaten by an opponent, had 9 paid 12.

When Cardiff were beaten 49-35 on 12 July, Long Eaton had won eight home matches in a row. The Archers, at this stage, were in seventh place in the ten-team Third Division and were tracking a reasonably settled team, although the management was still looking to strengthen. Stuart Hickman, who had started to make an impact at Sheffield before breaking a leg, was the latest recruit. The Owlerton track had closed by the time Hickman recovered and, after promising second-half displays at Station Road, he was signed by manager Charlie Lish.

The promotion was also seeking a bigger fish. *Speedway News* reported that Long Eaton were again trying to sign Lionel Watling on loan. The magazine said that, if the deal did go through, Long Eaton would have, 'a drawing card that could possibly save them from putting up the shutters.' This allusion to unsatisfactory gates at Station Road was the only suggestion in the media throughout 1951 that things were not altogether rosy.

The improvement in overall performances brought about by the run of home wins came to an abrupt end as August dawned. On the Thursday before August Bank Holiday, the fans were surprised when Aldershot, with New Zealanders Geoff Mardon and Trevor Redmond

Discovery Johnnie Jones looks to come under Vic Gent of Exeter in a 1951 Third Division match at Station Road, with Jack Winstanley on the outside.

both scoring maximums, triumphed 48-35. Two days later the Shots rubbed it in with a 57-27 win on their own tricky circuit.

On 8 August, the Archers had another unprofitable visit to the West Country, losing 59-25 at Plymouth, before returning home to a Midland Cup match against Second Division East Midland neighbours Leicester. What was described as a record crowd of around 16,000 packed into Station Road to see the Archers hold the Hunters to a reasonably respectable 52-44 victory, but Leicester won the Blackbird Road leg 75-21 to record a 127-65 aggregate. Eric Minall's motor stalled on lap three of heat four of the Archers' home leg and he was hit by the pursuing Johnny Carpenter. Neither man took any further part in the meeting.

By Saturday 18 August, Long Eaton had dropped two places in the Third Division table to ninth, with 16 match points to the 8 gained by the hapless Wolverhampton side.

There was considerable annoyance in the Midlands, said *Speedway News*, as both Long Eaton and Wolverhampton had been passed over as venues for the new junior test match series between England 'C' and the USA. The Control Board, no doubt, had their eyes on bigger gates than those likely at Station Road or Monmore Green.

The Archers' terrible away performances led most people to expect another terrific beating at Wimborne Road, Poole, on 27 August. But the visitors provided the winners of the first four heats on a rain-soaked track, and press reports said that, for a while, it looked as though Poole's unbeaten home record could be in peril.

Middleditch and Lewis then recorded a 5-1 and Poole gradually pulled away, although the 51-33 result reflected one of Long Eaton's best away displays. Winstanley (9 points) and Palmer (8) each recorded two heat wins.

Wolverhampton, too, put up some surprisingly stern resistance when they came to Station Road for a Third Division clash on 6 September, and the racing was described as being as good as any seen so far in 1951. Malouf, with 10 points, and Mason, Palmer and Winstanley, with 9 apiece, were solid for Long Eaton, and D. Harris (10) and Derek Timms (8) headed the Wolverhampton score-chart.

The visiting side included some interesting names. Ron Wilson, having lost form at Leicester, had been loaned to the Monmore Green side, and he scored 4 points. Ronnie Genz, a New Cross junior like Minall and Siggins, who was later to have a long career in British speedway at Oxford and elsewhere, scored 7. At the bottom of the list was Cyril Maidment, another man to reach the top of the speedway game with Wimbledon and Belle Vue.

Swindon were Long Eaton's bogey team at Station Road in this period, and the Robins recorded a 45-37 win on 13 September, mainly by skilful use of reserve Mike Beddoe, who collected 8 points. This match was notable for the Long Eaton debut of Wilf Plant, allowed to leave Coventry after some delay. The former Nottingham White City man scored a creditable 8 points.

Left: Australian Frank Malouf was one of the most spectacular Archers riders of the early 1950s era. He picked up 10 points as Long Eaton beat Wolverhampton in a Third Division match at Station Road on 6 September 1951.

Below: Eric Mason hugs the white line in a Long Eaton versus Cardiff Third Division match in 1951.

Narrow home wins against Rayleigh (44–40) and Aldershot (43–41) kept the fans on tenterhooks. The Shots' heat-leader trio of Basil Harris (11 points), Trevor Redmond (11) and Geoff Mardon (9) threatened to walk away with the latter match. Long Eaton kept their nerve and managed to restrict the visiting second strings and reserves and score the odd victory over the top men, with Winstanley registering crucial wins against Redmond in the first heat and Harris in heat twelve.

A 5-1 from Jones and Palmer gave Long Eaton a four-point lead going into the final heat. Redmond won easily, but Malouf held out Edwards to deny the Shots the four points they needed to draw.

The next evening Long Eaton were at Monmore Green for a Third Division fixture they must have fancied winning. Instead the Wasps recorded a convincing 50-33 victory – their first since they had met the Archers at home on 20 July. Long Eaton's weakness was the third pairing of Palmer and Moore, who scored only four points between them.

The Swindon hoodoo was laid to rest on 4 October, when the Archers rampaged to a 60-24 win. Moore and Winstanley recorded maximums as the home side won every heat.

'Winky' Winstanley was the only Long Eaton
rider to take part in the Third Division Riders'
Championship final at Cardiff, stepping in
as a reserve at the last minute in place of
Aldershot's Basil Harris. Winstanley scored 2
points from two rides.

A 42-40 home win over Plymouth on 11 October rang the curtain down on the league
season and was also the final Station Road meeting of the season. Peter Moore confirmed his
promise with four unbeaten rides, spoiling the maximum chances of the Plymouth top men,
George Wall and Alan Smith. Pedlar Palmer's variable season continued when he demolished
several feet of safety fence and a lamp standard. Fortunately, he escaped with a slight wrist
injury.

No Archer had qualified by right for the Third Division Riders' Championship Final, held
at Cardiff in recognition of the large crowds the Welsh track had enjoyed all season. But,
when Aldershot's Basil Harris was advised by his doctor not to ride, 'Winky' Winstanley was
summoned to Wales by telegram. He got two rides and scored two points. Ken Middleditch
of Poole was the eventual winner of the title.

Long Eaton's season was summed up as the efforts of, 'a team of possibilities which did not
come up to expectations.' All of the regulars had their share of the limelight at some stage of
the campaign, with maximums for Mason, Moore and Winstanley, and near misses, including
17 points from 18 in the *Daily Mail* National Trophy match against Swindon for Malouf.

But no single rider showed the consistency to score well week-in, week-out, home and
away. A rider with the consistency of Ken Middleditch, Trevor Redmond, or Alan Smith might
have inspired Long Eaton to a much more respectable placing. Lionel Watling might well have
done the trick, but he was almost an ever-present in Birmingham's First Division side.

Wilf Plant, riding in the final seven league matches, averaged more than seven points a
meeting, and Malouf and Winstanley managed six points a match. But Mason and Moore,
despite occasional match-winning performances, both averaged below five points.

With Moore expected to continue his progress in 1952, the Archers needed one or two
new heat leaders to balance the solid middle order scorers and turn a struggling team into
one capable of challenging for honours. At least the fans could go into the dark winter nights
in the knowledge that, according to the programme for the final 1951 meeting, another year's
racing at Station Road was virtually assured.

Riders off duty. Eric Minall (with cigarette), Johnnie Jones and Peter Moore with Irene, the daughter of skipper Ernest Palmer.

Two new sports were tried out on the speedway track at Station Road after the Archers' season had come to a close. A 'considerable crowd' was reported for a trotting meeting held under the floodlights in October while, a month later, an estimated 8,000 spectators saw midget cars make their Long Eaton debut. Lionel Watling was among the featured drivers.

13

Decline and Fall – 1952

The third post-war season of speedway at Station Road started with a washout. In both 1950 and 1951 the opening meetings had been rain-affected, but racing had gone ahead. On Easter Monday, 14 April 1952, however, a thunderstorm and a heavy downpour an hour before the scheduled starting time flooded the track and, after the steward and rival captains Frank Malouf of Long Eaton and Sid Clarke of Ipswich had walked the circuit, the match was called off.

Long Eaton was a small town and the local press reported that thousands of people had set off to walk to the Stadium for the scheduled match against newcomers Ipswich, only to meet others already returning home. Three thousand people who had already paid for admission when the downpour occurred queued up for re-admission tickets. To cap a disappointing evening, the fans had been told that Melton Mowbray garage proprietor Wilf Plant, expected to sign for the Archers on a permanent basis after his successful introduction to the side late in 1951, had decided to stay at Coventry.

The Archers lined up for 1952 in what was now the Southern League. Eight of their 1951 Third Division opponents were also in the new section – Aldershot, Cardiff, Exeter, Plymouth, Rayleigh, St Austell, Swindon and Wolverhampton – together with Ipswich, who had made their speedway debut the previous year riding challenge matches, and a reopened Southampton. Poole had been promoted to Division Two as champions.

Long Eaton had already raced two Easter away matches before the Monday washout: at Banister Court, Southampton and Swindon, being trounced 58-26 at Blunsdon. In these away matches, the two Australians – veteran Malouf and the promising youngster Peter Moore – comprised one pairing, together with Jack Winstanley and a fit-again Fred Siggins, Eric Mason and former skipper Ernest 'Pedlar' Palmer, and newcomer Charlie Oates, formerly of Liverpool, at reserve. Eric Minall and Johnnie Jones were also available again, although Ernest Palmer retired after one appearance, citing age, engine problems, and an invitation from Frank Varey to be team manager at Sheffield, where Owlerton Stadium had reopened for Division Two racing.

The team, if anything, looked weaker than the one which had finished next to bottom in 1951, particularly in the absence of the experienced Plant.

The new season eventually got underway with a visit on 17 April from Wolverhampton Wasps in the *Daily Mail* National Trophy competition. Long Eaton speedway queen Heather Rosling made a brief speech by the starting gate to open the season, and managing director Stan Lish also welcomed a crowd estimated by the local press at 8,000.

There was a pleasant pre-meeting surprise for the home fans when it was announced that Wilf Plant had, after all, decided to sign a contract for the Archers. The second piece of good news was the signing of former Leicester skipper Cyril Page, who had decided that the travelling in the Second Division was too much for his business interests.

A squad consisting of Plant, Page, Malouf, Moore, Minall, Winstanley, Jones, Mason and Siggins, with Oates also available, looked much stronger than the line-up which had raced away from home.

In the early stages of the match against Wolverhampton, the promise seemed to be fulfilled, with the Archers galloping into a sixteen-point lead at the halfway stage. Wolverhampton fought back strongly after the interval and cut the margin by half – not much of a lead to take to Monmore Green for the second leg. Frank Malouf scored 15 points, Page 10 and Moore 10 for the Archers.

The second leg of the National Trophy tie at Monmore Green was a disaster for Long Eaton. The eight-point advantage was soon lost, and the home side went on to win by an overwhelming 74-33 scoreline, with an aggregate advantage of 124-91 to Wolverhampton. Long Eaton were reduced to using the track spare and borrowed machines for most of the match. Eric Mason's bike was damaged in heat one, and there was subsequent damage to the machines of Jones and Plant, while Cyril Page had the misfortunate to break his frame.

The first home Southern League match, against Ipswich on a Saturday evening, brought a last-heat 44-40 victory, with racing described as, 'not of a particularly high standard'. Reasonably strong on paper, but unpredictable on the track, Long Eaton were going to have to do a lot better if they were to improve on their 1951 league placing.

In a strange contrast to the reservations expressed by the media after the first home victory, a 43-41 defeat at the hands of Cardiff in the next meeting at Station Road was welcomed as, 'the first sign of a promise of better things to come'. The strong Welsh side had been expected to win easily.

Above: A pleasant surprise for Long Eaton fans was the appearance of Wilf Plant, following initial reports that he had returned to Coventry after his 1951 loan spell. Here, the unmistakeable figure of the former Middlesbrough and Fleetwood star heads into the first bend at Station Road. Jack Winstanley is his partner.

Left: Former Leicester captain Cyril Page was another experienced addition to the team in 1952.

Roy Browning, a former mechanic at Birmingham's Perry Barr track, joined Long Eaton. Browning also rode for Birmingham and Leicester before going to live in South Africa.

Wolverhampton were again Saturday evening visitors, this time in the league, and the Archers, who had already lost twice at Monmore Green, turned the tables with a 54-39 victory. With injuries and loss of form preventing the development of a settled team, there were more newcomers in the side, in the shape of Bill Harris, signed from Stoke, and Roy Browning, a former mechanic to Australian test star Graham Warren, who came to Station Road on loan from Birmingham.

Harris made an immediate impact with a 12-point maximum and Long Eaton scored solidly through the ranks, Peter Moore scoring 9 points, with 6 apiece from Winstanley and Malouf and 5 from Plant.

There was no quick end to the team changes, as Plant broke a collarbone and, on Whit Monday evening, 1 June, was replaced by Lionel Watling, a favourite at Station Road during the initial open licence season in 1950. Watling, like Browning on loan from Birmingham, led the Archers to a convincing 59-31 win against St Austell, top-scoring with nine points.

Moore and Browning had 8 each, Harris 7, Page 6 and reserves Johnnie Jones and Frank Malouf 5 each. The only Archer to have an off night as the sequence of close matches ended was Jack Winstanley, who could manage only 2 points.

The St Austell meeting was run in a steady drizzle of rain, which kept many spectators away, and the following Thursday evening there was more disappointment for the management when the steward stopped the racing early on in the Midland Riders' Championship round, with the track reportedly 'churned into a paste'. Some 6,000 spectators were reportedly on the terraces, including contingents from Leicester, Stoke and Wolverhampton.

The Midland Riders' round was re-run on 12 June and the home riders gave a good account of themselves against Second Division opposition in the shape of Len Williams and Harwood Pike from Leicester, and Ken Adams from Stoke. At the end of heat twenty, Lionel Watling, whose First Division experience at Perry Barr was making him a real force in the Southern League, was level-pegging with Adams, both with 14 points from five rides.

Adams, later to captain the Archers in the Provincial League in 1964, gated faster than Watling in the run-off and went on to add a yard on every lap to take the meeting. Peter Moore, with 13 points, and Roy Browning, with 11, also cheered the home fans, but meeting favourite, Len Williams, leading with 6 points from two rides when the original meeting was abandoned, could only manage 8 points overall on this occasion.

Long Eaton Archers 1952, taken in the Station Road pits. From left to right, back row: Jack Winstanley, Peter Moore, Johnnie Jones, Charles Lish (team manager), Bob Ibbotson. Front row: Wilf Plant, Cyril Page, Roy Browning, Bill Harris, Lionel Watling, Frank Malouf.

Wilf Plant was back in the side for the late-June clash with Aldershot at Station Road. Visiting heat leaders Doug Papworth, with a maximum, and Ivor Powell were dominant, but the solidity of the Long Eaton side throughout the order carried them through to a 51-33 win. Plant top-scored with 10, Moore, Page and Watling had 8 points each, while the remaining riders notched at least 4.

With Watling allowed to remain at Station Road, despite the return of Plant, Long Eaton at last had the look of a side likely to win at home and capable of at least running opponents close on the long away journeys. Too often in 1951, the Archers had done their reputation no good at all by failing to put up much of a show on away circuits. The long journeys to places like Exeter, St Austell, Plymouth and Aldershot, in the days before motorways, did not altogether excuse some lame displays.

The question of travel now loomed large in the Southern League season, with the future of the section threatened by a dispute over the mileage allowance paid to the riders for away meetings. The Speedway Riders' Association (SRA) was looking for an increase in the allowance from 3d to 6d a mile. Archers' promoter Stan Lish told the local press that the Southern League promoters had 'turned the idea down flat'.

When the Archers visited Cardiff, the amount paid out in mileage allowances was £40. A doubling of that expense was impossible. 'We can't and won't pay it,' Lish declared. The Long Eaton riders were keen on an increase but had more realistic ambitions. Jack Winstanley, who was based in Lancashire, told the *Long Eaton Advertiser* that asking for the amount to be doubled was 'a bit foolish'. Winstanley added:

> There should be an increase, but to 4d or fourpence halfpenny. With the present rate, the riders can just about manage on some trips, but we are finding it difficult to avoid being out of pocket on travelling overall.

'Winky' Winstanley was one of speedway's real journeymen. Fading out of the sport in Britain during the lean years of the mid to late-1950s, he was certainly not reluctant to travel, making an impact on German tracks. When the Provincial League came about in 1960, he rode for Sheffield and later Newcastle, and was still in the saddle in 1968 with Division Two club Nelson.

Apart from the 100-mile round trip to Wolverhampton, each away match for Long Eaton represented a gruelling drive on the narrow roads of the day. For teams like St Austell, Plymouth and Exeter, there were at least local derby fixtures against each other as compensation for the trips to the Midlands. Almost every away match for Long Eaton was a marathon round trip of anything between 300 and 600 miles.

Trips were often slotted into the fixture list as mini-tours, with back-to-back away matches against Swindon and Cardiff, or Southampton and Poole. But rescheduled fixtures after washouts could mean a long trip for a single match.

Some teams used a bus as transport, with the bikes and spares carried in a van, and this at least encouraged the building of team spirit. The rail network, which then reached into every corner of the country, was also occasionally used. Ernest Palmer recalls a long rail trip to Exeter from his Sheffield home, with his machine in the charge of a not always co-operative guard.

Coventry were one of the last teams to travel as a unit by rail in the mid-sixties, but there were plenty of drawbacks, including the prospect of missing the train altogether if the meeting stretched out with re-runs or other delays.

The late forties and early fifties are rightly seen as a golden age for British speedway and, undoubtedly, the top riders could earn a good wage. Even so, the Nottingham-based Louis Lawson, a frequent guest in the pits at Station Road, whose entire career was with Belle Vue in the First Division, continued to run his coal haulage business as well. In the Southern League, few riders were making a financial killing.

Happily, the threatened strike was averted and an agreement was reached on expenses. The Archers were proving effective at home, thrashing Exeter (minus Goog Hoskins) 53-29 and thrilling the fans in an exciting draw with Rayleigh. At one stage in the match, Long Eaton were eight points adrift and seemed to be heading for defeat, but what followed were four of the best races seen at Station Road, with the crowd at fever pitch.

Bill Harris and Peter Moore got a 5-1 in heat eleven, and Cyril Page and Roy Browning a 4-2 in the following race, when Rayleigh's Applegate looped at the start. Harris and reserve Fred Siggins managed another 4-2 in the penultimate race and, with the scores level, the stage was set for a thrilling last-heat decider.

Peter Moore – unbeaten by an opponent up to this point – and the wily campaigner Plant looked to have a great chance to complete the turnaround in fortunes, but Rockets' Tom O'Connor gated first and completed four unblemished laps to ensure that the visitors shared the match points.

It was thrilling stuff and should have kept the fans happy. The local press reported a crowd of 6,000 for the Rayleigh match, but the reality was something different. Overall, Long Eaton were in much the same position as in 1951 – third from bottom of the Southern League – and looked a long way from being strong enough to win away from Station Road and challenge for some silverware.

The last-heat decider against Rayleigh was to prove the last truly competitive speedway match to be seen at Long Eaton for more than a decade. The truth was about to be revealed – that the track management was in deep financial trouble.

The track surface at Station Road was also causing concern among the riders. The press had reported, prior to the season opening, that cinders had been laid, 'to make for safer riding'. The new surface certainly had an initial impact on heat times, which were very slow during the opening meeting against Wolverhampton and, when wet in subsequent meetings, the surface became very heavy going indeed.

Australian Bill Harris, formerly with Stoke, was yet another of the experienced riders introduced by the Archers management for the 1952 season, in an effort to find consistent league form.

There was no fixture at Station Road on 19 July, with press advertisements telling the public that this was due to further track re-laying. The Archers riders had become more and more disgruntled with the surface as the season progressed and a group of them, led by Lionel Watling, carried out the re-laying themselves.

Station Road, to its demise, always had a reputation as a track with a great shape for encouraging close racing and plenty of overtaking. But, at many points in its history, not even the most ardent Long Eaton fan would have made any claims about the quality of the surface.

Ivor Brown, who rode in practice sessions at the track in 1951, '52 and '53, after its closure to league racing, later recalled that it had been even bumpier in that period than in the late 1960s, when there were continual complaints about preparing the circuit for speedway after the ravages of fortnightly stock cars.

A time was soon to come when there was a standing joke that if British Railways repainted a station, closure was inevitable. Long Eaton supporters, despite the danger signs of thinning crowds on the terraces, must have believed that no one would go to the length of completely re-laying a track if the club was in danger.

When the end came, however, it happened fairly quickly. On the evening of Tuesday 22 July, Stan Lish told a meeting of supporters that the match scheduled against Wolverhampton in the Midland Cup on the following Saturday might turn out to be the Archers' last fling.

Lish said the directors had invested £10,000 in the club over the past two years but were not willing to put their hands in their pockets any longer. Lish admitted that the track had so far made 'a very slight profit' in 1952, but the season had started with a deficit of £800, which was not being made up. In addition, there had been spending of £600 on transfer fees, and there was a further debt of £25 in payments to riders and staff and a liability (unspecified) of £3,000 at the bank. Management, Lish added, could not 'catch up with previous losses'.

The immediate response of the 600 supporters attending the meeting was to launch a Save Speedway Fund. Lish reacted by saying that the crisis point would be reached on the forthcoming Saturday. If the Wolverhampton match produced a satisfactory attendance, and if the supporters could raise a minimum of £500, racing would continue – at least for the time being. Any other promoter wishing to take over the running of the track would be welcomed. Long Eaton's only realisable asset was Peter Moore and, if a four-figure offer was made for the young Australian, it would be accepted, Lish added.

A group of novices take a break during a Station Road training session. The only riders identifiable are Ivor Brown, the future Cradley Heath star (far left) and Vic Hall of Leicester and Brafield (standing behind the group). Brown, a future Long Eaton promoter after finding stardom with Cradley Heath, remembered how rough the Station Road track was in the early 1950s.

Local councillor Harry Makins, who had supported the speedway project all the way and had formally opened the track in 1950, said every speedway had its good and bad times, but the bad times had predominated at Long Eaton. He had studied the question, he said, and found that an attendance of 5,000 left the promoters in debt. Makins added that at Long Eaton, the 'number of really profitable meetings could be counted on the fingers of one hand'.

The supporters' meeting at times sank into recriminations, with criticisms from the floor of too many free tickets, not enough publicity and loss of revenue caused by reduced rates of admission for members of the Supporters' Club. One of the wilder suggestions from the floor was that the riders should race without payment to 'square up the debts'. There have been suggestions, over the years, that the riders were willing to do this, only for the idea to be squashed by the Control Board. In reality, it is unlikely the riders even considered the idea.

Lionel Watling was certainly dismissive of the proposal during the meeting, saying that, first and foremost, every rider who kept his equipment in good condition spent about £10 a week doing so. He himself had spent some £900 in the past two years. In addition, every rider was a member of the Speedway Riders' Association, which would not allow such a scheme. But, as a parting shot, he said his name could be put down for £5 towards the Save Speedway Fund.

Responding to a further question from the floor, Watling said there were no problems between riders and management. The team had indeed complained about the state of the track and had decided to carry out the task of re-laying it themselves. 'We are now a 100 per cent team, and are beginning to work like one,' he added.

Team spirit or not, the Archers' riders were affected by the uncertainty surrounding the future of the track. In the first leg of the Midland Cup at Monmore Green, Long Eaton were swept aside 70-26 by Wolverhampton. When the second leg was raced at Station Road on Saturday 26 July, few fans expected the Archers to pull back the 43-point deficit, although most believed a home win was possible.

The impending doom surrounding the future of the Archers really seemed to have affected the performance of the riders. The team for the night looked strong, consisting of Bill Harris and Peter Moore, Jack Winstanley and Wilf Plant, Roy Browning and Lionel Watling, with Fred Siggins and new young hopeful Lionel Pugh as the reserves. Moore, later renowned as probably the fastest gater in speedway, simply flew from the tapes, putting on a flawless performance to record a 15-point maximum.

The final meeting before the 1952 closure. The Archers met a scratch Wolverhampton side at Station Road after Southampton's team coach had broken down en route. Frank Malouf leads from two Wolverhampton riders in front of a crowd of nearly 4,000 – not enough in 1952.

Moore was aware that he was in the shop window, as the only Archer likely to command a transfer fee, but his one-man show was in vain, with the only support he received being two heat wins by Watling. Long Eaton lost the home leg by 59 points to 37 – a whopping aggregate advantage for Wolverhampton of 128-63.

The Wasps gave a remarkable display of team riding and solid scoring. Their highest scorer, Eric Irons, had just 9 points from his five rides, but three of his teammates scored 8, 3 got 7, and the lowest scorer had 5 points.

Wasps' riders won nine of the sixteen heats and recorded no less than 11 bonus points for following their partners home, compared to just two bonuses for Long Eaton. On the terraces, the crowd was again way below the published break-even figure of 5,000.

Surprisingly, Stan Lish and his fellow directors decided to give it a further go at Station Road, and a Southern League meeting with Southampton was advertised for 31 July. The death of the track, in the end, was an inglorious one. Lish was forced to announce to the 3,882 spectators in the stadium – a precise attendance figure for once – that the Southampton team bus had broken down between Kettering and Leicester.

Fortunately, four Wolverhampton riders were already in the pits, having been booked in to race in the second half. With the loan of some Long Eaton juniors, the Wasps men agreed to provide the main attraction for the evening. Not surprisingly, under the circumstances, Long Eaton won the match 52-31. Equally predictably, the media verdict was that the racing had been the dullest ever seen on the track. At the end of the evening, Stan Lish told reporters: 'There will be no more racing after tonight. The last three weeks have been absolute hell. Our troubles are insurmountable.' Lish blamed insufficient support and high expenses for the failure of the Archers.

A decade later, crowds of almost 4,000 were a paying proposition in speedway and, when the sport finally came to an end at Station Road in 1997, an attendance of 1,500 was exceptional. But, in 1952, entertainment tax was at a punitive rate and the Chancellor of the Exchequer had ruled that an earlier reduction had to be passed straight on to the public through lowered admission charges.

The effort by the supporters, who had subscribed more than £100 to keep the Archers alive, was in vain. 'I would like to thank the supporters greatly,' Lish added, 'although the Save Speedway Fund has not come up to expectations. The final blow was the non-appearance of the Southampton team.'

The *Long Eaton Advertiser*, the weekly newspaper published in the town, appears to have consistently exaggerated the attendances over the two and a half seasons of speedway at Station Road. Match reports over the period talk of crowds as high as 12,000 and even 16,000. Ernest

Palmer, following a lifetime of watching speedway and having participated as a rider and later as the Sheffield team manager, believes the average attendance during his time at Station Road was around 4,000, although there were much bigger crowds for attractive derby matches against Leicester and Sheffield.

Attempts by the Supporters' Club to revive the track carried on into August, with a scheme to get 1,000 members to invest £10 each. Of this sum, £4,500 would buy the assets of the promotion, leaving £5,500 to run meetings.

The sum of £10 was a lot of money in 1952, far more than the average weekly wage, and the scheme was doomed from the start. Two final fundraising meetings were held. One, for supporters in general, attracted a much reduced attendance of 200, and the second, for those who had already given money to the fund, attracted only 'thirty-odd diehards'.

A cash receipt book with only a few counterfoils missing told the sad story. The costs of a takeover were beyond the means of the man and woman on the terrace. A booster fund to assist the then Long Eaton promotion in the late 1980s did prove to be far more successful, but the whole speedway business had changed almost beyond recognition by that time.

With the closure, the contracts of the Long Eaton riders became the property of the Speedway Control Board. Peter Moore, as predicted, was the main target for other clubs and he moved to First Division Wimbledon. His career encompassed a fourth place in the 1960 world final and team places at not only Wimbledon but also Ipswich, Swindon, Long Eaton and Kings Lynn. He managed the Australian team and died in May 1996 in his native Melbourne.

Speedway racing faced huge challenges as the 1950s moved forward, and the Long Eaton closure was to be the prelude to many other failures. Nevertheless, at the start of the 1953 season, some commentators predicted a boom year. The First Division looked solid and stable, with the five London tracks – Harringay, New Cross, Wembley, West Ham and Wimbledon – supplemented in a neat geographical pattern by Belle Vue and Bradford in the north, Birmingham in the Midlands, Norwich in the east and Bristol in the west. True, the arguments raged over whether or not some of the provincial sides really merited their top-class status, but this was an old dispute.

The Second Division meant lots of travelling as there were three Scottish sides, as well as Coventry, Leicester, Stoke, Liverpool and Wolverhampton (who had merged with Cradley, to ride at Monmore Green) roughly in the centre of the British Isles, and Yarmouth in the east and Poole in the south-west, both out on a limb.

The Southern League, now minus Long Eaton, was concentrated, as its name suggested, in the south and south-west, with only Ipswich in the east really removed from the section's centre of gravity. In all, twenty-nine sides began the season but only twenty-six survived at the end of a campaign which, according to the *Stenners* annual for the following year, effectively lost six weeks when gates were 'killed' by coronation celebrations and a spell of wet weather.

One side fell by the wayside from each section. The losses of Liverpool and Cardiff were regrettable, but perhaps not a huge surprise. What really rocked the speedway world was the mid-season withdrawal of New Cross, one of the London 'big five' and a glamorous side ever since the promoters had switched to the Old Kent Road venue from the Crystal Palace in the mid-1930s.

Practice sessions took place at Station Road in 1953 and a team labelled Long Eaton did in fact contest an away challenge fixture. This was staged at the Sports Stadium, King's Lynn (later to become the Saddlebow Road circuit), on Monday 6 April, in aid of the King's Lynn Flood Relief Fund.

King's Lynn beat Long Eaton 43-39 on a grass circuit marked out inside the greyhound track at the Sports Stadium, with sand on the bends. A crowd of 1,507 were reported to have attended.

Oxford and former Norwich rider Bill Codling (11 points), Wal Morton of West Ham (11) and Tip Mills of Norwich (9) led the scoring for King's Lynn. Joe Rodwell scored 4, Geoff Godwin and Malcolm Flood (later to be killed in a track crash) weighed in with 3, while Alan Stapleton scored 2 and Derek Hewitt 1.

Would Ivor Brown have broken into the Long Eaton Southern League team if the track had survived into 1953? He led a Long Eaton side in its only match in '53, a charity affair on grass at King's Lynn. In this picture, taken after a Station Road training session the previous season, there seems to be some dispute over times. Peter Moore and Johnnie Jones check their watches, while Ivor looks over their shoulders. Flanking the riders are Supporters' Club bus driver Cyril Smith (left) and another unidentified member of the track staff.

Long Eaton were led by Ivor Brown, who scored ten points. Ivor rode once or twice as a guest for the Archers in the Provincial League days and made a final track appearance for the Rangers side he promoted in 1969, scoring ten points in a challenge match at Station Road against, coincidentally, King's Lynn's second team.

The other Long Eaton scorers were Gordon Stevens (8), Don Briars (7), and John Cherry (5), while Barry East, Dennis Fletcher, Neville Gurney and John Wells each scored 2 points. Vic Hall scored a single point.

Ivor Brown, Barry East and Vic Hall were all Leicester juniors. Brown rode nine times in 1953 for the Leicester Hunters and rode in the team again in 1956 and 1957. East rode for Leicester in 1955 and 1956, and Hall in 1956 and 1957. Vic Hall was to make a surprise impact in pirate meetings at Long Eaton just over a year later.

The winter of 1953/54 saw more changes in speedway. The First Division was reduced to eight teams when Bristol voluntarily dropped a level. Division Two consisted of no fewer than sixteen tracks, incorporating the surviving members of the now defunct Southern League. In addition to the three clubs that had withdrawn during the course of the 1953 season, two, St Austell and Stoke, failed to make it to the tapes for the start of the 1954 campaign. Far worse was to follow as the season wore on.

The First Division clubs survived 1954 intact, but no fewer than five of the Division Two starters fell by the wayside. Promoters, press and fans had all welcomed the 'one big league' idea for clubs outside the top section. However, falling crowds put paid to Glasgow White City, Edinburgh, Yarmouth, Wolverhampton and Plymouth.

The twenty-nine starters at the beginning of 1953 had been reduced to nineteen at the end of the 1954 campaign. Over the next two seasons another five tracks disappeared, including London giants Harringay, West Ham and Wembley – the latter's closure a massive blow for the sport's public image – and, by 1957, the three division structure of the late forties and early fifties had been reduced to a single division of ten clubs, further reduced to nine in 1959.

Small wonder that riders from struggling sides like Long Eaton faced a major struggle to stay involved in the sport. Apart from Peter Moore and Jack Winstanley, whose widely contrasting careers have been mentioned earlier, few managed to stay in speedway for very long.

Lionel Watling, apart from his Long Eaton appearances in 1952, had nine matches for Birmingham and ten for Norwich in the First Division. In 1953, both he and Roy Browning linked up with Leicester in the Second Division, before Watling retired and Browning went to live in South Africa. Frank Malouf had some rides for Liverpool before returning to Australia for good. He was still riding at Kembla Grange, New South Wales, in the early 1960s and died at the age of eighty-eight in 2002. Eric Minall featured briefly for Exeter and Lionel Pugh and Fred Siggins rode at Stoke, but without making much impact.

Right: After Long Eaton closed its doors, Johnnie Jones lined up with Southern Area League side Brafield and is seen wearing the colours of the Flying Foxes.

Below: The pirate meetings in 1954 were promoted by former Norwich rider Paddy Mills (real name Horace Burke), pictured here, and Stadium lessee Tom Beattie.

For many of the former Archers' men, there were no team rides to be had at all in mainstream speedway. Johnnie Jones enjoyed some success at Brafield in the Southern Area League, but the modest rewards of Sunday afternoon speedway hardly allowed the upkeep of machinery.

It was against this background that the former Norwich rider Paddy Mills, having left his management post at Brafield after a dispute with the promotion, decided to reintroduce speedway to Long Eaton late in the 1954 season. Mills failed to secure a licence from the Speedway Control Board and the ACU, and the three meetings at Station Road in September of that year were effectively pirate events, with riders risking their individual licences if they were identified.

Earlier in 1954, Long Eaton had become one of the pioneer venues for stock car racing, presented by promoter Don Luck in front of large and enthusiastic crowds. Mills ran the speedway meetings on behalf of Tom Beattie, who leased Long Eaton Stadium from the actual owners, the Nottingham-based Home Brewery, and promoted greyhound racing at the track.

The former Norwich rider gathered together a collection of veterans, speedway journeymen, and novices. Some used assumed names while others, no doubt realising they had little future in what was seen by many as a dying sport, saw no risk in using their real names.

At least three identifiable former Archers' riders took part in the first meeting under the Tom Beattie/Paddy Mills banner. This took place on Saturday 28 August 1954, with a challenge match between teams representing the East Midlands and the North Midlands.

The East Midlands side consisted of Johnnie Jones (captain) and Bill Jackson, Frank Greasley and Ron Wilson, Wilf Plant and Jim Smith, with Peter Parkinson and Bill Billman as reserves. North Midlands tracked Harry Wardropper (formerly of Wolverhampton) and Arthur Hill, Alan Hailstone and Jack Winstanley, Rodney Armes and Clive Wasley, with Alan Pearce and Bob Cherry at reserve.

It is likely that the Ron Wilson named in the programme was the 1960s Archers' team manager and co-promoter. Wilson, a product of the Rye House training school in the 1940s, had been

Wilf Plant rode under his own name in the 1954 'pirate' meetings at Station Road. He is pictured in the Long Eaton pits with son Graham, later to become British Junior Champion, British League Division Two Riders Champion and a Leicester Lions star of the 1970s and 1980s. Graham made his competitive speedway debut for Long Eaton.

The programme cover for one of the 1954 'pirate' meetings at Station Road.

a high scorer for Leicester in the Hunters' early seasons, but had lost form and been transferred to Oxford, where he failed to make a major impact. Like many other riders, he was probably struggling for rides by 1954, which would explain an appearance on an unlicensed track.

Paddy Mills took the opportunity to introduce some innovations to the programme. Before the challenge match got underway, he staged curtain-raiser races for the heat-leaders, reportedly to give them an opportunity to 'get the feel of the track' before the principal events got under way. Why Mills should have felt the most experienced men in the meeting had a greater need to get a feel for the track than the second strings and reserves is a mystery.

He was also a great proponent of handicap racing and used the system in his second-half programme. Nearly all the necessary staff for the meeting were provided by the still-active supporters' club, led by stalwart Frank Exton, a Derby man who was to be a commanding pit marshal at Station Road in the 1960s.

The local press reported a crowd of 4,000 to see East Midlands gain a narrow 44-40 victory over their North Midlands rivals in a fourteen-heat match. Ex-Archers Jones and Plant scored 10 points each for the winning side, supported by Ron Wilson with 8, Jackson with 7, Greasley 4, Billman 3, and Parkinson with 2. Jim Smith failed to score.

The local press reports of the match give an incomplete list of scorers for the North Midlands. Published details record that the top scorer was the unknown Rodney Armes, who recorded a 12-point maximum, supported by Wardropper with 8, Hailstone with 7, Arthur Hill with 6 and Winstanley with 5. Reserves Wasley and Cherry failed to score. There is no mention of any score by Alan Pearce – listed in the team – as the reported team aggregate only totals 38.

Paddy Mills told the media that he planned to select the nucleus of a permanent Long Eaton team, to be known as the Black Panthers, from the riders who had competed in the match. He was also hoping to form a Midland Junior Speedway League. Promoter Tom Beattie, who also acted as timekeeper for the match, summed up the situation facing the new management team when he told the *Long Eaton Advertiser*: 'We have the riders, but not the teams.' He could have been speaking for speedway in general as the sport headed for its greatest-ever slump.

The idea behind the new promotion was that speedway would alternate with stock car racing on Saturday evenings at Station Road. The second meeting, on 11 September, was billed as an eighteen-heat Grand Handicap Challenge, with eighteen riders – mostly the same men who had taken part in the initial meeting – having five rides each.

An obvious indication of the real status and experience of the riders is given by the handicaps. Rodney Armes, unbeaten in the first meeting, started forty-five yards behind the starting gate, with Johnnie Jones, Bill Jackson, Arthur Hill, and Harry Wardropper going off forty-yard handicaps. Rather surprisingly, the highly experienced Plant and Winstanley were given thirty-five-yard handicaps, while the rest of the field varied from twenty-five and twenty yards to scratch.

Armes was once again unbeatable, recording a 15-point maximum, with Johnnie Jones runner-up with 13 points, and Wilf Plant, F. Forder and P. Harris each scoring 9. There was no mention of Ron Wilson in the line-up, at least under his real name, although former Archers reserve Lionel Pugh·was back in action, scoring seven points off a twenty-five-yard handicap.

The third (and final) meeting under the Beattie/Mills regime took place on Saturday 25 September 1954, and was billed as a double-header, featuring Young Stars versus Old Stars and a Best Pairs championship.

The *Long Eaton Advertiser* reported thrilling racing at the third meeting for a 3,000 crowd, but omitted to mention the result of the match! Rodney Armes, described by the paper as 'the invincible new boy who is to ride for Long Eaton Panthers next season', scored a maximum in the challenge match and recorded the fastest four-lap time of the season, 71.6 seconds.

Armes went on to partner Fran Forder to victory in the Best Pairs and appears to have gone through the three 1954 meetings at Station Road unbeaten.

Who was the unbeatable Rodney Armes? He was really Vic Hall, a second-halfer at Long Eaton during the 1950-52 Archers era, who rode in the April 1953 challenge match at King's Lynn and who was also associated with Southern Area Leaguers Brafield Flying Foxes, First Division Birmingham and Second Division Leicester in the period 1953-1957.

In 1954, he was a teammate of Johnnie Jones at Brafield – the side managed by Paddy Mills until his dispute with the promoter at the Northamptonshire venue and his move to Long Eaton. Hall was a great success at Brafield and was signed by First Division Birmingham, where he played a minor but decisive role in the Brummies' Midland Cup victory over Coventry.

Despite this success, Hall was not retained by the Perry Barr Club and returned to Brafield for the 1955 season, when he was the Southern Area League's most successful rider, finishing with an average of nearly ten points a match. Another link between Brafield and Long Eaton was through the Flying Foxes' mascot – Long Eaton Archer 1964 and 1965 vintage Kid Bodie, later to revert to his real name of Howard Cole.

Hall was also a regular second-half performer at Blackbird Road, Leicester, and rode in about a dozen matches for the Hunters in 1956 and 1957, vying with future Cradley Heath star and Long Eaton promoter Ivor Brown for team rides.

Vic Hall's success for Brafield had been matched by Johnnie Jones through most of the 1954 season. But, whereas Hall took the precaution of riding at Long Eaton under an assumed name, Jones was up front with his identity, something which was to cost him dear.

When the Speedway Control Board decided to crack down on the pirate riders behind the Long Eaton revival, Jones was made a scapegoat, losing his racing licence for two years and, with it, the chance to ride in the Southern Area League Riders' Championship final.

Jones and his family emigrated to Australia in June 1959, to live in the same suburb of Melbourne which was home to his former Archers teammate Peter Moore. Moore's brother took Jones out to practice day at Melbourne's own then well-established track, Tracey's Speedway, at Maribyrnong, run by former rider Fred Tracey.

Jones impressed at the practice session and was chosen to represent Victoria in an interstate match against South Australia on 17 October 1959. The line-up for the first race was formidable, with Johnnie partnering Junior Bainbridge against the South Australian combination of former World Champion Jack Young and Jack Scott, later of Southampton and Plymouth.

After the failure of the 1954 attempt to reintroduce speedway, stock cars took over at Station Road for the rest of the decade. In this pits shot, former Nottingham speedway riders George Dykes (white overalls) and Fred Strecker (far right) pose with their cars. Strecker's son Roger is in between.

Bainbridge made the gate and Johnnie had the crowd gasping as he rode around Jack Young going into the first bend. But, with the Victorian pairing seemingly in charge, disaster struck on the second turn. Jones recalled:

> Junior pulled a full locker, I clipped his back wheel and became airborne, hitting the fence very hard. I actually then went up into the air to inspect the track lights, or so I was told later.
>
> I regained consciousness some twenty minutes later when they were washing the blood out of my eyes. I had broken my pelvis on the left side and crushed an ankle on the right side and my goggles had tried to remove my nose. I was in hospital for a few days where they kept me until the bruising had gone down enough for them to be able to re-break my ankle.
>
> They did a good job of stitching my nose but, as you might have gathered, it was my last ride.

Johnnie took up flying and, in subsequent years, visited every state of Australia including Tasmania, notching up 3,000 hours in command and 1,200 as co-pilot. His son, Rob, later made the trip to England to ride for Wimbledon.

As former Long Eaton riders either made their mark elsewhere or faded out of the sport, the roar of speedway bikes was to be absent from Station Road for nine long years. Stock car racing, which attracted big crowds throughout the fifties and sixties, would keep the stadium alive and ripe for a possible, eventual revival.

14

The 1960s Revival

British speedway – still a three division-strong structure with more than thirty teams when the Long Eaton Archers pulled out of the sport at the end of July 1952 – had shrunk alarmingly by the last year of the decade. Three divisions in 1953 became two in 1954 and, at the end of the 1956 season, with three of the surviving fourteen clubs withdrawing, the unavoidable decision was taken to operate with just a one-section National League.

The eleven teams which finished the 1957 season shrank to ten in 1958 and nine in 1959. 'British' speedway had been a misnomer since the mid-1950s, with the demise of the four Scottish teams and Cardiff. Of the Division One clubs operating at the height of speedway's popularity, only Wimbledon and Belle Vue survived. The others had been 'promoted' as the lower divisions disappeared.

In 1959, league speedway on a national basis reached its lowest ebb since the mid-1930s, but it also saw the foundations laid for a major revival.

The roots of the revival were to be found in three distinct areas of operation. In 1959, in addition to the National League, four other tracks staged speedway on an irregular basis in southern England. Eastbourne, Rye House, Yarmouth and Aldershot comprised the Southern Area League (SAL), which had operated fitfully since the early fifties, and at times also included Brafield, California (near Reading), Ringwood, Hampshire, and a nomadic outfit called Southern Rovers.

In addition, a Manchester-based businessman and midget-car driver called Mike Parker decided to try to revive defunct tracks in the midlands and the north. The Speedway Control Board, seemingly content with the limited structure already in place, or perhaps concerned that the sport's image would suffer even more if the new ventures failed, refused to grant licences.

Undeterred, Parker and Jess Halliday of Bradford went ahead and ran pirate meetings on a similar basis to those operated by Tom Beattie and Paddy Mills at Long Eaton in 1954 – although considerably more successful. Meetings, sometimes also including the midget cars, were held at Liverpool and at the cavernous Odsal Stadium in Bradford. In addition, former Wembley rider Trevor Redmond staged a meeting at Cradley Heath.

The third strand of the revival comprised the tracks that, throughout the mid-to-late fifties, operated on a sporadic basis. These included Exeter, Bristol, Plymouth, St Austell, Motherwell and Edinburgh.

The Parker meetings were naturally frowned upon by the Control Board and the Speedway Riders' Association, and warnings were issued that any established riders taking part risked losing their licences. Some rode under assumed names, while many novices ignored the warnings, glad of any rides they could get, legal or otherwise.

The Southern Area League promoters, and others, watched the Parker/Halliday developments carefully, and the upshot was a late 1959 meeting between various interested parties, held in Mike Parker's flat above the hardware store he owned in Moss Side, Manchester. Present at these meetings were Parker himself; former England, West Ham, Stoke and Leicester rider Reg Fearman; Ian Hoskins, son of pioneer Johnnie and formerly promoter at Glasgow White City; pre-war Belle Vue star and one-time Sheffield promoter Frank Varey; Captain Fred Jephcott and his son Morris from Cradley; Charlie Dugard of Eastbourne; Fred Peachey of Rye House; Alf Weedon of Yarmouth; John Pilblad of Aldershot; journalist and speedway administrator John Wick, who was secretary of the SAL; and Trevor Redmond.

Parker told the southern promoters that he was prepared to enter his tracks into an expanded league, providing that the Control Board cooperated. That body eventually agreed to meet Parker, and the other promoters, to discuss the formation of what was already being called the Provincial League.

The Control Board moved quickly and, soon after Christmas 1959, announced that it would sanction the formation of the new league. Applications began to pour in from prospective promoters, including men interested in reviving tracks long lost to league speedway, including Bristol, Sheffield and Edinburgh.

Everything seemed to be going well until the Control Board turned down the applications of three of the four Southern Area League tracks that had been in at the very beginning of planning for the new structure! Eastbourne and Rye House were rejected on the grounds of the unsuitability of Sunday racing in the new league, while it was felt that the level of support experienced at Aldershot in 1959 would not sustain the extra expense needed to run in the new set-up.

Aldershot were granted an open licence to give them a chance to prove they could sustain Provincial League racing, while Eastbourne and Rye House were told to carry on with their Sunday training school and open meetings. It was a hard blow for men like Charlie Dugard, the former Wimbledon and Norwich rider, to have to sit on the sidelines and watch others realise the dream he had worked so hard to achieve.

The next obstacle to be overcome was the riders. The men who had ridden on the 'pirate' tracks in 1959 had done fairly well out of the season, with no strings attached. They would have to be persuaded to join the SRA, obtain ACU competition licences and become bona fide speedway riders.

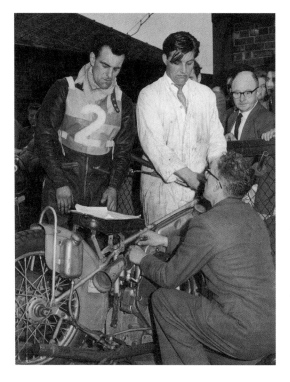

When the Provincial League revitalised speedway in the early 1960s, one of the top riders to emerge was Sheffield's Clive Featherby (wearing the number two race jacket), a former Norwich junior who had struggled to become established in the National League. Featherby's mentor was 1950s Long Eaton captain Ernest Palmer (kneeling to adjust machine) who had become the Sheffield team manager.

Former Long Eaton novice Ivor Brown, after struggling for many years to make an impact in the National League at Leicester, was one of many riders who found success in the new Provincial League, initially at Yarmouth and later at Cradley Heath.

This was eventually achieved and by Easter 1960 the Provincial League was ready to make its debut. Rayleigh, the eventual champions, Poole, who had stepped down from the National League (to be replaced by a revived New Cross), Bristol, Sheffield, Stoke, Cradley Heath, Yarmouth, Edinburgh, Liverpool and Bradford went to the tapes and were still competing when the season came to an end. John Wick, the former editor of *Speedway World*, was the first secretary of the new league until he was forced to step down owing to ill-health.

National League circles also welcomed back Birmingham, although the Midlands centre only ran a limited season of open meetings.

The Provincial League was a great success in many centres. Parker and Fearman's Potteries revival attracted a crowd of 10,000 on Good Friday evening, and there were consistently good crowds at Frank Varey's Sheffield, at Edinburgh, operated by Ian Hoskins, and at Cradley. Reg Fearman, in addition to his promoting activities, rode a full season for Stoke, averaging nearly nine points a match.

Elsewhere in the league it was more of a struggle, and although Bradford, Liverpool (another Parker/Fearman interest), Yarmouth and Bristol (where the stadium was sold for redevelopment at the end of 1960) fulfilled their fixtures, they all failed to reopen for 1961.

Other centres were, however, willing to give it a go, and new teams emerged at Plymouth and Exeter. In addition, the Mike Parker/Reg Fearman combination opened Newcastle, Middlesbrough and Wolverhampton, with former rider Bill Bridgett nominated as promoter at the latter track. The new centres ensured that the Provincial League had eleven rather than ten members for its second campaign.

The league was finding its feet, and in many ways starting to outshine its National League big brother. After the mini-revival to ten teams in both 1960 and 1961, the National League suffered a blow during the winter of 1961/62 when New Cross closed again and Leicester, faced with falling attendances, decided to drop down to the Provincial League. Eight teams started off the season, but Ipswich dropped out mid-term.

Long Eaton Stadium at the time of the 1963 Provincial League revival.

In stark contrast, thirteen sides embarked on the 1962 Provincial League campaign and thirteen sides completed the season. Only Rayleigh of the 1961 members withdrew, and the first Welsh team, Neath, operated by Trevor Redmond, was welcomed, together with the demoted Leicester and a revived Bradford (racing at Greenfield Stadium, rather than Odsal).

Both Leicester and Bradford came under the Parker/Fearman banner for 1962. Charles Ochiltree, better known for his long-time Coventry connection but also the effective promoter at Leicester, closed the Blackbird Road track after recording an average crowd for National League racing in 1961 of just over 3,000 people. Parker and Fearman had come to the rescue of Bradford during the open licence season in 1961, which lost money for Jess Halliday. Sadly, both Leicester and Bradford were unsuccessful both on the track and on the terraces in 1962.

'Leicester haemorrhaged money in 1962,' Reg Fearman recalls. 'At times we had less than 1,000 people for Provincial League racing.' Poole won the Provincial League championship for the second successive season, with Leicester and Bradford in the bottom two spots.

Struggling teams and consequent poor results go a long way towards explaining the low crowds at Leicester and Bradford but Neath, who finished second to Poole in the table, also failed to attract viable support and some PL fixtures were raced at Redmond's other interest, the Cornish Stadium in St Austell. Despite the lack of success in some centres, the PL now had a hard core of successful tracks, making it relatively easy to ignore the few failures.

Fourteen teams were to line up for 1963, the highest total to date, with nine of the 1962 finishers. The newcomers making up this record PL membership comprised St Austell, Rayleigh, once again, and two London teams in the shape of east-enders Hackney (taking Leicester's licence and appearing for the first time since 1939) and New Cross – these two tracks making a nonsense of the title 'Provincial League'.

The final new track announced in the speedway press, to the delight of East Midlands fans, was Long Eaton. Enthusiasm was high in the Derbyshire town as preparations for the 1963 season continued. What the vast majority of fans – not only in Long Eaton but in the other centres with tracks operated by Parker and Fearman – did not know was that the partnership between the two men was about to end acrimoniously, and at one stage looked like threatening the structure of the Provincial League.

'The dispute could have had a very marked effect on the 1963 PL season,' Reg Fearman recalls:

The promoting companies involved were Northern Speedways Ltd and Wolverhampton Speedway Ltd. At the end of the 1962 season, unbeknown to me, Mike Parker negotiated with the greyhound company which owned the Newcastle and Wolverhampton tracks for the leases to be made out in his own name.

When I discovered that he had converted a limited company's assets into his own name, I naturally went to a court of law. The Provincial League Promoters' Association was made aware of the situation at its annual general meeting in the winter of 1962/63, and the Speedway Control Board was also notified.

On the face if it, and what eventually became reality, was that Parker had Newcastle and Wolverhampton, and for 1964 he was to open at Newport, in partnership with the Knott family. I had Stoke, Middlesbrough and the new Long Eaton. But as my law suit against Parker dragged on, the Speedway Control Board said it would not licence any of the tracks for the 1963 season until a settlement had been reached.

A monetary settlement, including damages, was eventually made out of court, in my favour, and tracks were subsequently licensed.

The out-of-court settlement meant that the Provincial League fixtures could go ahead as planned, but it was not the last controversy involving the Parker and Fearman camps that year.

The rumours of a revival at Station Road had actually started to surface in the speedway press in late 1962, when it became obvious that Leicester was unlikely to continue to operate. Although Reg Fearman's name was well known throughout the sport, the majority of his career had been spent in the higher divisions and he had not appeared as a rider at Station Road.

Fearman had first come to prominence as an under-age debutant at West Ham in the late 1940s. He went to Australia as the youngest member of the England Test party in 1950/51 and had a successful career with Stoke and later Leicester, before spending some time in New Zealand. Despite his successful reappearance as a rider for Stoke in 1960, he suffered from back problems and rode only a few matches in 1961 and none at all in 1962.

With the track licensing problem resolved, Fearman set about putting together the Archers team. Various riders were touted as possibilities for Long Eaton, including Jack Winstanley, who with Swindon's Peter Moore was the only member of the 1952 side still active in the sport. Rick France, a Coventry junior who had been loaned to Provincial Leaguers Middlesbrough in 1961 and Leicester in 1962, was also the subject of speculation, which in the end came to nothing.

The Archers' opponents in their first match for nearly eleven years were, appropriately enough, Wolverhampton, who had provided the stand-in opposition when Southampton failed to arrive on the last night at Station Road in July 1952.

This time the venue was the tight circuit at Monmore Green, in the Midland Cup. Against most expectations, the Archers recorded a 40-37 victory – Long Eaton's first-ever away success in anything other than a challenge match. The match had an added piquancy as it was the first meeting between Parker and Fearman tracks since the legal dispute – and throughout 1963 these clashes were popularly believed to have that little extra 'devil'.

At Wolverhampton, the team that paraded in new-look Archers race jackets for the historic comeback – the green archer on a yellow background was a different model from the 1950s character – was drawn from several sources. Vic White had captained Leicester in 1962 and moved over to Station Road with team manager Ron Wilson, a former Hunters rider, and Tony Eadon, who with brother Eric had been around most of the Midland tracks.

Maurice 'Slant' Payling was a South Yorkshire coal miner and Belle Vue training school discovery who had forced his way into the Hyde Road National League team in the late

Above left: Ex-Wimbledon National League rider Gil Goldfinch had been a major success in the Provincial League at Newcastle. But he was to prove a reluctant Archer, despite his smile for the camera, and retired midway through 1963.

Above right: Former Belle Vue man Maurice 'Slant' Payling was an early Long Eaton signing for the comeback season and proved a real crowd favourite.

1950s, and was regarded as a highly promising prospect. The defining moment in his career came at The Firs, Norwich, on 23 July 1960, when Belle Vue met the Stars in a National Trophy match.

Payling and his teammate Derek 'Tink' Maynard were involved in an horrendous crash. Maynard lost his life and Payling was badly injured. When he returned, he was never again to be the same force. He appeared in eight matches for Belle Vue in 1961 but also linked up with PL newcomers Newcastle, scoring 166 points from 33 matches. In 1962, he began the season with Leicester but was then moved to the other Parker/Fearman track at Bradford.

Gil Goldfinch moved to Station Road from Parker's Newcastle. He was a Southern Area League discovery who became a Wimbledon asset, his moment of glory coming in 1960 in the second leg of the National Trophy final against Norwich at Plough Lane. In the first leg in East Anglia, Wimbledon, without the injured Ron How, had lost 62-46, with Goldfinch contributing just three points.

In the second leg at Plough Lane, the odds seemed stacked against the Dons making up the 16-point deficit, as skipper Ronnie Moore was by now also injured. But Goldfinch set about the opposition in no uncertain manner, winning races and scoring 12 points as Wimbledon won the match 69-39 and the trophy on an aggregate of 115-101. For Newcastle, in 1961 Goldfinch scored more than 200 points in all competitions, and was second to Brian Craven in the Tyneside club's averages for the Provincial League in 1962.

The Neath team of 1962 had been highly successful on the track, even if it failed to pull the crowds. St Austell replaced Neath in the 1962 Provincial League and acquired Chris Julian and Chris Blewett from defunct Plymouth, allowing Australian Charlie Monk – third in the Welsh club's averages – and Jon Erskine – a top grass-track rider whose father, Mike, had ridden for Wimbledon and was a noted bike constructor and tuner – to move to Station Road.

Above left: Grasstracker Jon Erskine, transferred to Long Eaton from defunct Neath, was the son of Wimbledon star and bike constructor Mike Erskine.

Above right: Australian Bluey Scott, who rode for Motherwell in the early 1950s, prepares to race for the new Archers, with Jon Erskine to his right.

Eric 'Bluey' Scott, thirty-three years old in 1963, was a red-haired Australian – hence the nickname – whose chief experience in Britain had been with Motherwell's Lanarkshire Eagles in the early to mid-1950s, then briefly with Southampton and Ipswich after speedway disappeared north of the border. Scott returned to the UK on a working holiday with his Scots-born wife. He wanted to ride for Edinburgh, but Ian Hoskins had a full squad and recommended the Aussie to Reg Fearman. The team was completed by Ken Vale, a rider with a reputation for being 'tigerish' but who was also decidedly injury prone. Vale had appeared in one match for Neath in 1962 and had also featured at non-league Weymouth. Dennis Jenkins, with Reg Fearman and Mike Parker at Bradford in 1962, and Tony Eadon, provided the Archers with potential alternatives for the reserve berth.

After the success at Wolverhampton, the new Archers made their home debut just four days later. St Austell, whose regular Tuesday race night was the same as Long Eaton's, took advantage of a late start to their own home season – timed to coincide as closely as possible with the peak Cornish holiday period – to race off the Provincial League fixture.

From this point on the author ceases to rely on research alone and has the added benefit of personal memory, being part of the Station Road crowd on the evening of 16 April 1963 when actor Kenneth Cope, 'Jed Stone' in ITV's *Coronation Street*, declared the circuit open. Staff had worked all day to get a muddy track into shape for racing, and their efforts paid an immediate dividend. Charlie Monk ensured that he would become an instant hero by beating not only his former promoter, the experienced Trevor Redmond, but also smashing Olle Nygren's twelve-year-old track record in a new time of 70.6 seconds.

St Austell steadily drew ahead as Scott and White suffered falls, Erskine and Goldfinch engine failures, and Vale an engine failure and an exclusion for tape breaking. At the end of heat nine, the Gulls had a seemingly watertight eight-point lead. The match exploded into life for the home

Above: Reopening night, Tuesday 16 April 1963, and promoter Reg Fearman (right) introduces *Coronation Street* star Kenneth Cope to 'Tiger' Ken Vale.

Left: The programme cover for the first meeting in 1963.

fans in heat ten, when Erskine and Goldfinch both came from behind to record a 5-1. In the next heat, Monk and Payling scored a 4-2 and the result was once again in the balance.

Bluey Scott fell again in heat twelve, but Ken Vale, brought in as a reserve replacement, delighted the crowd by holding off Blewett and Bob Warner to keep the dream alive. There was to be no fairy-tale ending, for although Monk won the final heat, his partner Vic White dropped out of the race with engine failure and the resulting 3-3 gave St Austell a 40-38 victory.

Monk (11) and Erskine (9) top-scored for the Archers, with Julian (10) leading the way for a solid-looking St Austell. No victory for the 3,000-odd spectators, who were joined for the occasion by riders like Louis Lawson and ex-Archer Lionel Watling, but exciting racing and the pleasure of speedway at Station Road once more.

The opening victory at Wolverhampton and the closeness of the St Austell match raised expectations, but these were dashed by the opening sequence of results for the new Archers. With a spate of injuries and engine failures, Long Eaton lost their next five matches, home and away, against Stoke and Cradley in the Midland League and against Edinburgh at Old Meadowbank in the Provincial League, on this occasion by the heavy margin of 58.5 points to 18.5.

The Archers had lined up against Stoke at Station Road minus gastric flu victim Bluey Scott, and Dennis Jenkins was included in the side. Erskine and Jenkins got a 5-1 in heat three and a 4-2 in heat five to give Long Eaton a four-point lead. But then Stoke's team-riding skills took over and they recorded five 5-1s in the next six heats, with Monk falling twice when well placed.

Four nights later, at Sun Street, the speedway press bemoaned the fact that tactical substitutes were not allowed in Midland League matches. Stoke won 50-28 in the absence of Monk, but Erskine (8), Scott (8) and Payling (6) fought hard and could have made the final score much closer with extra rides. It was a frustrating time for both supporters and Reg Fearman, who acted quickly to boost the side. Experienced former Harringay rider Danny Dunton, released by National League Oxford and originally tipped to sign for New Cross, came in against Cradley and showed promise of better things, although the team lost 34-44.

Reg Fearman had secured the services of the highly experienced and fluent Peter Arnold as the announcer at Station Road, and he played his part in getting the crowd, many of them new to speedway, attuned to the sport and its ups and downs. Arnold, who had been around speedway

Right: Quiet man Charlie Monk, initially reluctant to pose for photographs, did his talking on the track. He beat Olle Nygren's 1951 track record in Long Eaton's 1963 reopening Provincial League meeting against St Austell.

Below: A team shot taken at an away match early in 1963, with Australian Charlie Monk either absent or declining to face the camera. From left to right, back row: Ron Wilson (team manager), Gil Goldfinch, Ken Vale, Danny Dunton. Front row: Eric 'Bluey' Scott, Maurice Payling, Vic White.

in a variety of capacities almost since the birth of the sport in Britain, and who had founded the Veteran Dirt Track Riders' Association, also wrote programme notes for Long Eaton matches.

For the Wolverhampton match, following the five straight defeats, Arnold told the fans that Reg Fearman was usually a happy-go-lucky character, always ready for a laugh and a gag:

> As a friend of his of many years standing, I feel I know him well enough to 'score' off each other in a light-hearted way, and you may have heard this when we have the 'by-play' on the centre green microphone.
>
> But believe me, Reg was in no mood for 'funnies' after the third home defeat in a row. Reg so desperately wanted a home win for you, the regular supporters, to cheer. In Reg's own words, 'the public are the heroes' and by that he hopes you will have the patience to realise that things have just not gone right for the Archers. We are losing to teams who are having no ill-luck machine-wise, or with riders falling off, and are at full strength as a team. Get our lads fit and well and 'Robin Hood' Fearman will have due cause to be proud of his men in the Lincoln Green.

A 1963 portrait shot of Charlie Monk – not easy to find.

To a massive sigh of relief all round, Dunton scored a 12-point maximum as the Archers completed a Midland League double over Wolverhampton, again by the score of 40-37, to win their first home match of the new era. Long Eaton were losing 32-33 after heat eleven, but Dunton and Vale recorded a 4-2 over Graham Warren in the penultimate race, giving the Archers a slim 36-35 advantage going into the final race.

Charlie Monk and Jon Erskine lined up against Tommy Sweetman and Morrie Mattingley, and Sweetman tried the 'war of nerves' approach by turning back to the pits gate to get his mechanic to check a nut and bolt. Monk, riding with a badly swollen foot, and Erskine refused to be pressured. Monk emerged from a tight tussle on the first bend just ahead of Sweetman and managed to hold the lead, while Erskine won the battle at the back to hold on for the vital point. The tension was off and Long Eaton had won their first home match by 40-37.

The home win sparked something of a revival on the track, as the team paid two visits within five days to the north-east. A narrow 40-38 away defeat at Middlesbrough on 9 May could so easily have been a victory. Vic White seized up in his second ride but, with a solid performance down the order, the Archers led by two points going into the final heat. Sadly, this time it was Charlie Monk's turn to experience engine failure and the Bears stole a narrow match win. Jon Erskine top-scored with 10 points, and there were major contributions from Gil Goldfinch with 9 points, and Dunton, Monk and Scott, with 6 points apiece.

Four nights later at Newcastle, the Archers secured what looked to be their first Provincial League away victory. But, in yet another outbreak of Parker-Fearman warfare, the Newcastle promoter protested and claimed that the Archers were not entitled to use former Diamond Gil Goldfinch at reserve. Parker's protest was upheld and the match points the Archers had won on the track were lost in the committee room.

It later emerged that, at the date when Long Eaton were required to submit their team sheet to Newcastle, Goldfinch's average was sufficiently low to merit the reserve berth. But his nine-point return at Middlesbrough, after the team sheet had been submitted, made the difference to his average that cost the Archers the match, despite an appeal.

The better form was nevertheless continued at home, when Sheffield were beaten 41-37. Former Long Eaton captain Ernest Palmer managed the Tigers and spoke to the Station Road fans over the centre-green microphone at the interval. Lady Luck, however, continued to be fickle. Against Exeter at home, Long Eaton led by 5 points with two heats to go, but conceded a 5-1 and a 4-2 in heats twelve and thirteen to go down by 39-38.

The match could have been put out of Exeter's reach if Danny Dunton had not forgotten to turn on his fuel at the start of heat seven! Monk led the way with 10 points and Scott scored 7 but a worrying development was the loss of form of Erskine, who failed to score.

At Rayleigh, Long Eaton were again ahead, by 6 points after six heats, but Bluey Scott fell in heat seven and broke two ribs. Monk, with the help of an extra ride, got 13 points, backed up by Dunton (7) and Vic White, who also scored 7 and gave some hint of his Leicester form for the first time in Archers colours. Ivor Brown beat Norman Hunter in a run-off for the Archers Trophy, as Station Road staged its first individual meeting of the new era, with a subdued Monk (11 points) as the only home rider to impress. Brown was again influential as Long Eaton suffered a 53-24 defeat at Cradley, on a track described as being like a miniature lake in places. Five coach-loads of supporters made the trip to Dudley Wood for this match.

Vic White kept up his improved showing in a 41-37 home win over Edinburgh on 4 June, when the legendary Johnnie Hoskins made his first appearance at Station Road. On the following Saturday, Long Eaton put up one of their finest away performances of the season and finally got some tangible reward from their Provincial League travels.

On the season's previous visit to Sun Street, Stoke, Long Eaton, without Monk, had struggled to score points in a Midland League match, and the press had criticised the absence of the tactical substitute rule in the regional competition. This time, the Archers had Monk in the line-up, and it was Stoke who needed the tactical substitute, with the visitors six points in front with three heats to go.

Another large following from Long Eaton saw Charlie Monk and Slant Payling give the Archers a fine start with a first-heat 5-1. Pete Jarman and Colin Pratt each had five rides for Stoke and a last-heat 5-1 by Jarman and Hockaday over Dunton and Vale brought a 39-39 draw. *Speedway Star* described the Long Eaton performance as 'superb'.

Charlie Monk won the Long Eaton round of the 1963 World Championship, but there was a setback for the fans when Newcastle won 52-43 at Station Road in the first round of the Provincial League knock-out cup, future World Champion Ivan Mauger showing his growing influence with a 15-point maximum for the Diamonds in his British comeback season. There was another close away match at Wolverhampton, where good use of tactical substitutes kept the Archers in the hunt. Wolves eventually won 42-36, with Dunton top-scoring for Long Eaton with 11 points.

Home victories over Rayleigh (44-33) and Poole (46-32) kept the fans happy in early July. Charlie Monk recorded maximums against both sets of opponents and in the Rayleigh match, Jon Erskine, at reserve, had 10 points from four rides.

Despite his many successes, Monk was not having everything his own way. He had a bad night at New Cross, wrecking his machine and walking out of the meeting. The Rangers won 44-32 and left Long Eaton counting the cost of so many falls and engine failures that only Danny Dunton (13 points) and Slant Payling (5) completed all their rides.

Goldfinch, apparently never too keen on a switch to Long Eaton, had retired before the meeting at the Old Kent Road. With Monk and Erskine both absent for a difficult trip to Poole, Reg Fearman persuaded him to return but he was pointless in a 54-24 defeat in which only Dunton and Scott, with seven apiece, kept the Archers going. Monk had, in fact, taken a week off, 'to sort himself out', in the words of team manager Ron Wilson. The young Australian had suffered a succession of heavy falls, on each occasion damaging his machine, and the New Cross incident was his fifth ruined frame in half a season.

Tuesday 23 July and a visit from Hackney in the Provincial League had probably not been underlined by supporters as the most attractive home match of the season. It turned out, however, to be significant for the debut of a rider who was to remain a favourite at Station Road for the next five seasons.

Norman Storer, a twenty-nine-year-old car dealer with a reputation as a road racer, scrambler, trials rider and, since 1962, grass-track exponent, had been among the spectators for the opening match against St Austell. After the meeting, Storer bought a speedway machine from former World Champion Tommy Price. On 7 May, with the Archers facing Wolverhampton, he travelled again to Station Road, but this time with a bike on the back of his car. He was given his first competitive ride in the second-half 'Wolf Pack Scurry' and came third.

Derby-based Norman Storer, already an accomplished racer in other branches of motorcycle sport, watched the first match against St Austell in April. Three months later he was in the team, where he stayed until the Archers closed in 1967. The picture, as can be seen from the race jacket, was actually taken in 1964.

Reg Fearman spotted the promise and gave the Derby man plenty of second-half rides at both Station Road and Stoke. On 2 July, when the Archers beat Rayleigh at home, he got his first win, a reserve handicap in which he took advantage of his start to beat Jon Erskine, Tony Eadon and John Mills. Norman followed the win up with a second place in the second-half Rockets Orbits and third place in the final behind Monk and Dunton, with Slant Payling fourth.

The potential was obvious, but few fans could have predicted what would happen on the night of the Hackney match. The Archers were again struggling to track a side. With no Monk or Erskine, reserve Ken Vale was promoted into the team proper, and Storer was given a league debut at reserve.

Easily identifiable because of his red mudguard, Storer won his first ride in heat four, heading home teammate Vic White and Hackney's star in the making, future England international Malcolm Simmons. He won heat eight as well, took a third place behind partner Dunton in heat eleven and was second in heat twelve.

Norman's tally for the evening was 9 points and two bonuses – just one point short of a paid maximum in his first ever appearance. Long Eaton's 47-31 victory over the Hawks was almost an afterthought.

Storer was the first-ever truly local rider to make an impact for the Archers. Derby had always been more of a source of support for Long Eaton than Nottingham, and Norman was not short of admiring fans. Of course, such form could not last, but Norman kept his place in the side until the end of the season and shone on other occasions.

Charlie Monk returned to the side for a Provincial League home match against Middlesbrough on 30 July. The Bears had three riders missing, including the heavy-scoring Eric Boothroyd, but the Archers only managed a 41-36 victory, with Monk scoring a 12-point maximum.

Norman Storer had proved an unexpected
bonus for 1963. But the unremarkable debut
of sixteen-year-old Ray Wilson in the home
debacle against Stoke was, unbeknown at the
time, the beginning of a major international
career.

Two embarrassingly heavy home defeats followed, Stoke thrashing the Archers 50.5 points to 27.5 in the Provincial League, and the following week Sheffield won a Trent Trophy match by 48-30. The Stoke match, apart from the devastating scoreline, will be remembered by older fans for three reasons: a spectacular and frightening crash involving Bluey Scott and Jon Erskine, with both riders lucky to escape without serious injuries, a new track record of 69 seconds dead recorded by Colin Pratt of Stoke, and the debut in league racing of sixteen-year-old Ray Wilson, son of team manager Ron.

The young Wilson had first taken to the track at the age of fifteen at Rye House, where his father began racing in the late 1940s. Ron Wilson insisted that Ray should first concentrate on school exams, but by the latter part of 1963, the ex-Leicester rider prepared a new machine for his son and began to arrange second-half outings at Coventry and other tracks.

Those fans who bothered to watch the second-half reserve races could hardly have realised that they were watching the first efforts of a young man who would become a Long Eaton and Leicester legend, and one of England's greatest riders during the 1970s period of international success for the national team.

As the season continued, Charlie Monk won the Long Eaton Provincial Riders' Championship round on a difficult track, and with many riders refusing to take scheduled rides, Norman Storer went out five times in six heats and amassed 10 points. With Dunton now out of the side with a knee injury, there were further home defeats: 38-40 at the hands of a Provincial Select team, and 32-46 against Newcastle. With the closure of New Cross due to falling crowds, Long Eaton signed Geoff Penniket for the first of several spells at Station Road, and he was to contribute some useful points as a comparative purple patch got underway at Station Road, lasting to the very end of the season, raising the spirits of the fans.

There was another tense last-heat decider when Wolverhampton visited Station Road on 17 September. The Archers were 8 points behind after six heats, but team manager Ron Wilson used tactical substitutes to good effect and Bluey Scott's 11 points and 9 from Charlie Monk, backed up by Ken Vale (7) and Storer (5), gained the Archers an exciting 39-39 draw.

A 43-34 victory over Cradley in the final Provinvial League match helped to ensure the Archers missed the bottom spot. Monk scored another maximum, with Scott (9) and Storer (8) in support. Cradley were short of riders and Ray Wilson got an outing in Heathens' colours. Cradley's top scorer, predictably, was Ivor Brown with ten, but Monk beat Brown to win the Silver Sash – the season's last winner.

Away from home, Long Eaton undertook the first West Country tour of the new era, losing 30-47 at Exeter on 23 September and 29-49 at St Austell the next night. Monk (12) and Scott (10) kept things respectable at the County Ground, with Des Lukehurst, another casualty of the New Cross closure in August, taking the place of Slant Payling, who broke down en route to Devon. At the Cornish Stadium, Monk (9) and Scott (7) were again the top scorers. Payling arrived for this meeting but scored only two points and Lukehurst was again in the side.

A 40-38 win by an augmented side over Norwich and newly-crowned World Champion Ove Fundin kept the season alight until the third week in October. The actual finale to the season was a Long Eaton versus Provincial Select meeting, with a weak-looking Archers losing 28-49 to a side containing Ivor Brown, Eric Boocock from Middlesbrough and Ken Adams from Stoke. Amidst the string of heat wins for the visitors, Charlie Monk reigned supreme with a maximum.

As a comeback season, it had been enjoyable if not particularly successful from a results point of view. The Archers finished just above basement club Rayleigh in the Provincial League, while from an individual point of view Charlie Monk finished in the top ten of the PL riders' table, his 261.5 points from 27 matches giving him an average of 9.7 points a match.

In a final twist to the season, Mike Parker's Wolverhampton won the Provincial League from Reg Fearman's Stoke. The Potters were initially hailed as champions, but then Wolves managed to reverse the result of a defeat they had suffered at the hands of another Fearman track, Middlesbrough, giving them the title. The dispute was over the inclusion in the Middlesbrough side of future Long Eaton rider John Mills, which the authorities ruled was illegal. Mills was later to die when his gyrocopter crashed near Rockhampton in Queensland, Australia.

Overall, the end of the 1963 season, disputes and all, was overshadowed by the death of World Champion Peter Craven in a crash at Old Meadowbank, Edinburgh.

As far as Long Eaton's revival was concerned, racing was normally good on a track renowned for giving everyone a chance, and Reg Fearman's showmanship meant there was usually something to enjoy at the interval, whether it be Stanley Lindbergh diving into a flaming tank of water (Fearman himself was later thrown in by the riders!), or high-wire artiste Marcello performing on the centre green.

Quiet man Monk was the outstanding rider, Scott and Erskine a force when free from injury, Vale a never-say-die fighter who won the respect of the fans, Storer the major discovery and Payling a firm favourite with the crowd despite a modest average. Danny Dunton, given his experience, was something of a disappointment, and much more had been expected of Gil Goldfinch and Vic White, given their records at Newcastle and Leicester respectively. Most encouraging of all, in the longer term, was the promise of Ray Wilson.

The close season of 1963/64 saw British speedway in turmoil. In 1963, the National League had just about proved viable with seven teams, although the middle and lower rank riders complained bitterly about the lack of additional bookings over and above their guaranteed once-a-week meeting at their home track. But a real crisis loomed when developers moved in on Southampton's Bannister Court Stadium, and the Nationals were reduced to six members.

Today, it is an accepted part of speedway history that the formation of the Provincial League in 1960 was the catalyst for the great revival in the sport's fortunes in the 1960s and

'70s, another golden age which, in some respects, compared with the post-Second World War boom. However, at the time, not everyone in British speedway wholeheartedly supported the new venture.

Despite the success of the Provincial League over the four seasons from 1960 to 1963, the more established tracks to a large degree kept the newcomers at arms length. The National League, in the shape of Wimbledon promoter Ronnie Greene and the hugely influential and somewhat autocratic Charles Ochiltree of Coventry, had two representatives on the Control Board, to the Provincial League's one.

The National League tracks each received an equal share of the proceeds from the World Championship final, which up to then had always been raced in the UK at Wembley Stadium, compared to the one share which had to be divided between the PL promoters.

The National League men argued that they had kept speedway alive during its darkest years, and that the World final, apart from foreign qualifiers, was always contested by men under contract to them. The Provincial League response was that they had revived a sport which had shrunk to an almost unsustainable level, and that their riders were accepted into the World Championship competition, even if they did not make it to the ultimate round.

The crisis caused by the closure of Southampton came to a head when the Control Board ruled that Provincial League champions Wolverhampton, and one other track (apparently never named to this day), should be promoted into the National League. Wolves' promoter Mike Parker and the management of the other track in question declined the invitation, and were then told they had no choice!

Ian Hoskins – son of speedway pioneer Johnnie and, in 1963/64, promoter at the highly successful Edinburgh track – gives an insider account of what happened that winter and spring in his fascinating book *History of the Speedway Hoskins*:

> An emergency meeting was held by the Provincial promoters. We all decided to resist the directive. We were happy where we were. The Board then dropped its bombshell. Unless we agreed, every track and every rider who rode for us in 1964 would be declared 'black' and have to run outside of the Auto Cycle Union (ACU) and the Federation Internationale Motorcyclisme (FIM), the world controlling body. We would all have our licences revoked and be suspended indefinitely.

In Ian Hoskins' words, it was, 'the act of desperate men and a total abuse of power. But it became a reality.'

Faced with the prospect of running outside of authority, of being banned for life, the Provincial promoters made an appeal for a full investigation. As Hoskins describes, the PL promoters 'dug in'. They would not give away a single track and the National League promoters were obliged to reopen West Ham as a joint promotion, to keep their numbers up to scratch.

Hoskins adds: 'A move was then made to try and break us by working on our riders. Fortunately they too, with one or two exceptions, decided to remain loyal.'

As Long Eaton prepared for their second comeback season, the Provincial League had been banished by the vote of the Speedway Control Board, which was mainly made up of members of the Royal Automobile Club (RAC) and the Auto Cycle Union (ACU). But the vast majority of the men and women on the terraces cared little about the political upheaval as long as the bikes raced once a week. Reg Fearman explains:

> The Provincial League appointed their own referees, in some cases ex-riders and former Speedway Control Board licensed officials for 1964, and we simply ran outside the Control Board's authority. This made no difference to the organisation of the league or to crowd attendances.

There were, however, plenty of changes to digest at a team level. Southampton was not the only track to close its doors following the 1963 season. Reg Fearman's highly successful Stoke track also fell victim to redevelopment, leaving Fearman with Middlesbrough and Long Eaton.

The nucleus of the 1963 Archers squad was on the move from Station Road. Trevor Redmond had decided to move his St Austell team to Glasgow, where he reopened the White City track in partnership with Ian Hoskins. Charlie Monk was to be the spearhead of the new White City Tigers. Newport had become the latest Welsh venue to operate, and Jon Erskine, responsible for laying the track at the Somerton Park stadium, and Geoff Penniket moved to Wales. In addition, the inter-league dispute had placed Danny Dunton, as chairman of the Speedway Riders Association, in a difficult position.

The various situations combined to provide the replacements. Stoke skipper Ken Adams and the promising Kid Bodie were drafted in to Station Road from Stoke, and Fearman hoped to be able to add another ex-Potter, the highly-rated Colin Pratt, to the Station Road line-up. Adams was firmly in the veteran stage, having ridden since the post-war return of speedway, while Bodie was a teenager who had adopted the fairly obvious nom de plume (based on a TV western character) to hide from his mother the fact that he was racing at all!

Potentially the most important signing for 1964 was that of another veteran, high-scoring former Birmingham and England rider Eric Boothroyd. His former club, Middlesbrough, had switched race night from Thursday to Friday evening, making it impossible for Boothroyd to continue because of the demands of his greengrocery business. Long Eaton's Bluey Scott went to Teesside in a straight swap. Staying on at Station Road were 1963 discoveries Norman Storer and Ray Wilson, Slant Payling, Ken Vale and, initially at least, Vic White.

The 1964 speedway season began with home and away challenge matches between Exeter and Cradley Heath and, as a result, the riders from both sides who had taken part were solemnly banned.

Right: Bluey Scott's replacement was the highly experienced Eric Boothroyd, who switched from Middlesbrough to Long Eaton when the north-easterners moved their race-night to Fridays – Halifax greengrocer Eric's busy night!

Opposite left: Bluey Scott was transferred to Reg Fearman's other interest at Middlesbrough in exchange for Eric Boothroyd but appeared on one or two occasions in 1964 in Archers' colours.

Opposite right: Kid Bodie (later known by his real name of Howard Cole) transferred to Long Eaton with Ken Adams when Stoke closed at the end of 1963.

Long Eaton kicked off their season at home to Wolverhampton in a challenge match on 31 March, somewhat unexpectedly losing 41-37. Wolverhampton, struggling to build a team in the uncertain circumstances surrounding the split between the leagues, were allowed to use men from other Mike Parker tracks as guests: Provincial Riders champion Ivan Mauger from Newcastle and Maury McDermott from the new track at Sunderland.

Long Eaton's newcomers did not disappoint, Kid Bodie top-scoring with 11, while Adams and Boothroyd had 9 points each. But the remaining four riders, Payling, Vale, Storer and White, could only score eight points between them. Wolves were solid down the order, although Mauger had a poor night. The New Zealander looped at the gate in his first ride, suffered engine failure in his second, won his third and was then beaten by Bodie in heat twelve.

The Archers' first away match was at Cradley in the curtain-raising Southern League competition. Gilt-edged prospect Ray Wilson came in at reserve in place of Vic White. Cradley won easily, 48-30, and again Boothroyd (11), Bodie (7) and Adams (5) did the bulk of the scoring, with the main support coming from Wilson, who scored 4.

Cradley came to Station Road three nights later for the Southern League return. Wilson kept his place at reserve but Reg Fearman left the number two slot in the team vacant in the programme and announced that the match would be preceeded by a 'vultures race'.

Four riders – Slant Payling, Vic White, and two former Stoke men, Ray Harris and Hungarian refugee Sandor Levai – would compete over four laps, with the winner taking his place at number two in the Archers' line-up. Payling won the race and, clearly fired up by losing his automatic team place, went on to record his best ever performance in Long Eaton colours, scoring nine points in the match. His efforts were not quite enough to bring the Archers success, with Cradley winning 41-37. Boothroyd top-scored with 10 and Bodie had 7, but Adams was off colour with 4 points and the remaining three riders could manage only 7 points between them – a similar story to the Wolverhampton match.

Left: Slant Payling had to fight for a team place via a 'vultures race', but held his nerve to finish ahead of his rivals.

Opposite: The Control Board might not have liked the 'outlawed' Provincial League in 1964, but the fans lapped it up. The PL produced some all-action speedway at close quarters, as seen here, as Sheffield's Clive Featherby (on white line) tangles with Long Eaton skipper Ken Adams.

Vic White moved to Newport and should have faced Long Eaton in the Welsh team's opening meeting. Extra work needed on the track meant the meeting was deferred.

Long Eaton's search for a first win of the season moved on to a pair of matches against Exeter in the Southern League. At the County Ground on 13 April, the Archers, never happy visitors to Devon, collapsed to a 55-23 defeat. Adams (9), Boothroyd and Payling, with 5 points each, contributed all but 4 points of the Long Eaton total, and the Adams/Payling partnership got the only Archers heat wins, in the first and ninth heats. Len Silver got a paid maximum and Jimmy Squibb scored 11 (beaten only by Adams) for the rampant Falcons.

The tables were turned the next evening at Station Road, with Long Eaton managing a 39-37 victory. It looked ominous when Exeter led by 6 points after four heats but Len Silver fell in heat five, bringing partner Ray Wickett and Ken Vale down as well. Kid Bodie rode through the mayhem to win the heat and Vale remounted to give the Archers a 5-0.

Long Eaton took the lead for the first time in heat six when Boothroyd and Storer recorded a 4-2 against Squibb and Des Lukehurst, and further 4-2s in heats seven and eight put the Archers five points ahead. Amazingly, Exeter got their own 5-0 heat win in heat nine when Bodie and Vale dropped out, and heat ten was drawn. The decider came in heat eleven, with Adams and Payling proving quite a potent partnership, beating Silver and Wickett 4-2. Boothroyd and Adams took the first places in the last two heats to hang on to the lead, and Long Eaton had recorded a win in their fifth match of the season.

It sparked off one of the best winning streaks ever recorded by a Long Eaton side. Poole were beaten 41-36 on a wet track at Station Road on 21 April (Boothroyd – 12-point maximum, Payling and Storer – 7 points), and a week later Hackney were vanquished by 49.5 points to 29.5. Clive Featherby of Sheffield rode as a guest for Hackney. He was the only man to beat Ken Adams and collected half a point when he tied with Bodie in the last heat. In the meantime, Eric Boothroyd had completed yet another faultless maximum.

It was at this stage of the season that the Control Board published an advertisement in the *Speedway Star* informing all PL riders that they were banned. The Board had sent letters to all PL riders, but those addressed to riders at their tracks rather than their home addresses had been returned unopened.

Archers' target Colin Pratt had been one of the riders who initially decided to stay legitimate and try his hand in the National League, but a poor points return meant that, economically, he had to return to the PL. Long Eaton fans were disappointed when he signed for Hackney Wick after the East London side's visit to Station Road.

Long Eaton recorded a rare away victory when they won 40-38 at Wolverhampton. This was all the more unexpected because, Friday being race night at Monmore Green, Eric Boothroyd was absent. There was a last-heat decider, with Wolves needing a 4-2 to draw. Maximum man Tommy Sweetman had no trouble winning heat thirteen, with Bodie second. The real drama, as is often the case in speedway, was at the back, where Wolves reserve Chris Harrison led Slant Payling. The vastly more experienced Payling pressed hard and Harrison fell, giving Long Eaton the Southern League points.

Wolves protested about the use of the banned Barum tyre by Ken Adams, but the Provincial Promoters Association, who heard the appeal, decided both promoters had been negligent in allowing Adams to start the meeting using the illegal equipment. The result stood and eventually meant the Archers finished one place above the Wolves at the foot of the final Southern League table.

The fifth consecutive win came with a 42-36 victory over Newport at Station Road on 5 May. Visiting heat leader Dick Bradley, an England test rider against Australia in the early 1950s who had been with Southampton in 1963, was unbeatable, and Jon Erskine showed his knowledge of the Long Eaton track with nine points. Long Eaton were solid in the face of this, and 10 points from Boothroyd, 9 from Adams and 7 from Payling saw them home.

The winning run would undoubtedly have come to an end the following evening, when the Archers were due to race at Poole, but the meeting was rained off and win number six came at home against Newcastle. Again, the meeting was dominated by the visiting number one, this time Ivan Mauger, who scored a maximum. Long Eaton's solid scoring down the order, a great improvement on the opening few matches of the season when this had been the weak area, brought them the points in their first Provincial League match of the season.

Long Eaton Archers in 1964, before Slant Payling was switched to Middlesbrough. From left to right: Slant Payling, Kid Bodie, John Mills, Ray Wilson, Norman Storer, Eric Boothroyd, Ron Wilson (team manager). Skipper Ken Adams is on the machine.

Boothroyd (9) and Adams (8) were again the top men, but no fewer than three Archers, Payling, Bodie and the emerging Ray Wilson, scored 6 points. Payling's consistency in the middle order was a major factor in the run of success.

A seventh consecutive victory looked on the cards at Waterden Road, Hackney, when Long Eaton, described by the *Speedway Star* as the most improved team in the Provincial League, shot into an eight-point lead. Hackney fought back, led by maximum man Colin Pratt, showing Archers fans just what they had missed in failing to sign him, and the Hawks eventually won 41-37. Boothroyd was again consistent with 10 points and Norman Storer had one of his best nights so far away from home with 7.

It proved to be Slant Payling's last match in Long Eaton colours. Middlesbrough fans had been less than delighted in losing Eric Boothroyd to the Archers and did not consider Bluey Scott an adequate substitute. Boothroyd was continuing his 1963 Provincial League form and was close to the top of the league averages. Fearman, anxious to keep the balance between his two tracks, believed switching Payling up to Cleveland Park would help ensure parity.

The Station Road fans were upset. Payling had made consistent contributions to the Archers' recent run of success, ever since winning the 'vultures race' to keep his team position. Even when he was not scoring points, the former coal miner and steel worker had been a popular personality, who, together with his wife, was a regular at Supporters' Club functions.

The balance of the side did appear to have been upset when Wolverhampton won the return Southern League match 41-36 at Station Road on 19 May. Ex-Stoke man Ron Sharp came in for Payling, but scored just two points. The rearranged match at Poole was the next night, and Long Eaton crashed 57-21. The most significant feature of this match was the fact that Ray Wilson headed the Archers score chart for the first time. Boothroyd and Adams (who retired in his first ride with the recurrence of an earlier injury), scored two points between them.

The season got back on the rails in the next home match, with Glasgow, and the returning Charlie Monk, beaten 45-33. Monk scored 14 points from five rides, losing only to Boothroyd. Chris Julian scored 11 from five rides and between them Monk and the spectacular Cornishman accounted for 25 of the Tigers' points. Ray Wilson again top-scored for Long Eaton, this time recording 11 points. Boothroyd scored 10, but Adams, still struggling against injury, could manage only 3.

At this stage of the season, Long Eaton were occupying a respectable Provincial League placing, but it was not to last for a variety of reasons. The Friday absences of Eric Boothroyd, with several tracks racing on that evening, began to tell against the Archers.

A 49-29 defeat at Middlesbrough could have been reversed with Boothroyd, a Cleveland Park track specialist, in the side. On this occasion, the home fans got the better of the pre-season exchange, as Bluey Scott scored a 12-point maximum. The following evening, the Archers were at Edinburgh and Boothroyd scored ten points, but he had little support and the Monarchs won 53-22.

Edinburgh were riding high and came to Station Road on 9 June to record a thumping 42-36 victory. The Archers lost six of the first eight heats and, although they fought back with two 4-2s in heats nine and twelve, it was nowhere near enough to save the match. Boothroyd, with 12 from five rides, and Adams with 8 from five, tried to stem the tide, supported by Wilson with 6. Wayne Briggs got a faultless maximum for the visitors and reserve Jimmy Tannock got 5 from his two rides.

A heavy defeat at Newport was followed by a 54-42 success over Middlesbrough in the Knock-Out Cup round one on 16 June and a 40-38 win over Poole in the Provincial League a week later. Although crowds were never high at Station Road in the sixties, they were fairly consistent, and the closeness of most of the matches was a major factor. It was rare to see runaway home victories and racing was generally interesting, on a track which, although sometimes bumpy because of the regular stock car racing at the circuit, was a superb shape for speedway.

Cradley Heath's George Major won the first individual meeting of the season at Station Road, the 100 Guineas Trophy, with a 15-point maximum. Eric Boothroyd, who never recovered from a slow start in the first race, was second with 13.

In the league, the Boothroyd Friday night factor again told against the Archers. He was absent at Monmore Green as Wolves won 49-29, where Eric's replacement, junior John Mills, managed only two points, and again a week later at White City, Glasgow. The home side, spearheaded by a Charlie Monk maximum, managed a 44-34 victory, but it could well have been a very different story with Boothroyd in the Archers' team.

Long Eaton had slumped to second from the bottom in the Provincial League table, above Newport, but were level on points with Exeter and Cradley. In the individual averages, including Southern League matches, Boothroyd was a model of consistency, with 164 points from 16 matches and an average of 10.25.

The Archers got some revenge over Wolverhampton at Station Road on 7 July with a 40-38 victory achieved in the last heat. With the scores level at 36-36, Ken Adams was leading Sweetman, with Wolves' Australian newcomer Gordon Guasco, signed from Sunderland when the north-east track failed to stay the course of the season, in third. Archers took the points when Guasco fell and Ron Sharp moved up for the remaining point. Ray Wilson, now really beginning to make the speedway world take notice, was top scorer with 10 points, supported by Adams and Storer with 8.

Eric Boothroyd missed the match after tearing ligaments in his back while lifting a sack of potatoes at his Elland greengrocers' and was again absent the following night when Poole had a predictable 55-23 win.

Another Friday night saw the top scorer still missing and Archers lose 47-31 at Hackney, but Eric, although not fully recovered, was back in the saddle at Exeter the following Monday when Long Eaton put up a respectable performance in losing 48-30 (Wilson 9 and Boothroyd 7).

Only Boothroyd's high general level of fitness saved him from a slipped disc, according to the doctor who treated him. Reg Fearman was also getting pain at this stage from a back injury suffered during his riding career, which had included matches for Stoke in the earlier years of the Provincial League. The old injury was probably the only factor which prevented Fearman from donning his leathers again when the Archers were injury-hit.

Kid Bodie was contributing valuable points for the Archers and discovering that there were other rewards for good-looking teenage speedway stars.

There was no Ivor Brown in the Cradley side the next evening at Station Road, and Ray Wilson took advantage to record his first maximum, in the Archers' 43-35 victory.

Eric Boothroyd was still riding high in the Provincial League averages and he made an unprecedented Friday evening appearance at Newport. One can only imagine what the score would have been without his face-saving 11 points as the Wasps won 54-23. If Long Eaton had been forced to track a junior, it could even have been a complete 65-13 whitewash, something the Archers thankfully managed to avoid throughout the team's existence. The Long Eaton 'old boys' in the Welsh side all cashed in, with Penniket scoring 9 and Erskine and Vic White 8 each.

Boothroyd was again in top form at Cradley the following night, when the Archers' narrow 51-45 defeat in round two of the Knock-Out Cup represented a fine performance. Eric had first made his name at Cradley in the late 1940s, before going on to First Division success with Birmingham, and he collected 14 points, supported by 10 from Norman Storer and 7 from Ken Adams.

The Archers climbed a couple of places in the Provincial League table with a 44-34 win over Sheffield at Station Road on 22 July, inspired by Bodie (11), Wilson (9), Adams (8) and Storer (8). Boothroyd looked to be continuing his run when he won heat three but those were to be his last points for Long Eaton. He had engine trouble in his next two races and fell in the final race of the match.

Riding for an England side against Scotland at Sheffield, Eric was involved in an incident with former Archer Charlie Monk. Monk got into trouble near the fence on the first bend and Boothroyd, coming in wide and very fast, had no chance of avoiding an accident. He came off his machine and, before landing on the greyhound track, struck a lighting standard and the fence.

After X-rays at Sheffield Royal Infirmary, it was confirmed that Eric had a fractured pelvis and severe bruising. He sold his equipment and announced his retirement, and it looked like

Ray Wilson's injury at Weymouth was a worry for father Ron – for reasons relating to both family and speedway.

the end of an outstanding fifteen-year career in speedway. Happily for the sport, Eric did make a comeback when Reg Fearman opened up in Halifax, his home town, in 1965, and he went on to have his own promoting career.

If the Boothroyd injury was serious for Long Eaton, it was soon to be followed by more devastating news. Ray Wilson, rapidly becoming a consistent points scorer, had travelled to Weymouth, one of the non-league outposts of British speedway, to appear in an open meeting, together with Ken Adams, who ten years earlier had captained the Dorset side. Wilson had scored two second places when he became involved in a tangle with Adams and Jimmy Squibb which resulted in him breaking his leg.

The 1964 Provincial Riders Championship round at Station Road on 4 August was overshadowed for the fans by the gloom occasioned by the loss of Boothroyd and Wilson. Ivan Mauger was rapidly becoming unbeatable on the Derbyshire track, his 15-point maximum in defence of his PLRC title following a 12-point full house the week before when he rode for an Australasia team in a 39-38 challenge match defeat by the Archers. The Kiwi had also been unbeaten in Newcastle's Provincial League visit to Station Road. Kid Bodie kept the Long Eaton flag flying with 11 points and Norman Storer registered 10, and the crowd was reported to have been the highest of the season so far.

When league racing resumed, Long Eaton inevitably struggled. Even with Boothroyd and Wilson, they had hardly been the strongest of Provincial League teams. Exeter were the next opponents at Station Road and they won 42-36. Reg Fearman had been attempting to sign former New Cross star Cyril Roger, but he failed to materialise. The Archers in fact provided the first man past the post in nine of the thirteen heats, but engine troubles finally told against them. Norman Storer and Kid Bodie headed the scorers with 9 points each.

Long Eaton did contribute to a little bit of Provincial League history when they went down 44-34 at Sheffield on 13 August. The Tigers were also suffering from injury problems and were forced to include the fifty-one-year-old Wilf Jay, whose career had begun at Norwich before the Second World War. Jay took his place in the Sheffield team with two of his sons, Alan (twenty-three) and Derek (twenty-one)!

The Provincial League match against Newport at Station Road on 18 August was abandoned after seven heats with the Wasps leading 24-18. Long Eaton's line-up for the match included two Middlesbrough riders, Eric Boocock and former Archer Bluey Scott. The Bears' home league season had finished, and the track's entire future as a league side was in some doubt, with Reg Fearman committed to opening up at Halifax in 1965.

Once again, the Archers promoter was trying to balance his tracks and maintain interest at Long Eaton, which was in all probability a better financial bet than Middlesbrough. Some people criticise speedway for the juggling around which, even to this day, allows guest riders to appear for a team one day and then arrive with the opposition later on.

The truth is that speedway, unlike other sports, relies entirely on creating a good balance of team strengths if it is to be entertaining and competitive. As a terrace fan in 1964, I know I welcomed the strengthening of the side with the Middlesbrough riders. Had their inclusion had any effect on the league championship, then it might have been a different matter. As it stood, no one was adversely affected and the Station Road faithful had the rest of their season saved as a spectacle.

Boocock and Scott failed to make an immediate impression when Hackney won 40-38 in the next home league match, with both men scoring just five points. The Archers had looked to have the match sewn up, nevertheless, with an eight-point lead after heat nine. Hackney used the tactical substitute rule to good effect and recorded a 4-2 and two 5-1s in the next three heats. Long Eaton could still have won with a last-heat 5-1, and Kid Bodie was indeed first home, but Les McGillivray and John Poyser blocked out Ken Adams.

There was a touch of glamour at Station Road for the Coronation Street Trophy, presented to winner George Hunter by actress Pat Phoenix – 'Elsie Tanner' of *Coronation Street*, which was popular in the mid-sixties as it is today.

Left: Bluey Scott made an unexpected return to Long Eaton colours as promoter Reg Fearman introduced riders from his Middlesbrough interest to fill the gaps left by the Archers' injury crisis.

Opposite: Ron Sharp, on the left of this 1964 team group, was the main replacement for Slant Payling when he left for Middlesbrough. Also pictured in this informal pits shot are John Mills, Norman Storer, Eric Boothroyd, Ken Adams, Ray Wilson and Kid Bodie.

Nine points from Norman Storer and seven from Eric Boocock, together with an Ivan Mauger engine failure, helped the Archers keep the score to 30-30 at the heat ten stage when they visited Brough Park, Newcastle, but three 5-1s from the Diamonds in the last three heats were conclusive.

Middlesbrough arrived at Station Road on 8 September, presenting Reg Fearman with a team selection conundrum. He solved it adroitly by tracking Eric Boocock for Long Eaton and allowing Bluey Scott to ride for the Bears. The Archers had a comprehensive 54-24 win, Boocock losing only to David Younghusband in the first heat. Boocock and Kid Bodie each finished with 11 points, and Ron Sharp registered a season's best 10. Bluey Scott was best for the Bears with 9.

Ivan Mauger scored the inevitable maximum as he led Overseas to a 58-50 victory over Britain in a Station Road challenge on 15 September and Norman Storer, who as a reserve was Long Eaton's only qualifier for the Provincial League Riders' final at Belle Vue, scored three points.

The 1964 season of turmoil was coming to a close and it ended well for the Archers with a 44-34 home Provincial League victory over Newport which again helped the team to avoid bottom spot. Boocock (9) and Scott (8), in the Long Eaton line-up again, were the top scorers against the Wasps.

All that remained was a final open meeting, taking the form of a Four Team Tournament, involving Long Eaton, Wolves, Cradley and other home riders under the title of the Archers.

If 1964 had been traumatic for speedway as a whole, for Long Eaton it had been a mainly enjoyable season of consolidation. The final league placing could have been higher but for the injuries to key men, and Reg Fearman appeared to sum it up succinctly in his final programme notes. 'Crowd wise and team wise, Long Eaton has fared better than in 1963,' he wrote, sentiments which sent the supporters away from the last meeting in a happy frame of mind.

15

The British League

Few speedway teams have endured such a torrid season as Long Eaton experienced in 1965 and lived to tell the tale.

For British speedway as a whole, 1965 was a re-birth. Following an inquiry headed by eminent judge Lord Shawcross, the National League and Provincial League promoters came together to form one new and exciting eighteen-team competition, the British League. Sadly, Long Eaton was fated to become its basement team, an injury-ravaged chopping block for most of the other sides.

For the Station Road faithful, it was far from a vintage season. Management, riders and fans gritted their teeth and survived.

Fans across Britain had heaved a collective sigh of relief when the dispute between the leagues was finally settled. The National League promoters, in reality, had little choice but to be cooperative. Norwich, a consistently well-supported track ever since the 1930s, had fallen victim to property developers at the end of 1964. That the National League was again down to six teams and had no West Ham waiting in the wings on this occasion undoubtedly helped the senior promoters stomach the idea that, from now on, they would, at least in theory, have to share the spoils equally with the Johnny-come-lately Provincial League men.

It was not only some of the National League promoters who were metaphorically holding their noses as the new season got underway. One prominent Wimbledon supporter wrote a distraught letter to the speedway press, writing-off the new structure before it had even been launched. 'The thought of what we shall get in 1965 with all the mediocre Provincial riders, bar a very, very few, leaves my heart like lead and my hopes of a speedway boom very much dashed,' she said.

The vast majority of people who had experienced the sport's alarming decline in the mid to late 1950s regarded a new and strong league as speedway heaven. But, although the Long Eaton fans were full of the usual start-of-season optimism as Easter approached, they were to end up believing they were in speedway hell.

Norwich and Provincial League Middlesbrough were the only two of the 1964 teams not to start the 1965 season, constituting, in speedway terms, an admirable degree of stability. The surviving six National League and eleven Provincial League teams were joined by one new track, a reopened Halifax, promoted by Reg Fearman with the nucleus of the Middlesbrough riders. Norfolk was not a total loss to speedway; a new track was opened at Kings Lynn for an initial season of open licence meetings at a venue where a team labelled as Long Eaton had ridden a charity match in 1953, on what was then a grass circuit.

The National League teams had held all the top riders. The dispute which blackened the 1964 campaign, restricting the World Championship to National League men, had ensured there were practically no chances for riders from the two sections to compete against each other and see whether or not standards in the lower section were rising. Clearly, there had to be redistribution of riders to even up the eighteen teams as far as possible.

Despite the close season rider moves, when Long Eaton paraded at Old Meadowbank, Edinburgh, for their first taste of the new league, there were only two newcomers to boost a side which had hardly taken the Provincial League by storm the previous year. The most significant newcomer was Australian Ray Cresp, who had reached the 1961 World Final in Malmo, Sweden. A Wembley Lion in the season before the Empire Stadium team withdrew from league racing, he had subsequently ridden for Poole and Ipswich. Cresp had interspersed his British speedway career with motor racing and quit Ipswich when a conflict occurred between the four-wheel and two-wheel sports.

At Ipswich, Cresp had been regarded as a National League heat-leader and eyebrows were raised at the start of 1963 when Trevor Redmond was allowed to sign him for Provincial League St Austell. Redmond, never the man to miss an opportunity, retorted that no one else had tried to sign a man of clear ability. An official of the Speedway Riders Association, Cresp stayed legitimate in 1964 when he was an important part of the West Ham revival in the National League, again confirming his status as someone able to perform at the highest level.

The other newcomer was also from the Southern Hemisphere. The virtually unknown Rim Malskaitis, a New Zealander of Latvian origin, at first stood out from the crowd as the first rider resident in the UK to own and ride one of the new Czech machines – thus heralding a mechanical revolution in a sport in which the JAP engine had reigned supreme since the mid-1930s.

Malskaitis had a 1962 ESO DT500 with a two-speed gearbox. Halfway through the 1965 season, the gearbox failed and the rider, with the help of a Long Eaton mechanic called Cyril Clark who had previously worked for Peter Moore, welded the first gear to the second gear. When Malskaitis returned to New Zealand after just a single season at Station Road, he used the bike in that form for a season and then rode it the following year in Australia, where a countershaft and new engine plates were fitted. By then, the ESO was becoming the machine of choice.

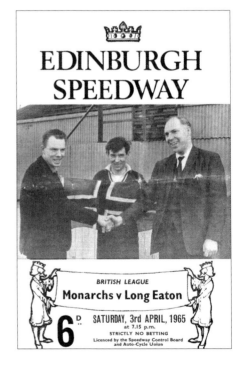

Above left: Aussie World finalist and former National League heat-leader Ray Cresp was allocated to Long Eaton after the Provincial League merged with the National League in 1965 to form the British League.

Above right: Long Eaton upset predictions by winning their first ever away match in the British League at Old Meadowbank, Edinburgh, in April 1965.

THE SHAY GROUNDS
HALIFAX

HALIFAX

SPEEDWAY
THE HOME OF THE 'DUKES'

1st MEETING   ∴   1st SEASON

BRITISH LEAGUE MATCH

HALIFAX 'Dukes' v.

LONG EATON 'Archers'

SATURDAY, 17th APRIL, 1965 at 7-30 p.m.

OFFICIAL PROGRAMME **9** d.

The Archers also upset the reopening party at Halifax with their second successive away victory in the new amalgamated league. Sadly, they spoilt the effect by losing at home to West Ham in between!

The five continuing Archers for 1965 were the two big Station Road discoveries: fit-again Ray Wilson, expected to continue the meteoric rise that had been cut short the previous summer by his broken leg, and Norman Storer, together with the former Stoke trio of Ken Adams, Kid Bodie and Ron Sharp. It looked, at best, a side which ought to be able to hold its own on its home track, but one which would probably struggle away, particularly against one or two of the former National Leaguers who had effectively maintained their superior riding strength.

But, at the end of thirteen heats of speedway at Old Meadowbank, Long Eaton had continued their tradition of opening-night surprises and confounded the pundits by winning their first away fixture in the British League. Despite injuries – Malskaitis looped at the gate and hurt his wrist, and both Sharp, who had broken ribs, and Bodie had to be stretchered off – Long Eaton were well ahead by heat ten. The Monarchs fielded top scorer Doug Templeton as a tactical substitute and he and George Hunter recorded a 5-1 to bring the home side back into the match. The Archers held on and sealed the win by the end of heat twelve, when they had a six-point lead. A further 5-1 for Edinburgh in the final race proved academic.

Monarchs' promoter Ian Hoskins was understandably upset by a home defeat against a Long Eaton side many believed to be the weakest in the league. On the other hand, few took seriously his presumably tongue-in-cheek claim that the Archers were too strong. The truth was that on the night both sides were below strength – Long Eaton were at least one heat-leader short and Edinburgh were missing Norwegian signing Henry Harrfeldt – and over the course of the season both would monopolise the British League's basement positions.

That was in the future, and an above-average crowd passed through the Station Road turnstiles on Good Friday, 16 April, for the Archers' first home British League match, an attractive fixture against West Ham. The fans were also cheered by what seemed a first-class solution to the heat-leader problem. When supporters opened their programmes, they found that the number four slot for Long Eaton had been left blank. It was to be filled by Peter Moore, the fast-gating Aussie world finalist who had first made his name at Station Road in 1951, and had gone on to a successful top-level career with Wimbledon, Ipswich and, latterly, Swindon.

Above: Peter Moore returned (reluctantly) to Station Road for the team's British League home debut, on the instructions of the Control Board. Moore was designated to spearhead the Archers in the new league together with fellow Aussie Cresp, but he soon dropped out through injury. The Archers' initial line-up, from left to right, back row: Ron Wilson (team manager), Ray Wilson, Peter Moore, Rim Malskaitis, Ken Adams, Norman Storer, Reg Fearman (promoter). Front row: Kid Bodie, Ray Cresp.

Left: After Long Eaton closed in 1952, Peter Moore rode for Wimbledon, Ipswich and Swindon.

Moore had missed the 1964 season through illness and injury, but flew into Britain in March 1965 on the advice of his former management at Swindon, 'probably expecting', as Reg Fearman put it, 'to take his pick of tracks, preferably in London'. But 'Piccolo Pete', as Moore was known in the sport, was surprised and none too pleased to learn that he had been allocated to Long Eaton in the rider distribution exercise. When the deadline for submitting copy for the programme for the West Ham match was reached, his position was still the subject of an inquiry by the new Rider Control Committee.

Speedway riders, even in the 1960s, were used to being switched from track to track. Clive Hitch, seen here in Swindon colours, rode for Halifax Dukes in their reopening meeting against Long Eaton, but later in the 1965 season he was at Station Road as one of the riders brought in when injuries hit the Archers. Clive made a big impression in a short time.

Reg Fearman actually revealed in the programme for the opening match that the Archers had originally been allocated the Oxford rider Colin Goody together with Moore, but this had come to nothing when Goody had asked for 'certain extraneous benefits over and above the other riders.' Fearman had put his foot down, and the result had been the signing of Ray Cresp.

In the interval between compiling the programme and the match, things had moved on, and when the Long Eaton promoter went out on to the centre green to introduce the riders, he had the pleasant task of welcoming Peter Moore back to Station Road. The Control Committee had stood by its decision, giving Moore, after the long flight from his Melbourne home, little choice in the matter.

With an away win under their belts, and two Aussies of proven ability in the line-up, the Station Road fans had some cause for optimism. But opponents West Ham, Reg Fearman's first track as a sixteen-year-old in the late 1940s, looked to be a powerful combination, spearheaded by former Leicester and Coventry man Ken McKinlay – a regular world finalist – the fast-developing Norman Hunter, and Norwegian star Sverre Harrfeldt. And so it proved, as the Hammers' heat-leader trio dominated, scoring 33 points between them, including a 12-point maximum for McKinlay. Cresp (9) and Storer (7) led the opposition, with Wilson, Moore and Adams each scoring 6 points.

Long Eaton had taken a first-heat lead with a 4-2 from Cresp and Wilson, and held it until heat five. Peter Moore started slowly, with a third place and a second, but in heat eight he inflicted the only defeat of the evening upon Hunter, and with Malskaitis beating future England international Malcolm Simmons for third place, the Archers were back in the lead.

They held this until heat twelve, with a succession of drawn heats, but in the penultimate race the strong pairing of Hunter and Harrfeldt proved too strong for Storer and Adams. The Archers needed a last-heat 4-2 to draw or 5-1 to win, but it was not to be. McKinlay beat Cresp and Hammers' reserve Ted Ede held out Kid Bodie for third place, to give West Ham a winning margin.

It had been an exciting, if ultimately unsuccessful, home debut for British League racing at Station Road. The fans went home reasonably happy in the knowledge that the home side had held their own against some of the strongest opposition they were likely to face.

They were happier still when the news filtered through of the result at The Shay Stadium, Halifax, the following evening. Long Eaton again confounded the critics, and the 11,000 home fans, by winning 41-36 in the first meeting in the Yorkshire town for many years.

It is impossible to keep ex-Station Road junior and future promoter Ivor Brown out of the reckoning. He made sure Long Eaton would not win three away matches in a row by scoring a maximum in Cradley's narrow victory over the Archers at Dudley Wood.

Halifax had lost their locally-born rider Bryan Elliott, signed from Coventry, in a crash when the new Dukes made their debut at Newport the night before, but still seemed strong enough to see off the Archers.

Kid Bodie, who had struggled against West Ham, top-scored with 10 for the Archers, and Wilson and Moore both scored 9, supported by Cresp with 6.

Halifax, without Elliott, were essentially the Middlesbrough Bears of 1964. Eric Boothroyd, injured after he had switched to Long Eaton, had returned to join young hopefuls Eric Boocock, David Younghusband, Clive Hitch, and two new Australians, Bert Kingston and Bob Jamieson, at The Shay – a huge, if primitive, Football League ground with a capacity of more than 30,000.

Halifax got the best possible start when Ray Cresp fell on the first bend and Wilson laid his machine down to avoid him. Long Eaton were not demoralised by the immediate 5-0 deficit and had taken the lead by heat four, taking an unassailable nine-point lead with a 5-1 from Bodie and Cresp in the penultimate heat. As at Edinburgh, a last-heat 5-1 from the home side was not enough to prevent the Archers taking the spoils.

The highlights of Long Eaton's season had come very early. After the euphoria of two successive away victories, never that common in speedway at the best of times, gradually at first and then with increasing momentum, the season went downhill, with a familiar tale of injuries and other misfortunes.

When Long Eaton went to Cradley Heath on 24 April, the cracks were beginning to show. It was reported that Peter Moore, after the two hectic meetings in two nights over Easter, had experienced back and leg pains and after examination by three London specialists was being admitted to St Margaret's Hospital in Epping, Essex, to undergo an operation on his spine.

The six-man Archers' squad managed to keep the result in doubt until the last race at Dudley Wood. The Heathens led 38-34, but a 5-1 could still give Long Eaton a draw. As it was, the home pair scored a 5-1, but Long Eaton had contributed to an entertaining match. Ivor Brown scored a maximum for the Heathens and Ray Wilson (9 paid 10) and Ray Cresp (7 paid 9) had kept the Archers in the hunt, with solid contributions from Adams and Bodie.

Reg Fearman, resigned to losing Peter Moore for at least a major part of the season, applied to the Rider Control Committee for Terry Betts – a former Norwich and Wolverhampton rider who had been on the sidelines for some time. Strengthening was urgently needed.

Hackney came to Station Road with Ray Wilson in hospital for the removal of the steel pin that had been inserted in his leg after the crash at Weymouth in the previous summer. On a wet track, the first of many in a damp summer, the Archers crashed to another home defeat, Hackney winning 40-38. To compensate for the absent riders, Long Eaton included John Mills and the former Norwich and Yarmouth man Tich Read.

Mills delighted the fans with two heat wins, in both cases after his teammate had suffered engine failure. Hackney's real break came in heat six, when Norman Storer's throttle came off as he was leading Pratt and Byford, giving the visitors an unexpected 5-1 victory. Read concluded after the match that his engagements clashed with the Archers' fixture list, and he became a one-match wonder – the first of several.

The Archers travelled to Newport with only five men – John Mills broke down en route – and, still without Wilson, collapsed to a 52-26 defeat. Cresp, proving extremely consistent, scored 11 points, and Kid Bodie registered 9.

Halifax Dukes came to Station Road for the next home match, in the first round of the Knock-Out Cup, and with Wilson back in the side and Mills continuing his good form, the Archers ran out 51-45 winners. On an atrociously wet track, Ray Cresp scored a 15-point maximum from his 5 rides and was well backed up by Norman Storer (10), Kid Bodie (9) Mills, who had two wins in his 8 points, and Wilson, back from his stay in hospital, with 7. Younghusband was the Dukes' top man with 14, losing only to Mills in the shock result of the evening, and the veteran Boothroyd had 10 points.

The Archers' season stayed on course when glamour side Belle Vue paid their first-ever visit to Station Road. Long Eaton's injury problems were balanced by the absence of the Aces' Dick Fisher, and another fluent maximum from Ray Cresp and good backing from Storer (8), Adams (7) and Wilson (5) produced a 41-36 home win. Despite the loss of Fisher, the Aces still had five men from the nucleus of their National League side, plus one-time Station Road second-halfer Sandor Levai – a revelation with 7 points – and the much-travelled Vic White. The Station Road fans went home celebrating the team's first victory over a former National League side. But Long Eaton had sunk to the bottom of the league table, despite being one of only three teams to have recorded two away victories.

There was to be no immediate improvement and no quick resolution to the injury crisis, which was actually worsening. Kid Bodie damaged a shoulder in a 50-28 defeat at Oxford, but lined-up in the Archers' side against Exeter at Station Road on 18 May. His brave effort came to nothing as the pain and discomfort increased after his first ride. He withdrew from the meeting and an X-ray revealed a cracked collarbone. Ray Wilson's front wheel lifted out of control along the Station Road back straight, dumping him into the fence, causing severe lacerations. Norman Storer was the star of another dismal evening for the Archers, recording his first ever maximum.

Some possible relief for the fans was the reappearance in the second half at Station Road, after thirteen years away, of one of the original Archers favourites, Eric Minall. Minall was still only thirty-two years old, and announced his intention to move back into the area and make a serious attempt at a comeback which, sadly, failed to get off the ground.

After a further heavy away defeat, 53-25 at Wolverhampton, Long Eaton got permission to sign Tommy Roper of Sheffield, who had been replaced at Owlerton by former Norwich man Billy Bales. He appeared in the Archers' colours in another home defeat – Poole winning 47-31 on 25 May – but scored just a point.

The pre-season predictions of real problems for the Archers away from home, initially confounded by the two opening victories on the road, were now being fulfilled. A 53-25 drubbing at Sheffield, with Roper scoring eight points in his only other appearance for Long Eaton (he subsequently

Reg Fearman persuaded ex-Norwich and Wolverhampton rider Terry Betts out of retirement to help the injury-hit Archers, but he broke his foot in his second appearance!

moved on to Halifax), seemed positively respectable compared to the trip to Glasgow the next evening, when a terribly weak team was massacred 60-18 by the Scots side.

Relief (temporary as it was to prove) was on the way. Reg Fearman at last managed to persuade Terry Betts back onto the track (with the help, it was reported, of a substantial signing-on fee for the rider), and the Archers gained some revenge for the terrible treatment they had received in Glasgow by beating the White City Tigers 41-37. Cresp recorded another maximum, Betts got 8 points from his last three rides after looping at the gate in his first heat, and a fit-again Kid Bodie contributed 7. The match saw the return to Station Road of former Archers favourites Bluey Scott (11 points) and Charlie Monk (10).

Monk had raised the profile of ex-Provincial League riders by winning the prestigious Internationale meeting at Wimbledon against world-class opposition including Briggs and Fundin. At the same meeting, Ivor Brown suffered injuries that were to keep him out of speedway for much of the season.

The evening after the Glasgow home match saw the Archers at Poole, never a favourite track. The outcome was almost as bad as the Glasgow debacle, with the Pirates winning 59-19 and, to make it worse, the Terry Betts comeback coming to a swift end. Betts fell in his second ride and broke two bones in his left foot. *Speedway Star*'s reporter at the match commented: 'It took eighteen months of coaxing to get Betts back in the saddle. It took just two British League meetings to put him out again!' The same reporter posed the rhetorical question: 'what is left for Reg Fearman and his Archers?' The answer seemed to be 'not a great deal' as Sheffield became the latest winners, by 40-37, at Station Road.

There was a brief respite from league racing when Barry Briggs made his first appearance at Station Road to win the World Championship round, and then Edinburgh, the only side Long

Eaton were likely to overtake at the bottom of the British League, gave an undistinguished performance at Station Road. The Monarchs' promoter Ian Hoskins did not make the trip south, but his legendary father Johnnie acted as team manager, surprisingly failing to use the tactical substitute option as the Scots side slumped to a heavy 52-26 defeat. Clive Hitch, another former Middlesbrough Bear, originally allocated to Halifax, came into the side at this stage of the season and scored some useful points.

Archers' fans had their first taste of international speedway since the visit of the Swedish tourists in 1951. Polish side Gornik were the visitors as part of a short British tour. The Archers, led by Bodie and Wilson, each with nine points, lost, but held the visitors to a respectable 35-43 scoreline. A Polish refugee who owned a café in Long Eaton, John Huc, acted as interpreter and entertained the tourists before the match. The author was present and remembers the palpable tension between the Pole, settled in England, and the visiting officials, who undoubtedly included minders briefed to prevent any of the Gornik riders defecting.

Perhaps the greatest shock of the Long Eaton season came on Tuesday 29 June. Former National League Coventry, whose formidable promoter and Control Board member Charles Ochiltree always seemed out of place and uncomfortable in the less-than-plush surroundings of Station Road, tumbled to an unexpected 50-45 defeat in the second round of the Knock-Out Cup.

Ochiltree ran a tight ship at Coventry, enjoyed good support, and staged superbly presented meetings. But, for once, things went wrong administratively for the Bees and the man known throughout the sport as 'the CO'. Alarmed by the non-appearance of key riders Ron Mountford and Rick France in the Long Eaton pits, Ochiltree telephoned the garage owned by Mountford. He was surprised to find France, Mountford's riding, travelling and business partner, on the other end of the line.

France told Ochiltree: 'We are tuning the bikes ready for Long Eaton tomorrow night [Wednesday]!' The pairing, for years the subject of humorous stories in the Coventry programme, had failed to read their booking slips and had thought that Station Road, which had recently staged a couple of Wednesday meetings, had switched permanently to that night.

Even without two key riders, forced to use junior Peter Gay and ride a man short, Coventry still ran the Archers close. The blue-leathered Nigel Boocock and Bees' skipper Jim Lightfoot both scored 14 paid 15 points from five rides, neither losing to an opponent. Long Eaton riders won only six of the sixteen heats, but kept their heads and got home in the end.

Coventry scored two 5-1s and a 4-2 in the first four heats to lead by nine points, before Long Eaton fought back to come within a point of the visitors by heat seven. Storer and Sharp got a 5-1 over the weak Bees pairing of Chris Harrison and Peter Gay in that race, but in the next heat Coventry were five points up again through Boocock and Col Cotterill.

In one of the most exciting matches at Station Road in any era, heat ten saw Long Eaton again take advantage of the lower-end weaknesses of the Bees to pull back to within a point of the visitors. Boocock and Cotterill stretched the lead to three points with a heat twelve 4-2, but the next two races saw the tables turn.

With the scores so close, Coventry were unable to give extra rides to their top men. Reserves Harrison and Gay were out again in heat thirteen, and Kid Bodie and Ken Adams had an easy task in recording a 5-1. With the Archers' fans beginning to sense an upset, the home side scored another 5-1 in heat fourteen, Storer and Cresp getting home in front of Cotterill after Les Owen fell.

Long Eaton now had an incredible five-point lead with just two races to go. Boocock, predictably, won heat fifteen and Lightfoot was first past the post in the last race, but the Long Eaton men in both instances took the minor positions to record a famous victory. Reg Fearman told the press:

What a shock for the critics. Long Eaton giving Coventry the old KO was certainly a turn-up, but the Bees' disadvantage in not having Mountford and France was no more than we have been racing under for weeks.

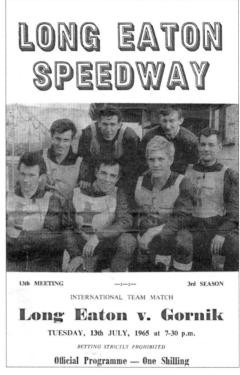

13th MEETING   —:—:—   3rd SEASON
INTERNATIONAL TEAM MATCH
Long Eaton v. Gornik
TUESDAY, 13th JULY, 1965 at 7-30 p.m.
BETTING STRICTLY PROHIBITED
Official Programme — One Shilling

Above left: Ken Adams played a role in the Archers' notorious Knock-Out Cup victory over Coventry. Adams was a reliable skipper and a steady influence on a struggling team in the first British League season.

Above right: The special programme cover for the tour match against Polish club side Gornik held a picture of the Long Eaton team before the start of the ill-fated match at Poole (complete with fairy lights round the track) in which Terry Betts (front row, second from right) broke his foot.

Long Eaton had become only the second former Provincial outfit to eliminate an ex-National League side in the Knock-Out Cup. It was a small beacon of light in a dark season, and doubly welcome for being over their aristocratic Midland rivals.

The Station Road fans would undoubtedly have appreciated the win even more if they had known what was to immediately follow. Long Eaton suffered thirteen successive defeats – seven at home – in the period from the end of June to the end of August. It is, even after a gap of more than forty years, almost as traumatic to write about it now as it was, as a reporter, to watch it unfold at the time.

It was, as already recalled, a wet summer, and the Station Road track was covered for much of the time by sawdust and shavings, which had been first put down to ensure that the tour match with Gornik could go ahead. There are several front covers of *Speedway Star* for 1965 that show riders in action in what appears to be a snowstorm.

Reg Fearman faced a hard public relations task as the summer unfolded. Sections of the crowd turned to heckling as defeat succeeded defeat at home, sometimes narrow and undeserved, on one occasion by a margin of 16 points. He never once flinched from going on to the centre-green microphone, not only to face his critics but, invariably, to face them down and silence them by some quick repartee.

In addition to the injury problems which hit the team, promoter Reg Fearman had to struggle against a far-from-perfect Station Road stadium. This shot shows the derelict totalisator, the sacking on the fence, and the heaps of tyres used for stock car racing barriers. Meanwhile, Kid Bodie, in second place behind Ivan Mauger and ahead of Bill Andrew, tries to keep Long Eaton in the British League hunt against Newcastle.

After the meetings, he usually faced another grilling in the speedway office from the journalists present. After they had been welcomed into the sanctum and largely disarmed by Reg's delightful wife, Joan, he would appear, calm and always immaculately dressed, and patiently answer their questions, which usually centred on the prospect of new riders and, inevitably, on the future of the track.

It is amazing that the hard core of supporters continued to turn out each week, often in imperfect weather, to face the likelihood of defeat for their team. Long Eaton may never have boasted the largest crowds, but what support there was demonstrated its loyalty – and the racing, despite the results, was good.

With Ray Cresp out from mid-July with an injured shoulder, the run of defeats inevitably included some away disasters. The worst was the 63-15 loss at Wimbledon, when only two second places, one for Norman Storer, who top-scored with five, and one for Ken Adams (three points), prevented a complete whitewash. Ray Wilson was the only other real contributor, with four third places.

There was some sympathy around the country for Long Eaton's plight, and also some admiration for the fight usually displayed by the riders. One of the better away results towards the latter end of the 1965 season came at Swindon. The Robins, with both Barry Briggs and

When New Zealander Rim Malskaitis was involved in a collision with teammate Ron Sharp in a match against Oxford, both riders had to withdraw from the meeting. Long Eaton's attempts to make up for the loss led to controversy. Malskaitis was the first British-based rider to use the new ESO machine on a regular basis in 1965.

Mike Broadbanks scoring maximums, won 44-34, but there was lavish praise in the *Speedway Star* for the Archers' performance:

> Hats off to the most courageous, grittiest, wonderful bunch of speedway riders in the country – the Long Eaton Archers. Battered almost to oblivion in previous matches and still minus heat-leaders Ray Cresp, Peter Moore and Terry Betts, the red and yellow Archers put up a magnificent battle at Swindon. Ray Wilson, Norman Storer, Kid Bodie – in fact, the whole darned lot of them – made a match of what could easily have been another runaway Robins victory.

Storer was Long Eaton's only heat winner, getting a 4-2 with Clive Hitch in heat two, but he also gained three second places.

There was another gutsy away performance to applaud at Coventry, when the Bees were only two points up with one heat to go. Boocock and Lightfoot, who both scored paid maximums, made no mistake in the final race, but a 42-36 defeat for the Archers was no mean feat in the circumstances. The run in the Knock-Out Cup came to an end at Exeter, with a 68-28 defeat.

By far the most controversial meeting of the season, and one that could have had an effect on the destination of the league championship, was the visit to Station Road of Oxford, the 1964 National League champions. The Cheetahs were now promoted by their former rider Danny Dunton, who had spent most of 1963 in the Archers' colours. Oxford were topping the British League table at this stage (they eventually finished fourth) but had recently been struck by injuries. The Archers were still without Ray Cresp and John Mills, to say nothing of Peter Moore and Terry Betts, and the task facing them was still a tough one.

Oxford paraded without heat-leader Ron How, hurt when his throttle jammed in the first Britain versus Russia Test match. Before the match, Danny Dunton had obtained permission from the British League Promoters' Association to ride himself, on the basis that two more of his men, former Archer Ken Vale and one-time Stoke man Jimmy Heard, were also out through injury.

Heard actually arrived for the match, but Dunton still went ahead and named himself at reserve in the visitors' side, with Stan Stevens being promoted into the team proper to ride in place of Vale. Despite some disquiet on Long Eaton's part, because this seemed to breach the Promoters' Association's special dispensation to Dunton, the match began.

The Archers took a two-point lead in heat two, but disaster struck two races later. Ron Sharp was well ahead and appeared to be untroubled, but he overdid it and slid off. Teammate Rim Malskaitis, close behind, hit his machine, and the Oxford riders took a 5-0, and then went further ahead with a 4-2 in heat six.

If the heat four incident was the catalyst for the controversy that followed – and dragged on for months – heat seven was when things really flared up. Sharp had suffered a broken finger and a cracked knuckle and did not ride again in the match. Malskaitis hurt his foot and also withdrew from the meeting.

Reduced to five men at the start of the seventh race, Long Eaton replaced Sharp with Clive Hitch, and the former Halifax man finished second behind Ray Wilson to give Long Eaton a 5-1 and bring them to within a point of Oxford. Danny Dunton, an experienced Speedway Riders' Association man, consulted the rule book and protested to the ACU referee that Hitch should not have ridden.

The injured Sharp had been designated for the match as the supplementary reserve, the rider who should have been introduced in a heat when the actual reserve (in this case Malskaitis, also injured) was unavailable. Because the points deficit was only five, rather than six, the Archers were not entitled to use a tactical substitute. Long Eaton, the referee confirmed, had indeed broken the rules and had actually been entitled to field only one man in heat seven.

Hitch's points from the race were deducted and the 5-1 to the Archers became a 3-3, with the match score now Long Eaton with 18 to Oxford's 23. To further complicate the situation, Reg Fearman claimed that Oxford's John Bishop had failed to complete four laps in heat seven and was not entitled to the point he had been awarded.

Hitch was allowed to replace Sharp in heat eight, without any further complaint being laid, and he came out with skipper Ken Adams to face Stan Stevens and Dunton himself. Dunton led for most of the race, but to the delight and derision of the home supporters, incensed by the earlier proceedings, he overslid and fell, leaving the home pairing to score a 5-1 heat win and again bring Long Eaton to within a point of the Cheetahs.

Gooch and Reeves restored Oxford's five-point advantage in heat nine when they got home ahead of Storer and Hitch, riding in his third successive race, but Bodie and Adams hit back with an immediate 4-2. Danny Dunton came out of the pits for this race but was unable to start his machine, again to the huge delight of the home support. A 4-2 to Oxford in heat eleven and a 3-3 draw in heat twelve meant that the Cheetahs, courtesy of the points deducted from Hitch and the disputed point won by Bishop, would take the match honours by scoring a single point in the final race. The Cheetahs' Danish star Arne Pander had engine failure and Norman Storer and Ray Wilson took the first two places but Jimmy Heard stayed on and stayed going to ensure an away victory.

Long Eaton protested against Danny Dunton's inclusion in the Oxford team and the Promoters' Association upheld the protest, awarding the Archers the match and two league points. Oxford appealed to the Speedway Control Board and eventually, well after the season had finished, the Board overturned the earlier decision and ruled that Oxford had, after all, won the match.

The Board said that, although Dunton had been undeniably unfair to the Promoters' Association in riding himself when one of the two men he had declared to be injured was in fact available, Reg Fearman had consented to his inclusion before the match, and Long Eaton were bound by this consent.

The gloom at home lifted somewhat when Cradley, still minus Ivor Brown – out since his Internationale crash – came to Station Road on 31 August, giving the Archers their first victory since the KO Cup win over Coventry on 29 June and the first league success since

22 June. On yet another wet track, Norman Storer's scrambles and grass-track experience showed through as he scored his second maximum and Ken Adams (9) and Kid Bodie (8) gave good support.

September was not to bring any great relief for the Archers. The team beat Swindon 40-37 at home – when Barry Briggs suffered engine failures in his last two rides – but lost heavily to Coventry in the final home match a week later and were also defeated in the last two away fixtures, by a respectable 44-32 at Exeter and a crushing 60-18 at newly-crowned British League champions West Ham.

When the curtain came down on the 1965 season at Station Road, a month earlier than in the two previous seasons, the overriding emotion for both management and the fans must have been relief.

For all the comings and goings at Station Road, and the disappointments over the injuries to Peter Moore and Terry Betts, Long Eaton fans could take some satisfaction from the performances of the home-produced riders. Norman Storer was an ever-present and top scorer, notching up more than 200 British League points, while Ray Wilson maintained his spectacular progress. Kid Bodie, Ray Cresp and Ken Adams were all steady scorers.

Clive Hitch was an underrated thrill-maker and New Zealander Malskaitis, while scoring few points, was always likely to do something unexpected on the track. Not only on the track either. When he recalls his Long Eaton season, he remembers travelling around the British League circuit with Ray Wilson, Kid Bodie and Norman Storer. They remember him too – particularly his habit of occasionally driving over rather than through traffic roundabouts!

Speedway as a whole had enjoyed the first historic season of the British League, which launched the sport on an upward trend that was to last for a decade or more. Although the start of a new boom time for the sport, 1965 was still a far cry from speedway of the twenty-first century. For riders like Kid Bodie, although pay rates had increased from the fifteen shillings a point plus a £3 10s machine maintenance allowance he received during his 1961 debut season at Wolverhampton, speedway's cash rewards were still meagre.

Bodie – the original heart-throb for Long Eaton's teenage female fans – reverted to his real name of Howard Cole after leaving Station Road, and eventually won the New Zealand Championship. He remembers a sport which in financial terms, even at the top level, was worlds away from the sponsorship and Grand Prix scene of today:

Only the very top riders received anything over and above the starts and points money. My first 'extra payment' did not come until I moved to King's Lynn in 1967, although with speedway doing well it increased every season I was there, and jumped enormously when I was allocated to Cradley in 1973, as I didn't want to go there. That was the most lucrative move I ever made, although I now cannot remember the full list of extra benefits.

You could not make a fortune at speedway in the 1960s and 1970s. I can remember one well established England international who rode for a former National League track telling me that in all the years he was the top man for his club, he never received a penny over the odds.

Costs were obviously a lot lower than they eventually became, although blowing an engine was still a major setback. Ray Cresp told me last time I saw him that in 1965 he spent only £25 on his machine, including the cost of his rear tyres. Ray was always careful with his equipment – he even used the valve springs the rest of us threw away!

If economy was the by-word for established team members, life was much harder for the juniors trying to break into the sport. There was no equivalent to the present-day Conference League or junior championships, and for most novices one or, at the most, two races after the league matches were over and perhaps a few spins around the track at the end of the meeting were the best they could hope for.

Howard Cole (Kid Bodie) pictured in New Zealand with a teammate and opponents from the 1960s. From left to right: Bob Andrews, Roy Trigg, Tommy Sweetman, Howard Cole, Rim Malskaitis. Cole recalls that it was unusual for a rider to make much money in the sixties.

Peter Wrathall was one of the local riders trying to make it in speedway in the mid-sixties. A farmer's son from Willington near Burton-on-Trent, he recalls that it took time to save up for his first machine and a vehicle to transport it to meetings:

> Most young riders were really desperate for a chance and would go to great lengths to get a ride. I remember finishing a day's work and driving all the way to Middlesbrough, without even having a firm second-half booking. It was a question of pleading with the promoters for a ride, and they didn't always have room in the programme.

The author once wrote a feature for *Speedway Star* about a Hampshire-based youngster called Syd Whatley, who had won (with a 15-point maximum) a special meeting for juniors staged by promoters Wally Mawdsley and Pete Lansdale at Exeter. Even that proved no passport to a team place, and Whatley for a while made the 400-mile round trip to Station Road – 'Just for a Second Half' as the *Star* sub-editor headlined the piece. The fifteen shillings paid for the article was probably more than Whatley earned for risking his neck on the track.

Much of this sort of background information was, at the time, out of reach of the average supporter. They, particularly at Station Road, were more concerned about the future of their team than about the plight of the juniors. Relief, and an early Christmas present for the Long Eaton fans, came with a story in the local press on 26 November that Reg Fearman, following a promoters' meeting in London, had confirmed that the battered Archers would resurface for another season in 1966. The promoter had also visited Station Road for talks with the stadium management about arrangements for the new season.

The *Long Eaton Advertiser*'s review of the 1965 season, also published in November, reflected all the injuries, controversies and disappointments of the soggy summer. But it also revealed that the gates at Station Road, boosted by the appearances of world-class former National League riders, had been up on the previous season. Speedway fans do not go to meetings just to see their team win.

Speedway is a sport full of superstition. Long Eaton reverted to the original 1950s archer motif for the 1964 season after trying a new design in the comeback year of 1963. Later on, after deciding that the original colours of green and yellow had brought ill luck with injuries, the team switched to red and yellow.

16

Flattering to Deceive

1966 was heralded at Station Road as the year of Ove Fundin. For the first time, the Archers would have in their ranks not only their first ever European overseas rider, but a fully-fledged world superstar.

Like many of the news stories to break at Station Road, this one quickly went sour. When the time came to tell the story of the season, it was not a tale of the inspirational exploits of one super Swede, but a chronicle of bitter disappointment, centred around not one but three Scandinavian speedmen.

Fundin himself did virtually all that was expected of him in an all-too-brief association with the Archers. His two replacements, Leif Enecrona and Nils Ringstrom, did not meet expectations of overseas men. In truth, it would have taken another rider of the very highest quality to replace the five-times World Champion, and by the time Long Eaton finally accepted that Fundin had gone for good, there was no one available.

When the story broke that Fundin was to join Long Eaton, an eternal Cinderella side, many fans felt it was too good to be true. Ove appeared in the Station Road pits on 5 April 1966 for an opening challenge match against Belle Vue and supporters had to rub their eyes as they saw a speedway legend buckle on an Archers' race jacket. It was not quite Beckham joining Hartlepool United, but for a track like Long Eaton, where the fans were used to, in the main, journeymen speedway riders, it was not far off.

The Archers-Fundin partnership was to prove a brief one, but it was good while it lasted. Throughout his years at Norwich in the National League, Fundin had used a machine owned and maintained by the management at the Firs Stadium. 'When he signed for Long Eaton, a similar arrangement was the only extra that he asked for,' Reg Fearman explains. 'We supplied the machine and Ray Wilson and his mechanic prepared it for Fundin for each match.'

In his debut against Belle Vue, Fundin got off to a less-than-perfect start in his first race at a rain-drenched Station Road. He was slow away from the gate and was unable to catch Belle Vue's Dick Fisher. But the Swede made up for it by winning his next three races and seemed to inspire his riding partner, Vic White, who scored a solid seven points.

White had returned to Station Road for his second spell as an Archer and, mounted on an ESO, was to enjoy by far his best season in Long Eaton colours. The third new man in the Archers team for 1966 was Dennis Newton, who had been around British speedway for many years, appearing for Norwich before moving to live in South Africa.

Skipper Ray Cresp, Ray Wilson – whose father Ron was now co-promoter with Reg Fearman at Station Road – and Norman Storer remained from 1965, but the former Stoke trio of Ken Adams, Kid Bodie, and Ron Sharp, together with Clive Hitch and Rim Malskaitis, had left. Local junior Peter Wrathall, who had made a couple of team appearances in 1964, was given the reserve slot for the Belle Vue opener, but this was to prove one of only two chances for him in 1966.

Ron Wilson, who had a motorcycle dealership in Leicester, had been keen to move into promotion. When his application for planning permission to run the sport at Peterborough Greyhound Stadium was refused, Reg Fearman offered him a half-share in Long Eaton under the banner of Disofast Ltd.

Above left: The sight of multi-World Champion Ove Fundin in a Long Eaton race jacket brought the fans through the Station Road turnstiles at the start of the 1966 season.

Above right: The programme cover for 1966 was a completely new look and reflected what promised to be a lively season for the Archers, with a World Champion in the ranks.

Left: Vic White (with Long Eaton in 1963) returned to Station Road for 1966 and was paired with Ove Fundin, to good effect. White was later to become co-promoter at Station Road with Ivor Brown. Now secretary of the World Speedway Riders' Association, he still lives in Long Eaton.

The first really competitive action for the new-look team came at Coventry the Saturday after the Belle Vue curtain-raiser, and the author was in the Brandon press box to witness it. A large contingent of Long Eaton fans made the comparatively short journey, full of expectation, and gave Fundin a rousing reception when he paraded with his teammates for his first British League match as an Archer. Again riding a borrowed JAP machine, Fundin top-scored with 11 points from five rides, as Long Eaton lost 48-30 to the Bees, twice finishing behind home star Nigel Boocock. In the second half, Fundin borrowed an ESO, which he had previously fought shy of, and cleaned up, beating Boocock twice.

Three days later, the action had switched to Station Road again, and a league meeting with Sheffield. This time there was no mistake, as Fundin cruised to his first 12-point maximum. Home-grown talent also shone on the night, as Ray Wilson also recorded a maximum and Norman Storer scored eight points. Lower down the order, the Archers struggled and the 40-38 victory was only secured by a last-heat 5-1 from Fundin and Cresp.

Cresp scored 5 paid 8 points in the match, twice tucking in behind Norman Storer to secure drawn heats, and his team riding experience was as vital a factor in deciding the result as the points scored by Fundin and Wilson. Cresp had scored 8 points in the challenge match victory over Belle Vue and 8 points at Coventry, suggesting that he would continue to be one of the most consistent riders in the side.

Edinburgh were the next visitors to Station Road and the fans were full of expectation. The result did not disappoint, with Long Eaton winning 49-28, but the absence, with only three matches ridden, of Ove Fundin caused raised eyebrows. Fundin had been suspended in his native Sweden, apparently for refusing to ride in a match. Nigel Boocock guested for Long Eaton and made up for Fundin's absence points-wise by scoring a 12-point maximum, well supported by Cresp (10 points) and Storer (7 paid 9). Ray Wilson broke a footrest in his last ride and tried to complete the race without it, but eventually fell.

Long Eaton Archers with Ove Fundin. The team shot that raised the hopes of fans. From left to right: Ray Cresp, Vic White, Ove Fundin, Ron Wilson (team manager), Norman Storer, Peter Wrathall, Dennis Newton, with Ray Wilson on machine.

There was no Fundin either for two away league matches, which brought heavy defeats at Sheffield (31-47) and Belle Vue (27-51). The Swedish star also missed the Station Road round of the Midland Riders Championship, won by Nigel Boocock, and the doubts began to grow on the terraces.

Belle Vue returned to Station Road on 3 May, this time with league points at stake. The good news for the Archers was that Fundin was back in the side, with the troubles in Sweden apparently amicably sorted out. Out on the track it was almost a repeat of the Sheffield match, with another last heat 5-1 from Fundin and Cresp proving the decider. Ove scored his second maximum for Long Eaton, Cresp scored eight, and the Archers might have won more convincingly had Ray Wilson not suffered two engine failures.

Fundin got revenge for his defeats at the hands of Nigel Boocock in the Brandon British League opener when Coventry visited Station Road on 10 May for a Midland Cup match. In the opening race, Fundin inflicted Boocock's only defeat of the night and shattered Colin Pratt's track record of 69 seconds, which had stood since August 1963. Fundin shaved nearly a full second off Pratt's time, recording 68.2 seconds. Given a full season of British League racing in 1965, it was a surprise that Pratt's record had lasted so long. But, in the winter of 1965/66, the track had been relaid with granite and shale and was in first-class condition.

Although Fundin scored his third maximum, he had little support, even from the normally reliable Cresp, and Coventry won the match 41-37. Archers' reserve John Mills, the man at the centre of the dispute over the 1963 Provincial League title, recorded a 5-1 with Vic White in heat four to give Long Eaton a two-point lead, but a 5-1 for Mountford and France in the next race tipped the balance Coventry's way. Fundin and White levelled the scores in heat seven but a 4-2 for the Bees in heat ten gave them a two-point advantage and they sealed the match in heat twelve, when Boocock and Lightfoot outpaced Wilson. Fundin and Cresp got a 4-2 in the final race, but it was too late.

Ove Fundin's presence in the side for the visit of Exeter on 17 May was reassuring for the fans, and Station Road that night also staged a clash between Nigel Boocock and Barry Briggs in the *Daily Mirror* British Match Race Championship. The opening weeks of the

Not the sharpest ever study of Ove Fundin in action, but a rare shot of him racing in Long Eaton colours on the way to a last-heat 5-1 with Ray Cresp. Sadly, Fundin's stay at Station Road was all too brief.

season had seen some dreadful weather, with meetings across the country plagued by both rain and snow. Long Eaton had not suffered a cancellation, although for two successive weeks the second half of the programme had to be cancelled. On the afternoon of the Exeter match, staff watered the track for a couple of hours early in the afternoon, only for the rain to start at 4p.m.

It was Fundin's worst performance for the Archers, scoring just six points and coming off worse in a clash with Exeter's Tommy Sweetman. For once, it was the lesser lights who impressed, with both Vic White and Norman Storer scoring paid 11 points. In the match race, Boocock was suffering from the effects of an ankle injury sustained the previous week in Coventry's Midland Cup win at Long Eaton, and he proved no match on the night for Briggs.

Ray Wilson, who had again broken a footrest in the Exeter match, was right back to his best form in the World Championship qualifying round at Station Road, taking the cheque with a 14-point return that saw him lose only to Ivan Mauger. Mauger was unbeaten with 12 points, but a failure to start in his first race cost him the meeting. Second place went to former Archer Eric Boothroyd with 13 points, and there were also good displays from Ray Cresp and another ex-Long Eaton man, Peter Moore, who each scored 11.

As the end of May approached, Long Eaton had won all four of their home British League matches and were respectably placed in the table. They lined up against Cradley on 31 May, well set to extend the winning run. The meeting started half an hour late, as the Cradley management and the Speedway Riders' Association argued in the pits over whether or not Coventry's Rick France was eligible to ride as a guest for the Heathens.

Archers' skipper Ray Cresp, as the national secretary of the SRA, was at the forefront of the negotiations. The pugnacious Cresp, a former middleweight boxer, won the bout, France stayed on the sidelines, and Long Eaton won the match 50-27. Fundin and Wilson recorded maximums, Cresp scored ten points, mainly from the back (surprising for a man with a reputation as a fast gater), and Vic White and John Mills had six points apiece.

This evening was to prove to be the high water mark of the 1966 season. Ove Fundin had scored three maximums in his four home British League matches and twice his inclusion

Ray Cresp had an interest in the controversy surrounding Ove Fundin both as Long Eaton captain and as a highly efficient and outspoken secretary of the British Speedway Riders' Association (SRA). Cresp was Long Eaton's 'Mr Consistency' in the first two British League seasons of 1965 and 1966.

(as the team's number one) in the crucial last heat had proved conclusive. But the Cradley meeting was to be his last appearance for Long Eaton. Reg Fearman explains:

> The partnership between Ove Fundin and Long Eaton was dissolved by SVEMO, the Swedish governing body for speedway. SVEMO in fact withdrew Ove's licence when he refused to take part in championship events in Sweden. That was the end of his brief spell in Archers' colours, but not the end of his career in British speedway. He came back for a short time with Belle Vue in 1967 and, of course, won his fifth World title.

Through no fault of their own, the Archers had once again flattered to deceive. With Fundin in the side, Long Eaton looked capable of seeing off most opposition at Station Road, while the former World Champion's experience of many of Britain's speedway circuits would have ensured respectable away performances – and for once would have made the Archers attractive away opposition. Fundin had proved to be a crowd-puller at home too, and the difference soon began to show on the Station Road terraces.

The row that had erupted before the Cradley match brought action by the British League to ban substitute or guest riders, although by the time the new ruling came into effect on 27 June, Long Eaton had made ample use of guests to try and compensate for the loss of Fundin.

Bill Andrew of Poole came into the side for the visit of West Ham on Saturday 4 June – the fact that the Hammers also rode on Tuesdays gave Long Eaton a rare weekend meeting. Andrew was a failure on the night, contributing only three points, and Long Eaton were beaten 40-37. Dennis Newton, who had taken a long time to settle, was a revelation, winning his two scheduled reserve rides and a further outing when he replaced John Mills.

Newton and White had given the Archers a boost with a 5-1 in heat four, levelling the scores after two 4-2s from the Hammers, and when Ray Wilson beat Ken McKinlay in heat six, with John Mills in third place, a surprise Long Eaton victory was on the cards.

In the next race, both Bill Andrew for the Archers and Sverre Harrfeldt for the Hammers suffered engine failure, but Vic White got home ahead of Malcolm Simmons to extend the lead to three points. Although a tight finish looked certain at that stage, West Ham won the last three heats by 4-2 as Norman Hunter and McKinlay proved too powerful and were backed up by their second strings.

Charlie Monk guested for Long Eaton on 14 June and although he kept the Archers in the hunt with 12 points from five rides, Halifax exploited the Long Eaton second-string weaknesses to win 42-35.

Fundin had appeared in only one away match during his nominal two-month stay on the Archers' strength and guests had been used to replace him all the way through. Ivan Mauger rode twice, at Belle Vue and at Glasgow, but in the match at the White City he struggled and Ray Wilson kept the flag flying in a 50-28 defeat, with a fighting 13 points from five rides. Other guests before the ban included ex-Archers Betts and Boothroyd, Brian Brett and Eric Boocock.

In general, the guests did little for the Archers' cause. The month of June saw six consecutive British League defeats – three at home – before a 44-33 win against King's Lynn at Station Road when, against the trend, Roy Trigg of Hackney contributed ten points. Oxford also lowered the Long Eaton colours at home with a 46-32 victory in the Midland Cup.

The general pattern of the season was indicated by the next four matches. The fixture list had thrown up a number of back-to-back fixtures against the same opposition and, in the first half of July, Long Eaton raced twice against Newport and twice against Hackney. Both away fixtures resulted in predictable heavy defeats for the Archers – 57-21 in Wales and 51-27 in East London – but the home matches were won, 43-35 against Newport and 41-37 against Hackney.

Guest riders had by this time been replaced by a new rider replacement rule, allowing nominated riders to have a total of six rides, including one as a tactical substitute, where a heat

A classic speedway quiz question. How come both these riders seen tussling for the lead at Station Road were former Archers, but when the picture was taken in 1966 neither man was contracted to Long Eaton – the answer is that Charlie Monk (left) was guesting for the Archers against Halifax, who featured Eric Boothroyd (right).

leader was missing due to injury or international appearances. It was not a lot of immediate use to Long Eaton, as Fundin was missing because of suspension. The British League promoters' meeting in June that approved the new rule, with the backing of the SRA, also gave the Archers the go-ahead to sign a new Swede, the relatively unknown Leif Enecrona, provided agreement could be reached with the Swedish governing body.

The red tape took a long time to sort out, and Enecrona did not make his debut until Saturday 30 July, when he scored two points in a 44-34 defeat for the Archers at Swindon, followed by a more encouraging seven points at Exeter two nights later. In the meantime, Long Eaton had been beaten convincingly at home by Wimbledon (34-44), and had crashed 27-51 at Oxford, with the home fans' spirits being raised somewhat by a 54-40 home win over Edinburgh in the second round of the Knock-Out Cup.

Enecrona made his home debut in a thrilling 39-39 draw against Wolverhampton on 2 August, recording his best score of ten points. It was a creditable performance, all the more so as it was his third match in four days, including a long trip to Devon – a schedule he was unlikely to have faced before.

Sadly, it was the high point of his stay with the Archers, which was to last for only five more matches, through to the end of August. Fundin's five British League appearances for Long Eaton had produced an average of nearly ten points a match. Enecrona's eight matches brought an average of just over seven – creditable, but not the consistent heavy scoring the team needed.

Long Eaton also used Australian Greg Kentwell, who had formerly been placed by Reg Fearman at Halifax. Again, Kentwell was a useful performer who would have been at home in a more successful side. The rest of August brought away defeats at Edinburgh, Poole, Newcastle and West Ham in the league, plus a 31-47 Midland Cup loss at Coventry, with the Archers losing at Station Road by a single point to Swedish tourists Vargarna, and recording narrow victories over Poole, Newcastle and Glasgow.

The run of home victories was extended to four when Oxford were beaten 50-28 in the first home meeting of September, with Ray Wilson scoring a maximum. Long Eaton had

been allocated another Swedish rider, Nils Ringstrom, who alternated with Enecrona and then stayed around for most of the rest of the season once his fellow countryman had left. Ringstrom achieved a high of a six-point score against Hackney at Station Road, but struggled at British League level and averaged only just over four points a match.

The Archers' passing interest in the Knock-Out Cup ended when they lost 53-43 at Belle Vue, and the attention turned to another competition. Long Eaton's dreadful record in their Midland Cup group – bottom of the eastern section with no points from home and away matches against Coventry and Oxford – meant that they 'qualified' to ride in the consolatory Midland Shield final against Cradley, bottom club in a western section which had also comprised Wolverhampton and Swindon.

Cradley came to Station Road for the first leg on 13 September and Long Eaton's 50-28 success not only extended the winning home run to five matches but gave the Archers the chance of some silverware. After league defeats at Coventry and King's Lynn on consecutive nights, the team went to Dudley Wood and held Cradley to a 36-42 scoreline, giving Long Eaton the shield with an aggregate score of 86-70.

It was not a great deal of consolation for another hugely disappointing season which, in contrast to the early shutdown in 1965, stretched on until 16 October with challenge matches. When the final league table was published, Long Eaton had risen just one place, finishing eighteenth out of nineteen clubs. Cradley assumed the mantle of wooden spoonists.

The links between Long Eaton and Brafield, which dated back to the early fifties when Johnnie Jones appeared for the Northants team in the Southern Area League, were revived towards the end of 1966. Archers reserve Ian Champion, who also raced for the Brafield club in challenge matches, won the Midland Junior Championship with a 15-point maximum at the Northamptonshire track on 14 August, when the trophy was presented by Ray Wilson. In October, Long Eaton sent a junior side to the Sunday afternoon track for a challenge match, with the young Archers losing 29-47.

Greg Kentwell was to have been the spearhead of the Long Eaton side, but was late arriving and had just two pointless rides. Ian Champion, who represented his parent club on the day,

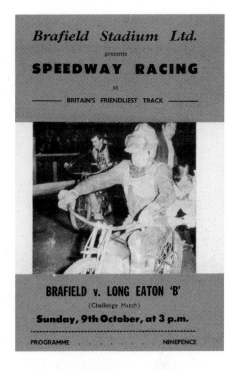

Right: Long Eaton's junior strength got a rare chance for a team match, when they rode at the Northamptonshire Sunday track Brafield, better known as a stock car circuit.

Opposite: Long Eaton without Ove Fundin. Leif Enecrona (left) was the first Swedish replacement for Fundin and was later followed by Nils Ringstrom. Australian Greg Kentwell was also drafted in mid-season. From left to right: Enecrona, Newton, Ray Wilson, Ron Wilson, Kentwell, White, Storer, with Ray Cresp on the machine.

Whatever the results, Long Eaton fans had the consolation of a regular chance to see two home-grown products in action. A contrast in styles is evident between Ray Wilson (inside) and Norman Storer as the Archers duo head for a 5-1 at Station Road.

rather than the home side, was, not surprisingly, the top scorer for the Archers with 11 points, losing only to another junior with Long Eaton connections, Peter Wrathall.

Wrathall had slipped out of the reckoning at Station Road after two pointless British League matches at reserve earlier in 1966, but on the 335-yard Brafield circuit he scored a 12-point maximum in the match. The track record fell twice in the match. First Ian Champion knocked more than four seconds off Peter Wrathall's time of 69 seconds, lowering it to 65.7, but Wrathall then shattered the timing once again, with a fast 63.2-second ride.

The Long Eaton side was largely composed of second-halfers from Station Road and the scorers were Champion (11), Dai Evans (8), Trevor Chamberlain (5), Steve Waplington (4),

Ray Wilson was fast becoming a major rider in 1966. Here, he tussles for the lead on the first turn at Station Road in a World Championship qualifier.

A. Greaves (1), Barry Bostock (0) and Greg Kentwell (0). Bostock made one British League appearance for the Archers in 1966, scoring one point and one bonus.

Looking back on 1966, the major gain from the season had been the rise in stature of Ray Wilson, particularly after Fundin's departure put the responsibility of being top man on to the teenager. Wilson finished the season with 342 British League points and an average of just over 8, although there were still nights when he looked far from being the finished object. He accepted the burden of expectation, however, and avoided injury to be a league ever-present, recording ten double-figure scores at home and seven on the road, including mature and face-saving performances at West Ham and Wimbledon. At Custom House, he scored 14 out of the Archers' 26-point total, and at Plough Lane his share was 13 out of 27. Although his riding style was still robust, he matured considerably in 1966, and the possession of a real potential star gave the fans something at least to be proud of.

In what, in many ways, was a season of remarkable stability by Long Eaton standards (apart from the saga of the Swedish trio), three other riders, Ray Cresp, Dennis Newton and Vic White, escaped injury to be ever-presents in British League matches. Cresp, who returned home to Australia with his wife after the season, scored nearly 250 points, bringing his total in two seasons at Station Road to more than 400.

17

Archers' Finale

It is difficult to know exactly how to write about the 1967 speedway season at Long Eaton. When the fans turned up for the first meeting of the season, the Station Road venue was as dilapidated as ever, with precious little comfort for the hardcore support of between 2,500 and 3,000 Archers fans. When the last wheel had turned in October, and the story of the season came to be written in hard, statistical facts, it could be said that nothing much had changed on the track either.

Despite the lack of serious team success, the Long Eaton line-up for 1967 was – at least for rather more than half the season – without a doubt the most successful combination ever to have worn the Archers' colours. Long Eaton as a team hit new heights in 1967, at least for a while, and two members of that team, Ray Wilson and newcomer Anders Michanek, blazed a trail of unprecedented individual success around the British speedway circuits, in international competition and in prestigious open meetings.

As the fans left the stadium at the end of the last meeting, they had a store of memories to mull over during the dark winter months, and seemingly much to look forward to once the 1968 campaign got underway.

The season began on 28 March, going straight into British League action against old rivals Cradley. When Long Eaton lined up for the photographer in the Station Road pits, the eight-man squad included an impressive roster of close-season signings including a new Swede, a new Australian, a new Englishman and, uniquely for the Archers, a Scotsman.

The first-meeting introductions may have lacked the 1966 excitement caused by the debut of Ove Fundin, but the 1967 Archers had a solid look down the order that had been lacking at any time in the past. The new Englishman, former Coventry captain Jim Lightfoot, was not at Station Road as the result of rider reallocations. Unsettled after many seasons at Brandon, Lightfoot had been transferred to Long Eaton, with promoters Ron Wilson (now taking the lead role at Station Road) and Reg Fearman paying a fee to the Bees.

The new Swede was Michanek – destined to be World Champion in 1974, but in 1967 an unknown late replacement for the original target, Karl-Erik Andersson. Michanek, who had ridden only once outside Sweden, was still unproven in British speedway but was recommended to Reg Fearman by Ove Fundin and regarded as a much more promising prospect than either of the 1966 disappointments, Leif Enecrona and Nils Ringstrom. The Aussie was a twenty-one-year-old Queenslander, John Boulger, joining the Archers on the recommendation of Ray Wilson, who had spent the winter down under and spotted the young man's potential.

Perhaps the least expected signing of them all was the fourth member of the new quartet, the highly experienced Gordon McGregor, who had been in the sport, usually at the top level, since his debut in 1947 for Glasgow White City. McGregor, most recently with Belle Vue, was approaching the veteran stage but was expected to add solidarity to the lower half of the line-up.

Still at Station Road, poised to become a top-flight rider in 1967, was Ray Wilson, together with the reliable Norman Storer and Vic White, who had scored solidly in 1966. The team picture was completed by the nominated number eight, Ian Champion, the 1966 Midland Junior Champion. As the season progressed, Ron Wilson also introduced John Poyser, no longer wanted by King's Lynn.

Above: Long Eaton 1967. The team that took on Cradley Heath in the first match of the season, plus the then unknown John Boulger, who at that stage was confined to second halves. From left to right: Ian Champion, Vic White, Ron Wilson, Norman Storer, Anders Michanek, Ray Wilson, Gordon McGregor, John Boulger. On the machine is new skipper Jim Lightfoot.

Left: Future World Champion Anders Michanek was virtually unknown at the start of the 1967 season but went on to win three major track championships and make a huge contribution to the Archers.

Missing from the previous year were Ray Cresp, who in many ways had held the Archers together over two difficult seasons, Dennis Newton who, although having experienced a patchy 1966, had nevertheless finished fourth in the team's averages, and Greg Kentwell.

Cradley were crushed 50-28, with Wilson completing a flawless maximum. Lightfoot – chosen to captain the side – was not far behind with 11 points, Michanek impressed with 9, and there was solid support from Storer and White with 6 points each, and 3 from Ian Champion. Gordon McGregor had been given the final team place ahead of the untried Boulger, and he weighed in with three points.

Above left: John Boulger, seen here on parade in front of the Station Road grandstand, had a dream debut, scoring a paid maximum against Exeter at Long Eaton. Ian Champion is the rider to his right.

Above right: Boulger was a protégé of Ray Wilson, who had seen the rider in action during a racing visit down under in the winter of 1966/67. Here, Wilson gets down to work, in the Station Road pits, on Boulger's machine.

In the first away match of the season, Wilson and Michanek both scored 12 points as the Archers restricted Hackney to a 42-36 victory. Lightfoot's nine points showed that the Archers at last had a heat-leader trio of high potential, but the tail was not so impressive. Vic White and Norman Storer collected only two points between them and Gordon McGregor and Champion failed to score.

When the team returned to Station Road and set about visitors Exeter, Ron Wilson excluded Champion and dropped McGregor to reserve, bringing in John Boulger for his UK debut, and what an introduction to British League racing it proved to be. Exeter were crushed 52-26 and Boulger had the fans gasping with a paid maximum.

These early season excitements were the prelude to an unprecedented run of success, at least at home, during which Long Eaton rose to the dizzy heights of third place in the British League table at one stage – achieved on 12 July after a home win against Hackney. Altogether, the Archers rode sixteen home matches unbeaten, from the Cradley opener on 28 March through to 27 July, when Oxford won a Midland Cup match at Station Road.

During this period, Long Eaton won two away matches, a 44-34 success at Belle Vue in the league and a 51-45 victory at Cradley Heath in the Knock-Out Cup. Along the way, there were no fewer than three drawn home matches but, with points being taken for the first time in the history of the British League from glamour sides West Ham and Wimbledon, and some nail-biting finishes, no one was complaining unduly at Station Road.

The pessimists on the Station Road terraces, deeply sceptical after the Fundin episode, once again considered that it was all a little too good to be true – and eventually their fears were to prove to be justified. The comparative slump in fortunes more or less coincided with the loss of Jim Lighfoot through retirement as July came to an end, coupled with an injury to Michanek in the Sweden versus Russia international series.

Waiting for the start of a pre-meeting parade at Station Road in 1967 are Jim Lightfoot, Norman Storer and Ray Wilson. Sadly, Lightfoot never completely settled at Station Road after being a one-club man at Coventry for many years. Behind the riders is long-serving pits marshall Frank Exton of Derby, who was heavily involved in the 'pirate' meetings of 1954.

Lightfoot, despite his willingness to be transferred from Coventry to Station Road, never seemed totally at ease in Long Eaton colours. He had some machine troubles and missed some matches through injury, before another injury prompted him to quit. He rode, in all, in twenty British League matches, averaging just over seven points. It was perhaps not quite the return that Ron Wilson had envisaged, and his departure was a total loss for the team, which was effectively given no replacement and, initially at least, was not allowed to use the rider replacement rule.

Lightfoot must be given credit for the part he played in Long Eaton's run of success up to the end of July in 1967. Had he been completely free of injury and machine troubles, he might have been the means of pushing the Archers right up into the top half of the British League table. As it proved, and all things being considered, he was sadly another Station Road disappointment.

There were some outstanding matches at Station Road during the record-breaking run of home successes. When Swindon were the visitors, on 2 May, Ray Wilson shattered both the track record and the seeming invincibility at Long Eaton of World Champion Barry Briggs. Wilson scored a maximum in the match and then took the Silver Sash from Briggs, the holder.

Long Eaton beat the Robins 41-37 in the sort of tight contest that was a Station Road trademark. The match was not without controversy, as Swindon team manager Norman Parker, the former Wimbledon and England star, protested about the bumpy state of the racing surface. 'We are not making excuses, but the track was diabolical,' said Parker.

Wilson's new record time of 67.6 seconds indicated that not everyone found it impossible to go flat out that night.

Mechanical failings also had a strong influence on the result. Barry Briggs, who finished the night with just seven points, had engine trouble throughout the match and contested the Silver Sash race on teammate Peter Munday's machine. To balance matters, Anders Michanek and Jim Lightfoot for the Archers also had machine failures.

As usual, good gating was no guarantee of a win at Station Road. When Michanek and Briggs clashed in heat six, the world champion led out of the traps, only for the hard-pressing Swede, mounted on junior Tom Leadbitter's ESO machine, to dive underneath him on the fourth bend of the first lap.

LONG EATON SPEEDWAY

9d Official Programme

30th MEETING   FIFTH SEASON

GRAND FINALE OF 1967

LONG EATON v. SHEFFIELD

TUESDAY, 10th OCTOBER, 1967 at 7-30 p.m.

BETTING STRICTLY PROHIBITED

The final programme cover of the Archers era threw the spotlight on young star Ray Wilson.

With Briggs subdued and Broadbanks enigmatical – two wins and two last places – Long Eaton won because their heat-leader trio of Wilson (12), Michanek (8) and Lightfoot (8) proved more successful on the night, and in Storer (6) they had the most consistent second string. Bob Kilby and Martin Ashby (9 points each) were best for the Robins. The match might have gone to the wire had it not been for a Briggs retirement in the penultimate race, cancelled out when Lightfoot shed his primary chain when lying second to Wilson in the last heat.

The one man who might have had most reason to complain about the state of affairs that evening was Barry Briggs. He had just flown into the UK from a weekend's sand-tracking in Germany – during which he had sustained a black eye – and blew his motor in heat twelve. When interviewed in the pits after the meeting, Briggs refused to make excuses. He said he would have had difficulty holding Ray Wilson, even if his bike had been perfect: 'It was a young man's track tonight.'

There was more controversy when the Archers held on to their unbeaten home record by the skin of their teeth on 25 July against Wimbledon. The 39-39 draw gave Long Eaton their first ever point against the Dons, but another close and exciting match was marred by a bitter controversy over the result of heat four.

After the first three laps, the Archers led by four points. Heat four saw the first appearance of the reserve riders, which always offered the chance of something unpredictable and/or spectacular. Vic White and John Poyser lined up for Long Eaton, with Jim Tebby and New Zealander Murray Burt starting for the visitors.

White, who was riding against his doctor's advice, chased Tebby, who had made the gate, and eventually passed him on lap three. Unknown to White, Murray Burt had fallen on the far straight and White ploughed into the young Kiwi's bike, which was in the centre of the track. Tebby and Poyser managed to avoid the debris and finished the race in that order.

Announcer Peter Arnold gave the result as a 3-2 to Wimbledon, but after protests referee G.H. Reynolds ruled that there should be a rerun. Dons' team manager Vic Gooden then protested that this was against the rules, and Tebby refused to take part in the rerun. The eventual outcome, after much wrangling, was that Vic White should be awarded the other point, making the heat result a 3-3. Had the race been completed without incident, it is likely the Archers would have recorded a 4-2.

A healthy crowd is still evident at Station Road for the visit of West Ham in 1967. West Ham and Long Eaton riders are distracted by Reg Fearman's centre-green showmanship. The Hammers riders are, from left to right: Stan Stevens, Norman Hunter (standing up), Tony Clarke, Ken McKinlay (concealed by the flag and mascot). The Archers visible are Anders Michanek, John Boulger and, behind the flag, new skipper Jim Lightfoot, signed from Coventry on a full contract.

In the end, both team managers, Gooden for Wimbledon and Ron Wilson for Long Eaton, accepted the situation. Gooden said after the match:

> The race should have been stopped when it was clear to the referee that Burt's machine was causing an obstruction. I agreed, however, to give White the point because it was the only fair way. I was quite satisfied with a draw. If there are disputes in a match and these lead to arguments, surely a draw is the best result? It removes all the 'ifs'.

It was an impressive result against a strong Wimbledon team, which had won every previous encounter with Long Eaton. Wilson (14 points) and Michanek (13) had extra rides, with Long Eaton, at this stage of the season, being allowed to use the rider replacement rule for the missing Lightfoot. Olle Nygren, who had held the track record at Station Road from 1951 to 1963, spoilt Ray Wilson's maximum.

The solitary away win at Belle Vue, by 44 points to 34, was Long Eaton's best performance on the road, points-wise, during the whole of the Archers' era. The 51-45 success at Cradley Heath in the Knock-Out Cup in June was more controversial, with a police guard on the referee's box after a controversial last-heat decider which saw a clash between Anders Michanek and Tommy Bergkvist, in which Long Eaton's Swede came off better. Both Michanek and Wilson scored 15 points.

Sadly, neither league nor cup away success led to any repeats and, at the start of August, Edinburgh won 52-44 at Station Road in the Knock-Out Cup quarter-final. Rider replacement was again utilised by the Archers in what was virtually a four-man effort. Wilson (17 points), Michanek (11), Boulger (8) and Storer (7) scoring all but one of the Archers' points. Edinburgh, led by Bernt Persson (14), and George Hunter and Reider Eide (11 points each), were much more solid down the order.

A Midland Cup defeat by 35 points to 43 at Oxford deserves mention as it marked the competitive debut of Graham Plant, the future British Junior Champion and Division Two Riders' title winner, and provided the first instance of the son of a former Archers' rider (Wilf Plant 1951/52) wearing the Long Eaton colours.

West Ham were always attractive
and welcome visitors to Long
Eaton – even when they won!
Here, Ray Wilson takes the inside
line against Norman Hunter in
a shot by teenage photographer
John Sumpter.

When the final league table was published, Long Eaton were third from the bottom, the highest any Archers side had finished in five completed seasons of league racing in the Third Division, the Provincial League and, from 1965 onwards, the British League. There were just two home defeats in the British League, again a record, but the solitary away success prevented any hopes of a higher placing in the table. Ironically, the Archers side that was forced to withdraw at the end of July 1952 because of falling crowds was on course to finish halfway up the Southern League.

Nevertheless, most fans' memories of 1967 would be happy ones. The ability of the team to win the majority of home matches, the continued high standard of racing, despite the sometimes bumpy track, and the huge achievements of star riders Wilson and Michanek had brought pride back to the East Midlands.

The individual achievements of the two leading Archers during the season were phenomenal, at least by Long Eaton standards. Both made international appearances for their respective countries. Ray Wilson made three appearances for Great Britain against Sweden, at Wimbledon, Coventry and Belle Vue, in a series which the Swedes won 3-2. Wilson scored 17 points plus four bonuses. Jim Lightfoot had a scoreless reserve ride in the match at Coventry. Anders Michanek also rode in three of the matches, at Newport, Glasgow and Belle Vue, outscoring his teammate to total 30 points with six bonuses, ending with a calculated match average of 8 points.

Wilson had three matches for England in the England-Poland series, which England won 3-2. He was pointless in two of the matches, at Wolverhampton and Halifax, but scored eight in England's 59-49 success at Poole.

In the winter of 1967/68, Ray Wilson was part of the English Lions' Test squad in Australia, and played his part in a 3-2 series win against the Kangaroos. Ray scored 6 points at Sydney, 7 in Brisbane, 9 in the second Sydney test, 3 in the third meeting at Sydney, and a superb 11 points when England clinched the series with a 62-46 triumph in Adelaide. Wilson was not the only current or former Archer taking part in the series. Terry Betts rode in all five Tests for England, averaging just less than 4 points a match, while for Australia John Boulger rode in four of the five Tests, averaging just over 4 points. Greg Kentwell rode in all five, averaging 8 points, and Charlie Monk was the top scorer for the Kangaroos in the Adelaide match, with 12 points.

In the World Championship, Anders Michanek took sixth place with 9 points, Ray Wilson finishing eighth with 7 points. Former Archer Ove Fundin was World Champion, for what was then a record-breaking fifth time.

When it came to the most prestigious open meetings around the British circuits in 1967, Michanek and Wilson shared five titles. Anders enjoyed an incredible three-day run, winning the Olympique at Newcastle on Monday 18 September, the East Midland Open

Ray Wilson made his World Championship final debut and scored a satisfying 7 points.

Anders Michanek, recommended to Reg Fearman by Ove Fundin, is seen in action at Long Eaton. He took sixth place in the 1967 World Final with 9 points. Michanek went on to win the World Championship in 1974.

John Poyser, who scored some useful points in 1967.

Championship at Long Eaton on the Tuesday and the Brandonapolis at Coventry on the Wednesday! Ray Wilson won the Tadeusz Teodorowicz Memorial Trophy at Swindon and The Laurels at Wimbledon. Wilson completed a memorable season by finishing third behind Barry Briggs and Nigel Boocock in the British League Riders Championship final at Belle Vue, showing his mastery of both small (Wimbledon) and large (Hyde Road) tracks.

In the British League, Wilson scored 412 points for a calculated match average of 10.36, and Michanek totalled 261 points for an average of nearly 8.5. John Boulger's tally of 211 points (including 28 bonuses) and an average of almost 6 a match was a solid return for a first-year rider. Norman Storer was the only ever-present in the 1967 team.

It was, in many ways, a heady time to be a Long Eaton fan, and as thoughts turned to spring and the 1968 season, there was a feeling that speedway was established in Long Eaton. Then, in March, came the bombshell. The Long Eaton licence and the core of the Archers' team were to be transferred lock, stock and barrel down the road to Leicester's Blackbird Road.

National League Speedway had operated continuously at Leicester from 1948, initially in the Third Division and then in the Second Division, until the shrinking number of teams meant a merger and one big league for 1957. Despite some success – the Hunters were second in the 1959 National League and boasted the consistent brilliance of Ken McKinlay, aided for three years running by top Polish riders – the crowds fell at Blackbird Road.

The Leicester promotion called it a day at the end of 1961, and Mike Parker and Reg Fearman, as Northern Speedways Ltd, stepped in at Blackbird Road, introducing, as mentioned in an early chapter, Provincial League speedway for 1962. The lower level proved unacceptable at a venue accustomed to seeing the best. Leicester finished next to bottom of the league, with just six wins, and I remember paying my first visit to Blackbird Road to see the home side ride against Neath in September, when it was already obvious that the shutters were going to go up.

With National League riders struggling for open bookings in 1963, the man behind Leicester, millionaire Alan Sanderson, staged a short series of all-star open meetings, but these were ultimately unsuccessful too. Leicester lay fallow for four seasons.

Reg Fearman and Ron Wilson clearly took stock of the situation from all angles at the end of the 1967 season. Long Eaton, since the reopening in 1963, had attracted only modest crowds to a stadium which was visibly deteriorating. The racing surface required a huge

Leicester Lions 1968 (including five of the 1967 Long Eaton Archers), from left to right, back row: Wilson, George Major, White, Michanek. Front row: Boulger, Storer, John Hart. George Major and John Hart were the additions.

amount of attention after fortnightly stock car meetings, promoted by a management which, to put it mildly, was not always stable or wholly co-operative.

The 1967 stock car promotion was a strange affair, with several people having a financial interest, ranging from former driver Reg Saul, who managed the meetings, to the wrestling tag-team partnership of Bert Royal and his younger brother Vic Faulkner. The Author vividly remembers attending a pre-season planning meeting amid the somewhat faded splendour of the huge Palace Hotel in Buxton, Derbyshire on a winter evening.

The journey there, in a Jaguar driven fast by a stock car driver, was hair-raising enough. The partners, in those pre-breathalyser days, accompanied their talks with a lavish supply of whisky. The lounge at the Palace was furnished with chintzy sofas and as a youngster unused to strong drink, the author managed to push most of the glasses under the loose covers. The journey home, down the steep and winding Taddington Dale, was not for the faint-hearted.

Stock cars operated at Leicester too, but on the basis that the four-wheel sport had always proved so successful at sister track Coventry, with well-spaced-out meetings and immaculate track maintenance.

The Leicester switch was perfectly understandable in business terms. The British League itself had proved remarkably successful, and there were signs that speedway was on the verge of another boom period. The Long Eaton promoters had the nucleus of a highly successful team under contract. Put that team in one of the best stadiums outside London, with a first-class grandstand and concrete terracing rather than Station Road's grass and cinder banking, and in a city where, in its heyday, the sport had attracted genuinely large crowds, and logic suggested that you had the makings of a major success story.

The author's memory of the happenings in March 1967 suggests that the majority of Long Eaton activists, including stalwarts of the Supporters Club, while bitterly disappointed with the closure, were realistic enough to accept that it made a lot of sense. The protests were muted, and the Supporters' Club made arrangements for buses to run to Leicester on speedway nights.

Clearly, taking speedway back to Leicester after the failure in 1962 was still a gamble. It paid off handsomely.

Reg Fearman's promoting career in speedway took in success not only at Leicester but also at other tracks, perhaps most notably Reading where, after the loss of the original Tilehurst Stadium, he and his associates built a new track, Smallmead, from scratch. Today, he lives in the South of France, but is active in the World Speedway Riders' Association, of which he was president in 1992, and keeps in touch with riders throughout the world.

The Long Eaton years 1963 to 1967 sadly do not rank among the happiest of Reg Fearman's speedway memories, and his recollections, forty years on, form a gloomy epitaph to the history of the Archers era:

> I realise now, reading this account of those years, what a horrendous five seasons I had at Station Road.
>
> At the time, of course, each problem that arose was just another one to surmount. I was thirty years of age in 1963, an eternal optimist in that I believed things would come right. Perhaps in 1963, if I could have foreseen the next four or five seasons, I would have thrown in the towel.
>
> There were so many adversities, season after season. And in addition to the injuries, stock car racing was a continuing problem. The stock car people were impossible to work with. They didn't need a good track for the stock cars.
>
> On the Sunday morning after a Saturday stock car meeting I would work, with a small gang, from 7.30 in the morning, filling giant craters on the bends with shale and cement. One winter I completely relaid the track base with limestone, which did improve matters somewhat, and in 1966 Ron Wilson and I actually took over the running of the stock cars, so that we could control the number of meetings.
>
> But the expense of trying to keep the track in a fit condition was always down to me and the speedway.

In the 1960s, the Long Eaton fans, like Reg Fearman, took one season at a time and continually hoped that things would improve. There was always huge optimism at the start of a new campaign and it would be entirely wrong to end this account of an era on a note of gloom.

Although the results often disappointed, there was always entertainment at Station Road. 'I always thought that speedway was first and foremost entertainment,' Reg Fearman concludes.

A drab and run-down Long Eaton Stadium after the closure of the Archers. Some improvements were eventually carried out but the site is now completely derelict.

1950s stars Ernest Palmer (left) and Jack Winstanley have retained their love for speedway in the twenty-first century. They are pictured together at Sheffield's Owlerton Stadium.

'I got that from two of the most important influences on my career – Johnnie Hoskins and the great Australian and West Ham star Aub Lawson.'

It's not a bad thought with which to bring the story to a close, or at least to a temporary close. For, as it was to prove, Station Road was to return to the speedway circuit after just one year's lay-off, when Ivor Brown and Vic White brought British League Division Two racing to the town in 1969.

From that point until the purchase of the stadium by developers and the enforced closure after the 1997 season, Long Eaton operated fairly consistently, winning a championship in 1984. That, as they say, is another story, and although there was a temporary return to the Archers name and motif in 1974, most fans would agree that the true Archers era ended in 1967, never to return.

If you are interested in purchasing other books published by Stadia,
or in case you have difficulty finding any Stadia books in your local bookshop,
you can also place orders directly through the Tempus website

www.tempus-publishing.com